THE SCULPTURE OF
GIOVAN ANGELO MONTORSOLI
AND HIS CIRCLE

THE SCULPTURE OF
GIOVAN ANGELO MONTORSOLI
AND HIS CIRCLE

MYTH AND FAITH IN RENAISSANCE FLORENCE

Edited by Alan Chong and Lorenzo Principi

with contributions by

Kurt Sundstrom and Sergio Ramiro Ramírez

CURRIER MUSEUM *of* ART

This book is published in conjunction with the exhibition
*The Sculpture of Giovan Angelo Montorsoli and His Circle:
Myth and Faith in Renaissance Florence*, presented at the
Currier Museum of Art, Manchester, New Hampshire,
October 13, 2018, to January 21, 2019.

This catalogue is made possible by a generous grant from
Rose-Marie and Eijk van Otterloo.

The exhibition is sponsored by
M. Christine Dwyer and Michael Huxtable, and by
Thomas Silvia and Shannon Chandley.

Copyright 2018 by the Currier Museum of Art
Manchester, New Hampshire
www.currier.org

ISBN 978-0-929710-44-0

Library of Congress Control Number: 2018958013

Exhibition curators: Alan Chong, Lorenzo Principi,
and Kurt Sundstrom

Published by the Currier Museum of Art, Manchester
Designed by Geoff Kaplan, General Working Group
Copyedited by Kristin Swan
Printed by Pristone, Singapore

FIG. I
Giovan Angelo Montorsoli, *Prophet Jeremiah*, 1542–47.
Marble, height 156 cm. San Matteo, Genoa.

INTRODUCTION

Alan Chong

THIS EXHIBITION PRESENTS A NEWLY DISCOVERED TERRACOTTA of John the Baptist (FIG. 2) by Giovan Angelo Montorsoli in the wider cultural context of the 1530s, a period of fevered artistic and political upheaval in Florence. Recently acquired by the Currier Museum of Art, the sculpture measures more than four feet (130 cm) tall. In its musculature and intense gaze, it reflects Michelangelo's influence on Montorsoli, absorbed while working at the New Sacristy (Medici Chapel) of San Lorenzo. But the terracotta was not made under Michelangelo's scrutiny, which allowed Montorsoli greater artistic freedom. The Baptist strides forward in a manner distinct from other works of the period, and the sculpture demonstrates Montorsoli's deep understanding of ancient art, gained through his restoration of celebrated sculptures at the Vatican. The subject of the terracotta is significant, as John the Baptist, the object of artistic obsession for centuries, was the patron saint of Florence and thus a contested figure in the ongoing battle for control of the city. Finally, the sculpture dates to the period when Montorsoli also produced important work for the Hapsburg court, and through it for Holy Roman Emperor Charles V, the dominant political force in Italy in the 1530s and 1540s. The exhibition thus considers Montorsoli's work in relation to expansive themes that reveal networks of meaning. We consider the subject of John the Baptist in sixteenth-century Florence, the influence of Michelangelo's New Sacristy, the impact of ancient sculpture both artistically and conceptually, and Montorsoli's response to the Hapsburgs.

We should not underestimate the political turmoil in Italy around 1530. The struggle between France and the Holy Roman Empire for hegemony in the peninsula led to the Sack of Rome in 1527 and the virtual imprisonment of Pope Clement VII, the leader of the Medici family, which was quickly expelled from Florence. A head-spinning reversal then took place when Emperor Charles V formed an alliance with the pope, which led to imperial armies restoring Medici rule in Florence and the emperor marrying his daughter Margaret of Austria to Alessandro de' Medici, the city's new hereditary ruler. These events brought chaos to the arts in Italy. Several artists died during the Sack of Rome or saw their work destroyed. The projects funded by the papacy and the Medici family ground to a halt. Michelangelo even joined the Republic of Florence in their fight against the Medici, his erstwhile patrons. His artistic importance and friendship with Clement VII led to a pardon, and Michelangelo returned to work on the shrine to the Medici family – the New Sacristy – until the pope's death in 1534.

Montorsoli emerged as an artist amidst all this chaos. He was born in 1499, just north of Florence, with the name Angelo di Michele da Poggibonsi; he later took the surname Montorsoli, after a village northeast of Florence. After an apprenticeship and work as a stonecutter at the New Sacristy, in 1530 he entered the Servite order at the church of Santissima Annunziata in Florence. He became a priest in 1532 with the name Giovan Angelo, and was often called *Frate* or *Fra* (friar). However, his religious career was diverted a few months later when he was called to Rome to restore the ancient sculptures at the Vatican, namely the *Apollo Belvedere*, *Hercules and Telephos*, and *Laocoon*. Montorsoli's reimagined limbs and gestures, which remained in place for the next several centuries, greatly influenced the perception of these ancient works. In July 1533, Montorsoli, now excused by the pope from his duties as a priest, returned to Florence to work on the New Sacristy with Michelangelo. He was assigned the task of carving the marble figure of Saint Cosmas that flanks Michelangelo's *Virgin and Child*. The agonized pose and grimace of Cosmas (FIG. 3) are strongly dependent on ancient sculptures like the *Laocoon*. Giorgio Vasari carefully described the collaborative process of making the sculpture, lending insight to our consideration of the malleable materials of clay and plaster. Montorsoli made a large terracotta model of Cosmas that was retouched by Michelangelo, who made the head and arms himself. Montorsoli also assisted Michelangelo with the marble statues of the dukes in the New Sacristy "in executing certain difficult undercuttings."[1]

FIG. 2

Montorsoli, *John the Baptist*, 1530s. Terracotta, height 130 cm. Currier Museum of Art, Manchester. CAT. 8.

FIG. 3
Montorsoli, *Saint Cosmas*, 1533–37/38.
Marble, height 202 cm. New Sacristy,
San Lorenzo, Florence.

FIG. 4
Montorsoli, Apse of the church of
San Matteo, Genoa, 1542–47. Marble
and stucco.

Michelangelo's permanent departure from Florence in 1534 deprived Montorsoli of a mentor and protector. He thus became an itinerant artist, working in Paris, Bologna, Genoa, Naples, and Messina, before returning to Florence at the very end of his life.[2] With his major projects scattered, Montorsoli lost an intimate identification with his native Florence, where today only *Saint Cosmas* in the New Sacristy is easily visible. His most public monuments – the two grand fountains dedicated to Orion and Neptune in Messina, Sicily – have been ravaged by weathering and the devastating earthquake of 1908. These factors partially explain why Montorsoli is not better known.

Vasari's description of Montorsoli's sojourns in various cities is full of drama and political intrigue. The artist abandoned his appointment at the French court because of condescending court officials who acted against the interests of the king. His work in Naples was interrupted by the Turkish invasion of Puglia.

FIG. 5
Montorsoli, *Bust of Charles V* (detail),
1539–41. Marble. Museo Nazionale
della Certosa di San Martino,
Naples. CAT. 11.

And his marble sculpture of Hercules and Antaeus was ruined through the political maneuvering of the sculptor Baccio Bandinelli, which caused Montorsoli to leave Florence in disgust, to return only when his rival had died. In Genoa, Montorsoli received generous commissions and reportedly established a close relationship with the ruling prince, Andrea Doria. He produced work for the cathedral and for the Doria church of San Matteo (FIGS. 1, 4).

Montorsoli also worked extensively for Spain, although he never visited the country. His remarkable portrait of Charles V (FIG. 5) was commissioned by Andrea Doria as a gift to a Hapsburg courtier, and two fountains designed by the artist were also sent to Spain. Montorsoli's Fountain of Orion in Messina, Sicily (FIG. 6), begun in 1547, is also an integral part of the Hapsburg world. Created to permanently celebrate Charles V's victory in 1535 over the Ottomans at nearby Tunis, the fountain proclaims the supremacy of

FIG. 6
Montorsoli, Fountain of Orion,
Messina, 1547–53. Photograph of
1867.

FIG. 7
Medal of Giovan Angelo Montorsoli, ca. 1556.
Lead, diameter 4.5 cm. Museo regionale
interdisciplinare di Messina. A. 4319-431.
Obverse: Emblem of the Servite Order.

the Hapsburgs and confirms their rule of Sicily. After a decade of successful work in Messina, a medal was struck in Montorsoli's honor (FIG. 7).[3]

Montorsoli has been well served by scholars, beginning in 1568 with Giorgio Vasari, who devoted to the artist one of the longest biographies in his *Lives of the Artists* (FIG. 8). This may have been because Montorsoli's career served Vasari's primary goals of celebrating both the "divine" Michelangelo and the magnanimity of Medici patronage in Florence. As Michelangelo's principal follower in sculpture, Montorsoli disseminated the master's style throughout Italy. In addition, Montorsoli was a founder and the main funder of the Accademia del disegno in Florence, a society of eminent artists established in 1563 under Duke Cosimo I de' Medici. Montorsoli's figures of Moses and Saint Paul were placed in the painters' chapel at Santissima Annunziata, and he designed the seal of the Accademia and carved the design onto the marble slab covering the crypt of the chapel (FIG. 9).[4] Pontormo was the first artist to be buried there, and Montorsoli himself was interred under the plaque on September 1, 1563.

More recent studies of Montorsoli include Carla Manara's dissertation of 1959 on Montorsoli's work in Genoa. Sheila ffolliott published a nuanced study of the artist's fountains in Messina in connection with triumphal entries, and Birgit Laschke in 1993 provided a substantial survey of Montorsoli's work.[5] Still missing is a full consideration of Montorsoli's collaborative network, which included the sculptors Silvio Cosini, Niccolò Tribolo, Bartolomeo Ammannati, and a substantial workshop. The discovery and restoration of ancient sculpture in Rome around 1500 has been extensively surveyed, although a number of inaccurate claims persist.[6] The role of John the Baptist in Florentine art has yet to be comprehensively studied.[7]

We hope that this book provides avenues for understanding several aspects of Montorsoli's *John the Baptist*. Lorenzo Principi advances the work's attribution and dating here for the first time. The sculpture responds to a long tradition of representations of the saint, visible in public settings in Florence. At the same time, it departs from previous poses and gestures – he strides forward, and rather than pointing to a cross, toward heaven, or to Christ, Montorsoli's figure grips the cross like a lance. As Kurt Sundstrom suggests, this seems no less than a reference to ancient warrior gods like Mars, the Baptist's predecessor as patron of Florence. Thus, Montorsoli is not simply a restorer of antiquities or a borrower of ancient styles; he responds to the universal ideal of a divinity as protector of one's homeland. Sergio Ramiro

FIG. 8

Portrait of Giovan Angelo Montorsoli.
Woodcut from Vasari 1568.

FIG. 9

Montorsoli, *Tomb Cover*, 1562. Marble,
110 × 94 cm. Cappella dei pittori,
Santissima Annunziata, Florence.

Ramírez considers Montorsoli's work for the Hapsburg court, especially through the rich imagery of fountains, although many of the artist's creations in this genre were ephemeral constructions, and others have been damaged or lost. Montorsoli's great Eagle Fountain, which once adorned Madrid's Casa de Campo, unfortunately remains in storage.

Another goal of this exhibition has been to highlight little-known works of sixteenth-century Italian sculpture in American museums, many rarely exhibited and previously attributed incorrectly. For example, a work by Francesco da Sangallo in the Chrysler Museum of Art has never been publicly shown. Besides the terracotta by Montorsoli, Lorenzo Principi presents new attributions to Benedetto da Rovezzano (CAT. 2), Sandro di Lorenzo (CAT. 16), Zaccaria Zacchi (CAT. 26), and Silvio Cosini (CAT. 27). Other works have only recently been correctly attributed (CATS. 4, 9, 10, 17). Despite being the subject of scholarly endeavor for many generations, Italian Renaissance sculpture continues to hold many uncertainties of connoisseurship, patronage, and interpretation. One indication of this is the fact that no fewer than five sculptures exhibited here have been attributed (incorrectly) to Michelangelo in the recent past. May such mysteries and ambiguities continue to delight all audiences.

1.   Vasari 1966, vol. 5, pp. 493–94.

2.   On the concept of the traveling artist in the Renaissance, see Kim 2014.

3.   Inscribed: IO. ANGELUS MO/NTURSULI FLORENT. Reverse: emblem of the Servite order, "NON TIMEBO MALA QUONIAM TU MECUM ES." Sarica 1997.

4.   For the drawing of the Accademia seal, see Laschke 1993, figs. 177–79.

5.   Manara 1959; ffolliott 1984; Möseneder 1979; Laschke 1993.

6.   Brummer 1970; Haskell and Penny 1981; Bober and Rubinstein 2010; Rome 2006.

7.   Lavin 1955; Lavin 1961.

FIG. I

Giovan Angelo Montorsoli, *John the Baptist*,
1530s. Terracotta, height 130 cm. Currier
Museum of Art. CAT. 8.

MONTORSOLI'S TERRACOTTA *JOHN THE BAPTIST*

THE INFLUENCE OF MICHELANGELO AND ANDREA DEL SARTO

Lorenzo Principi

GIOVAN ANGELO MONTORSOLI (1499–1563) IS GENERALLY REGARDED AS A TALENTED pupil of Michelangelo, an assiduous imitator of the monumentality, pathos, and muscular *terribilità* (or "ferocity") so closely associated with the master. Through his work in Genoa, Naples, Messina, and Bologna, Montorsoli was considered the standard-bearer of Michelangelo's style.

Michelangelo must have believed deeply in Montorsoli's ability, as it is through him that Montorsoli was summoned to Rome in 1532 to restore the celebrated ancient sculptures in the Vatican, namely the *Apollo Belvedere*, the *Laocoon*, and *Hercules and Telephos* (see essay by Chong). Michelangelo likewise entrusted Montorsoli with important work in the New Sacristy (known as the Medici Chapel) in Florence, in particular the *Saint Cosmas*, which Montorsoli carved to stand beside Michelangelo's own *Virgin and Child*.[1] Montorsoli worked on the figures of the two dukes for the New Sacristy,[2] and in August of 1533 was named supervisor of the Medici tombs. In 1539 or 1540, the artist moved to Genoa, where he became official sculptor to the powerful Doria family. There, he carved a monumental statue of Andrea Doria and a *Saint John the Evangelist* for the city's cathedral; between 1542 and 1547, Montorsoli designed and executed marble and stucco sculpture for San Matteo, the Doria church in Genoa (see p. 8).[3]

A recently discovered work by Montorsoli, a terracotta representing John the Baptist (FIG. 1), sheds new light on the artist's work in Florence in the 1530s, in particular his response to Michelangelo's art.

The sculpture is remarkable for its monumentality, suggestion of movement, and sense of space. Cloaked in a camel-skin tunic and a flowing mantle, the Baptist is portrayed with a severe frown, bristly beard, and intensely concentrated gaze. He strides confidently forward. In his left hand, he grasps a staff surmounted by a cross, while his muscular left arm anchors the composition. The statue is composed of at least five pieces of separately fired clay.[4] Montorsoli's modeling of the legs and the left arm was inspired by ancient art, in particular the *Apollo Belvedere*, which he had recently restored. The earliest Renaissance analogies are with the work of Jacopo Sansovino (1486–1570), one of the most influential sculptors of the sixteenth century. There are similarities between the terracotta *Baptist* and Jacopo Sansovino's two statues of Saint James in Florence's cathedral (1511–18) and in Rome (see FIG. 24), but Sansovino's work lacks Montorsoli's emphasis on musculature.

Such athleticism also appears in Montorsoli's *Saint John the Evangelist* in the cathedral of Genoa (FIG. 2). This work shares with the Currier Museum's *John the Baptist* a minutely chiseled beard, thick eyebrows, rounded and incised pupils, and a flattened jaw that grows more fleshy at the sides of the mouth (FIGS. 3–6). Circular, flattened, and elongated folds, which seem to be blown by the wind, define the cuffed sleeves of both figures (FIGS. 7, 8). The folds of their drapery are depicted with a thin and tubular hollow that ends with a rounded profile (FIGS. 11, 12).

The physiognomic traits of the sculpture in the Currier Museum appear in other works by Montorsoli, such as the bust of *Charles V* in Naples (FIG. 9), whose visage is marked by the same technical and stylistic characteristics found in *Saint John the Evangelist*. The face of the *Baptist* shares with Montorsoli's *Saint*

FIG. 2

Montorsoli, *Saint John the Evangelist*, 1540–41. Marble, height ca. 250 cm. Cathedral of San Lorenzo, Genoa.

14

FIG. 3
Detail of FIG. 7.

FIG. 4
Detail of FIG. 8.

FIG. 5
Detail of FIG. 7.

FIG. 6
Detail of FIG. 8.

FIG. 7
Montosoli, *Saint John the Evangelist*,
1540–41. Marble. Cathedral of San
Lorenzo, Genoa.

FIG. 8
Montorsoli, *John the Baptist*, 1530s.
Terracotta. Currier Museum of Art. CAT. 8.

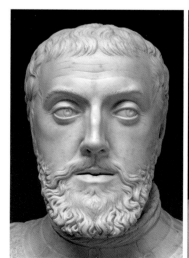

FIG. 9
Montorsoli, *Bust of Charles V* (detail),
1539–41. Marble. Museo Nazionale della
Certosa di San Martino, Naples. CAT. 11.

FIG. 10
Montorsoli, *Saint Andrew* (detail),
1542–47. Marble. Church of San Matteo,
Genoa.

15

FIG. 13
Detail of FIG. 8.

FIG. 11
Detail of FIG. 8.

FIG. 12
Detail of FIG. 7.

FIG. 14
Detail of FIG. 23.

FIG. 15
Detail of FIG. 16.

Andrew in San Matteo, Genoa (FIG. 10) facial proportions, wispy hair, and beard patterns. The *Saint Cosmas* in the New Sacristy displays the same protrusion above the arch of the eyebrows and irregular nose with a pronounced bump at its center.

The Baptist's pose is closely related to the *David* in San Matteo, Genoa, where the lightly flexed left arm creates a right angle, while the right arm points downward, parallel to the body. The sharp-edged folds in the Baptist's garments resurface in *Saint James the Greater* on the tomb of Sannazaro, and in the *John the Baptist* in San Matteo (FIGS. 13–15). The drapery of this last work provides a striking analogy to the mantle of the terracotta, which descends from the shoulder in delicate but full folds (FIGS. 8, 16). In Montorsoli's figures of the Baptist, there is a marked similarity in the manner in which the heavy, rigid camel skin falls; such surfaces are often treated with a network of light scratches, as can be seen in the terracotta *Baptist* as well as in the marble sculptures of the saint in San Matteo (FIG. 16) and in the Santissima Annunziata (1562–63).[5]

The powerful arms of the Currier Museum's *Baptist* betray a direct link to the tradition of muscularity in Florentine art. The pronounced veins are another typical characteristic of Montorsoli's sculpture, recurring in the *Triton* and *Saint John the Evangelist* (FIGS. 17, 18, 19), as well as the *Prophet Jeremiah* in San Matteo.[6] Montorsoli's careful depiction of the sinews and blood vessels in these hands shows his familiarity with anatomy. In fact, Vasari records that in Genoa, Montorsoli made anatomical dissections with the help of medical friends who provided him with "many anatomical specimens of human bodies."[7]

The sculpture in the Currier Museum provides a useful model for attributions to Montorsoli. He was above all a formalist who gave priority to *disegno*, witnessed in the importance of line in his sculptures. The facial expressions of his figures have an intensity that can be interpreted as sullen or grim, while the upper portions of his heads are powerful and rugged. The arms have a tense power, as robust hands clutch an object – often a mantle.

FIG. 16
Montorsoli, *John the Baptist*, 1542–47. Marble, height 146 cm. Church of San Matteo, Genoa.

FIG. 17
Detail of FIG. 1.

FIG. 18
Montorsoli, *Triton* (detail), 1540–43.
Marble. Villa del Principe, Genoa.
See p. 68.

FIG. 19
Detail of FIG. 2.

FIG. 20
Montorsoli, *Sheet of Studies* (detail), 1530s.
Pen and brown ink on paper, 27.4 × 20 cm.
Gabinetto dei Disegni e Stampe degli Uffizi,
Florence. 14526 F.

FIG. 21
Montorsoli, *Moses*, 1535–36.
Painted terracotta and stucco,
height 143 cm. Cappella dei pittori,
Santissima Annunziata, Florence.

FIG. 22
Montorsoli, *Saint Paul*, 1535–36.
Painted terracotta and stucco,
height 155 cm. Cappella dei pittori,
Santissima Annunziata, Florence.

The larger surfaces of drapery are frequently modeled with thick, clearly defined lines that produce subtle shading. Montorsoli tended to work his material deeply, notable especially in his marble sculptures, as already noted by Vasari, who praised Montorsoli's carving of marble. Vasari stated that the artist had helped Michelangelo with the statues of the two Medici dukes in the New Sacristy by "making certain difficult pierced undercuttings."[8]

The terracotta sculpture of John the Baptist is unique in Florentine sculpture from the first half of the sixteenth century, because large standing terracotta figures finished on all sides were nearly always glazed (predominantly by the Della Robbia or Buglioni workshops). Remnants of gesso (plaster) undercoating with lead white (see CAT. 8) indicate that Montorsoli's *Baptist* was painted, though in the early sixteenth century, terracotta sculptures of this size were rarely polychromed. Montorsoli modeled two other sculptures in terracotta and stucco in the 1530s – figures of Moses and Saint Paul made between 1535 and August 1536 for the Santissima Annunziata (FIGS. 21, 22).[9] These were painted white to simulate marble, and it is likely that the *John the Baptist* was similarly treated. The remnants of gesso would appear to contradict the idea that the *Baptist* was a model for a work in marble or bronze; the terracotta is more likely to be a finished work in itself.

No other works by Montorsoli besides these testify to his activity as a modeler. However, Vasari describes a number of ephemeral works made around this period, such as clay figures of Faith and Charity for a fountain that the artist created when the entire Servite order met in a general chapter, held at Budrio, Emilia, on April 29, 1535. These were said to be life-size and painted to imitate white marble.[10] The artist also produced decorations for the triumphal entry of Charles V into Florence in April 1536, and made a Neptune in stucco for Genoa (1543–47).[11]

In 1767, Ignazio Enrico Hugford (1703–1778), an English painter and dealer living in Florence, displayed three terracottas

by Montorsoli in the exhibition of the Accademia del disegno, held at the Santissima Annunziata. The works, which represented Christ, Saint Peter, and Saint Paul, are now lost, but they may have been connected with one of Montorsoli's sculptural projects – for example, the cathedral of Messina (1550), the high altar of the Servite church in Bologna, or an uncompleted project for Santissima Annunziata (the last two, 1558–62).[12] Hugford seems to have had a special interest in Montorsoli since he also owned a drawing that bears old inscriptions identifying the artist as Montorsoli.[13] The drawing shows two cornucopias, tree branches with detailed color indications, the head of an eagle, and a seminude figure in a mantle whose composition and heavy folds of drapery recall the terracotta *John the Baptist* (FIG. 20).[14]

PROVENANCE

We know nothing of the original setting of the terracotta *John the Baptist*. However, the work appears to be connected with a transaction of 1791, when the Florentine painter Tommaso Gherardini (1715–1797) sold two terracotta sculptures to Giovanni degli Alessandri, who would become president of the Accademia di belle arti of Florence in 1799, and director of the Uffizi in 1811.[15] The receipt states that Gherardini received 35 lire for "two statues about two braccia [117 cm] high in terracotta by Montorsoli, one depicting Saint John the Baptist and the other Saint Paul."[16] It is unlikely that this attribution was proposed simply to make the works more saleable, as Montorsoli was not an artist to whom works were commonly attributed in the eighteenth century. Gherardini probably had information about the creation and original context of the sculptures.

The two works are again recorded with the Alessandri family in 1828 when an inventory was drawn up of the oratory of San Francesco in the Villa Petroio near Vinci, which the family owned. They are described as "two white wood bases with gilded molding that support two statues, one depicting Saint John the Baptist and the other Saint Paul, the two situated in the middle of the two walls of the chapel, and which are in terracotta."[17] The two sculptures were valued at 80 lire. In 1879, Archbishop Eugenio Cecconi made note of them: "I observed in the middle of the church two statues in gesso or stucco, one on each side, representing Saint Paul and Saint John the Baptist."[18] It seems that the sculptures had been replaced with plaster copies. In addition, we know that a painting by Jacopo da Empoli of Saint Francis had been removed from the same villa by 1877, and replaced by a copy.[19] Two terracotta reliefs depicting the Adoration of the Magi and the Preaching of John the Baptist from the villa appeared on the London art market in 1965 and were later attributed to Girolamo Ticciati (1671–1744).[20] They must have been two of the "five bas reliefs in terracotta with stucco frames representing holy acts" listed in the 1828 inventory.

THE ORIGINAL CONTEXT OF THE TERRACOTTA BAPTIST

While stylistically datable to the 1530s, a peripatetic decade for the artist, the *John the Baptist* in the Currier Museum was likely made in Florence, where Montorsoli was based at Santissima Annunziata. The sculpture shares a similarity of style and material with the figures of Moses and Saint Paul that Montorsoli made for the church. It is also very likely that the *Baptist* was paired with a figure of Saint Paul, as they are recorded together in the Alessandri collection between 1791 and 1828, as noted above. These two saints form a natural pair as holy figures who come immediately before and after the Apostles – John the Baptist as the precursor of Christ, and Paul as a founder of the wider church. John and Paul were often added to series depicting Christ and the Apostles. The Compagnia di San Giovanni Battista dello Scalzo in Florence possessed a pair sculptures of John the Baptist and Saint Paul in the late sixteenth century.[21] We could imagine that Montorsoli made the terracotta figures of John the Baptist and Saint Paul for Santissima Annunziata or its subsidiary spaces, or perhaps for a patron connected with church.

MONTORSOLI IN FLORENCE

The probable Florentine provenance and the close affinities with Montorsoli's work of the 1530s and early 1540s allow us to date the terracotta *Baptist* to the artist's activity in Florence in the 1530s, an especially intense and eventful phase of his life. In October 1530, Montorsoli became a Servite monk at the monastery of Santissima Annunziata in Florence, and in March 1532 he was ordained as a priest.[22] In July of that year, he began his collaboration with Michelangelo.[23] In September, he moved to Rome to restore antiquities at the Vatican, where he remained until the early summer of 1533.[24] On July 25, 1533, Sebastiano del Piombo writes that Montorsoli "was at work on the figure of Duke Giuliano" in the New Sacristy in Florence.[25] In August, Montorsoli was made "overseer [*soprastante*] of the double tombs of the sacristy."[26] He remained in Florence until the end of September 1534, when, on the death of Pope Clement VII, Michelangelo left Florence permanently, interrupting work on the Medici tombs. After finishing a wax portrait of Duke Alessandro de' Medici for the Annunziata church in the autumn of 1534, Montorsoli joined Michelangelo in Rome, where he assisted with the tomb of Julius II.[27]

Between the end of 1534 and the beginning of 1535, he travelled to France at the behest of Cardinal François de Tournon, who wanted to introduce an Italian sculptor to the court of Francis I.[28] However, Montorsoli was so disillusioned by the Parisian court that he immediately left to visit Lyon, Provence, Genoa, Venice, Padua, Verona, and Mantua. In April 1535, he attended the general chapter of his order in Budrio.[29] Between May 1535 and the summer of 1536, Montorsoli worked in Arezzo on the tomb of Angelo d'Arezzo in the church of San Pier Piccolo.[30] He prepared ephemeral decorations for the triumphal entry of Charles V into Florence in April 1536, and in August completed statues of Moses and Saint Paul in terracotta and stucco for the Annunziata.[31] He may have visited Urbino in the same month, and shortly afterward went to Naples in hopes of receiving the prestigious commission for the tomb of Jacopo Sannazaro.[32] He worked on that project in Naples until July 1537, when the Turkish invasion of Puglia forced him to move to Carrara or Florence.[33] In October 1537, Francesco Ferrucci del Tadda, a friend and collaborator of Montorsoli's, sent architectural elements for the tomb from Carrara to Naples.[34] At the end of the summer of 1537, Maria Salviati, the mother of Cosimo I, asked Montorsoli to finish the figure of Saint Cosmas for the New Sacristy, and shortly after, in April of 1538, to carve a *Hercules and Antaeus* for a fountain at her Villa di Castello.[35] In April and May the sculptor went to Carrara to extract marble for the fountain and to continue work on the Sannazaro tomb.

While he was working in Florence and Carrara, Montorsoli was asked (perhaps around April or May 1538) to make a monumental portrait of Andrea Doria in Genoa, a commission that had been given to Baccio Bandinelli in the 1520s but was never completed. According to Vasari, this brought Montorsoli and Bandinelli into a heated conflict. Bandinelli convinced the ducal majordomo, Pierfrancesco Riccio, that Montorsoli's marble *Hercules and Antaeus* was not going well (an opinion disputed by Vasari). Feeling badly treated, Montorsoli decided to leave the work unfinished and move to Genoa, where he is first recorded on March 27, 1539.[36] However, in December 1538 he was already in contact with the Lombard sculptor Giovan Maria da Passalo who was working in Genoa.[37] Montorsoli remained for the most part in Genoa until 1547.[38] Between October and December 1541, he installed the Tomb of Sannazaro in Naples.[39] There is no evidence that Montorsoli was ever in Florence in the 1540s, a decade when he was receptive to influences from Michelangelo, Sansovino, Cosini, and Tribolo.

MONTORSOLI AND MICHELANGELO: A REASSESSMENT

The terracotta *Baptist* provides an opportunity to reassess Michelangelo's influence on Montorsoli, especially on sculptures made for cities more resistant to the celebrated artist's style. For example, Montorsoli's *Saint James* in Naples (FIG. 23) possesses a pictorial treatment of drapery, a wistful expression, a delicacy of the hair, and subtly spiraling locks of the beard that betray a strong debt to the work of Jacopo Sansovino (FIG. 24).[40] Appreciation of the complexity of Montorsoli's sculptural language allows us to move beyond the idea that he was wholly dependent on Michelangelo. In this respect, attention to Giorgio Vasari's biography of Montorsoli helps in a reassessment of his sculpture.

Vasari seems embarrassed at first to recount Montorsoli's beginnings, before the artist fell under Michelangelo's influence. Lacking information on works made in the 1520s and early 1530s, Vasari begins with a description of the *Saint*

FIG. 23
Montorsoli, *Saint James the Greater*, 1536/37–41. Marble, height 155 cm. Church of Santa Maria del Parto, Naples.

S·IACOBVS AP.

Paul and *Moses* in the chapel of Santissima Annunziata, made in 1535 to 1536, when the artist was already more than thirty years old. Vasari then offers a vague list of Montorsoli's early travels, his friendship with Francesco Ferrucci del Tadda, an apprenticeship with Andrea di Piero Ferrucci, work at Saint Peter's in Rome, and the tomb of Raffaele Maffei in Volterra, a collaboration with Silvio Cosini.[41] Finally, we come to the New Sacristy in Florence, where Montorsoli most likely started work in October 1524.[42]

Vasari's account becomes clearer once Montorsoli joins the Servite order in October 1530. The artist, we are told, aspired to a religious life because of an earlier sojourn at the hermitage of Camaldoli, and his decision to become a brother in the order of the Jesuates (Gesuati).[43] Montorsoli's subsequent association with the church of Santissima Annunziata indelibly marked his career. Vasari specifically states that as Montorsoli was preparing to become a priest, he studied the works of Andrea del Sarto at the church as inspiration.[44] Painted between 1509 and 1514, Sarto's frescoes in the Chiostrino dei Voti, the entrance atrium, depict the life of Saint Filippo Benizi, as well as the Birth of the Virgin and the Journey of the Magi (FIG. 25). Sarto's art had considerable effect on sculptors, including Jacopo Sansovino and Silvio Cosini, in addition to Montorsoli. The spiral form and subtle contrapposto of the terracotta *John the Baptist*, as well as its dense drapery (realized in broad crests that converge on the surface of the fleece), all testify to the influence of Andrea del Sarto, in particular, the *Madonna of the Harpies* made for the church of San Francesco dei Macci in 1517 (FIG. 26). Sarto's rendering of John the Evangelist, on the right, is an important source for Montorsoli in its controlled muscular energy beneath the billows of heavy drapery. With one foot on the dais, the figure has a sense of movement, while the powerful forearm is a dominant feature, just as in Montorsoli's terracotta.

The *John the Baptist* should also be examined within the pictorial impulse of Florentine sculpture at the beginning of the sixteenth century, as led by Giovanfrancesco Rustici and Jacopo Sansovino, under the influence of Leonardo da Vinci.[45] Sansovino's sculptures share with Montorsoli's terracotta the rendering of heavy drapery, the turn of the shoulder, and the hand that grasps the cloak to facilitate forward movement. Many of these features are also found in Andrea del Sarto's work, not least in the Annunziata frescoes, which is unsurprising since Sarto and Sansovino were close friends.[46]

FIG. 24
Jacopo Sansovino, *Saint James the Greater*, 1518–20. Marble, height ca. 260 cm. San Giacomo degli Spagnoli, Rome.

FIG. 25
Andrea del Sarto, *The Journey of the Magi* (detail), 1511. Fresco. Chiostrino dei voti, Santissima Annunziata, Florence.

FIG. 26
Andrea del Sarto, *Madonna of the Harpies*,
1517. Oil on wood, 207 × 178 cm.
Galleria degli Uffizi, Florence.

Such affinities demonstrate that during the 1530s, Montorsoli looked intently at the work of the preceding generation. At the same time, the influence of Michelangelo can be strongly felt, especially in the *Baptist*'s sullen and threatening countenance, and most of all in the powerful arms – all reminiscent of Michelangelo's sculptural program in the New Sacristy. The hypothesis that the *John the Baptist* was a model for a work in marble seems highly improbable, and it is more likely to be an independent object. However, Vasari reminds us that the media of terracotta and marble were closely associated, in the description of Montorsoli's work on the *Saint Cosmas* (FIG. 27). Montorsoli, we are told, "made a large model of this figure, which Michelangelo retouched in many parts, then Michelangelo made the head and the arms in clay, which are kept today in Arezzo by Vasari among his most prized possessions, in memory of the man," that is, Michelangelo.[47] The arms modeled by Michelangelo must have struck Montorsoli profoundly because they are directly linked to the Medici tombs, in particular *Day*, in which the arm is powerfully flexed (FIG. 28). This gesture appears in many of Montorsoli's sculptures, in particular the *Saint Cosmas* and the *Baptist*.

The intervention of Michelangelo in the making of the *Saint Cosmas* was therefore providential, as much for the sculpture itself as for Montorsoli's later career. Vasari states: "And in truth, whether it was his own study and diligence, or the assistance of Michelangelo, it proved in the end to be an excellent figure [*ottima figura*] and the best that Montorsoli ever made of the many he produced in his entire life, so that it was

FIG. 27
Montorsoli, *Saint Cosmas* (detail),
1533–37/38. Marble. New Sacristy, San
Lorenzo, Florence.

FIG. 28
Michelangelo, *Day*, 1526–31. Marble,
length 285 cm. New Sacristy, San Lorenzo,
Florence.

truly worthy to be placed where it was."[48] Is it because of Montorsoli's close collaboration with Michelangelo, or because of his own diligence that his statue of *Saint Cosmas* was superior to any of his later work? Perhaps both are true, but in the absence of the model by Montorsoli, or of the head and the arms made by Michelangelo, it is impossible to know how much the intervention shaped the outcome. Nonetheless, as Vasari anticipated, the *Saint Cosmas* remains Montorsoli's masterpiece, and one can certainly agree that it represents an *ottima figura* – an excellent figure – even if this judgment betrays Vasari's exaltation of Michelangelo above all else, a bias that underlies the entire project of the *Lives of the Artists*.

We do not know if Michelangelo or Vasari ever saw the terracotta *John the Baptist*, but perhaps they would have concurred that, even if it is less rhetorically Michelangelesque than *Saint Cosmas*, it is of exceptional quality, worthy of comparison to Montorsoli's best work as yet another *ottima figura*.

1. There is presently a consensus that the sculpture to the left of the Virgin (from the viewer's perspective) is *Saint Cosmas* by Montorsoli, although in the past there was some disagreement about this. For example, Gilbert 1961 and Verellen 1979 suggested that the sculpture on the left was in fact *Saint Damian* by Raffaello da Montelupo. Confirmation that Montorsoli's work is on the left is furnished by the second state of Cornelis Cort's engraving of the group (Sellink 2000, no. 219; see CAT. 13 for the first state of 1570). This print, published in Rossi 1711 (Sellink 2000, pp. 145, 147, incorrectly states it is from 1621), identifies the statue on the left as "S. Cosimo / Scultura di Agnolo da Montorsoli" and that on the right as "S. Damiano / Scultura di Raffaello da Monte Lupo."

2. Vasari 1966, vol. 5, p. 493: "nel condurre la statue del duca Lorenzo e Giuliano si servì molto del frate nel rinettarle e fare certe difficultà di lavori traforati in sotto squadra." This is also implied in a letter from Sebastiano del Piombo to Michelangelo, July 25, 1533 (Poggi 1965, vol. 4, no. CMXIII).

3. The statue of Andrea Doria was initially entrusted to Baccio Bandinelli, who between 1529 and 1536–39 had two blocks of marble excavated, the second of which is today in the square of the cathedral of Carrara (F. Loffredo in Florence 2014, pp. 574–75).

4. The sections appear to be: the head; from the right shoulder to the waist; the left arm and shoulder; from the waist to the knees; and the lower part of the legs and the base. See under CAT. 8.

5. The *Baptist* in the Santissima Annunziata: Laschke 1993, fig. 172. See also the relief of the Baptism of Christ in San Matteo, probably executed with a collaborator; the statue on the altar of the church of the Servites, Bologna; and a relief in the same church: Laschke 1993, figs. 75, 144, 162.

6. The attribution and dating of the *Triton* in the Villa del Principe are based on a letter from Anton Francesco Doni to Montorsoli of June 3, 1543 (or August 9, 1543), recording "il dignissimo mostro marino, che getta in tanta copia l'acqua nel bel giardino del Principe" (Doni 1543, pp. 2r–2v; Doni 1970, pp. 92–96). Vasari 1966, vol. 5, p. 501, also records that Montorsoli "avendo in ultimo fatto, dalla parte dinanzi di detto palazzo [Villa del Principe], un vivaio, fece di marmo un mostro marino di tondo rilievo, che versa in gran copia acqua nella detta peschiera." The correspondence between the description and Montorsoli's style led Laschke 1993, pp. 62–64, 153, 161, no. 11, and others to classify the *Triton* as by Montorsoli. The attribution can also be confirmed thanks

to similarities with the three putti playing at the top of the Fountain of Orion in Messina; Laschke 1993, fig. 111.

Doubts regarding the attribution have arisen from a record in the Doria-Pamphilij archive, Rome (Filza mandati 1581, no. 220), which states that in April 1581, 6 scudi "to the account for the figure that goes above the fountain" (a buon conto et per capparro della figura che va sopra la fontana) were paid to Giovan Giacomo Parraca da Valsoldo (ca. 1546–1597). Another account indicates that the payment was for "del satiro." These records suggest (Merli and Belgrano 1874, p. 57) that the current *Triton* on the fountain might be a later copy by Parraca. However, the *Triton* on the Villa Pallavicino delle Peschiere attributed to Parraca is quite different from that at the Villa del Principe. The attribution of the Peschiere sculpture to Parraca is based on a 1562 commission by Tobia Pallavicino for several unspecified works for his villa, which might have included the fountain (Poleggi 1972, p. 138).

Montorsoli's *Triton* immediately enjoyed great popularity in Genoa as well as in Spain. The fountain of the Peschiere copies that model, and Parraca may also have used the same model for three figures in the Triton Fountain (Fuente de los Tritones) in the gardens of the Palacio Real, Madrid, which came from the Palacio de Aranjuez (see the essay by Ramiro, note 33). In Genoa, other replicas of Montorsoli's work include a late 16th-century fountain with Tritons and Nereids at the Villa Imperiale Scassi a Sampierdarena (Giannattasio and Quartino 1982, pp. 38, 40, fig. 3; Magnani 2005, fig. 170); a fountain at the Villa Balbi Durazzo Gropallo Castelbarco allo Zerbino (A. Lissoni in Cazzato et al. 2002, pp. 91–92), as Giacomo Montanari kindly pointed out to me; and the two Tritons above the cornice leading to the grotto of the Villa Di Negro Rosazza of 1556–66 (Magnani 2005, p. 52, pl. IV). Furthermore, Montorsoli's *Triton* is reproduced in a drawing by Gerard ter Borch the Elder of 1614–16 (Rijksmuseum, Amsterdam, RP-T-1887-A-1180). The statue by Montorsoli was so well known in Genoa that Federico Peschiera (1814–1854) copied it in his *Rinaldo in the Garden of Armida* (Galleria d'Arte Moderna, Genoa).

7. Vasari 1966, vol. 5, p. 499: "molte notomie di corpi umani."

8. Vasari 1966, vol. 5, p. 493: "fare certe difficultà di lavori traforati in sotto squadra."

9. Laschke 1993, p. 159, nos. 2, 3; Pizzorusso 2013, pp. 219–20, 224.

10. Vasari 1966, vol. 5, p. 495: "fece in un dì et una notte due figure di terra grandi quanto il naturale, cioè la Fede e la Carità; le quali, finte di marmo bianco, servirono

per una fonte posticcia, da lui fatta con un gran vaso di rame, che durò a gettar acqua tutto il giorno che fu fatto il Generale, con molta sua lode et onore."

11. Vasari 1966, vol. 5, p. 496, on the decorations for the entry of Charles V on Apr. 28, 1535. Stucco Neptune: ibid., p. 501: "Fece un gran Nettunno di stucco, che sopra un piedistallo fu posto nel giardino del principe."

12. Fleming 1955a, p. 206, no. 44; Borroni Salvadori 1974, p. 105: "Nostro Signore, S. Pietro e S. Paolo." On Hugford, see Fleming 1955 and Fleming 1955a. The connection with Montorsoli's projects was suggested by Laschke 1993, pp. 147, 168, no. 18A.

13. The recto is inscribed: F Gio Angelo Montorsoli; the verso: F. Gio. An.lo. Petrioli Tofani 2003, p. 156, note 29; Petrioli Tofani 2014, pp. 1141, 1144, no. 25. Hugford also provided the portrait drawing of Montorsoli, derived from Vasari 1568, for Serie 1773, after p. 56.

14. Another drawing related to Montorsoli's work in clay is a sketch of his *Saint Paul* in the Annunziata, which is not a preparatory study but a record of the finished work. Uffizi, inv. 14367 F. Laschke 1993, p. 159 [as a later drawing by an unknown hand]; Petrioli Tofani 2003, p. 151 [uncertain]; Petrioli Tofani 2014, p. 1027, no. 12.

15. On Tommaso Gherardini and his collection of Renaissance sculpture, see S. Coltellacci in *Dizionario biografico degli italiani* (Rome, 2000), pp. 616–18; and Tormen 2015, pp. 107–8, 110, 111, 114. On Giovanni degli Alessandri, see Bertini 2005 and Gioli 2012.

16. Archivio di Stato di Firenze, Alessandri 117, Ricevute di Giovanni di Cosimo degli Alessandri, 1790–1791, receipt of Jan. 7, 1791: "Io sottoscritto ho ricevuto dall'Illustrissimo signore Cavaliere Gio. degli Alessandri lire trentacinque per valuta fissata d'accordo di due statue alte circa braccia 2 di terracotta del Montorsoli esprimenti una S. Gio. Battista e l'altra San Paolo. / A me sottoscritto dico in contanti £. 35 / Tommaso Gherardini." The expenditure by Giovanni degli Alessandri is also recorded in his account book for the fiscal year 1790–91; Archivio di Stato di Firenze, Alessandri 499, Entrata e uscita di Giovanni degli Alessandri, 1787–1791, c. 97s: "A spese diverse. Fiorini 5 portò contanti il signor Tommaso Gherardini pittore per valuta di 2 statue di terracotta del Montorsoli alte braccia 2." One florin equals seven lire. Davide Gambino kindly informed me of the documents relating to Alessandri.

17. Archivio di Stato di Firenze, Alessandri 55, ins. 4, Stato patrimoniale di Giovanni degli Alessandri al momento della sua morte, Sept. 20, 1828: "Due basi di legno bianche con filettatura dorata che sostegno due statue, uno esprimente S. Gio. Battista e l'altro San Paolo, situate ambedue nel mezzo delle due pareti della cappella, quali sono di terracotta."

18. Archivio Arcivescovile di Firenze, Cancelleria arcivescovile, Visite pastorali, Documenti di visite pastorali, 47, ins. 36, cc. 122–25: "Ho osservato a metà della chiesa due statue di gesso o stucco poste uno per lato e rappresentanti S. Paolo e S. Giovanni Battista."

19. Paci 1877, pp. 15–16. On the removal of the painting by Empoli, see Ferretti 2000, p. 18, note 5. On the paintings depicting Saint Francis at the Mount of Vernia and Saint John Gualberto Forgiving His Enemy, see Marabottini 1988, p. 284, nos. P23a–b.

20. Colnaghi 1965, nos. 11, 12. The reliefs later belonged to Arthur M. Sackler (Avery 1981, nos. 35, 36) and John Winter; his sale: Sotheby's, London, Dec. 10, 2015 (lots 35, 36).

21. There are other references in Florence to terracotta sculptures of these subjects. Two terracottas of John the Baptist and Saint Paul were in the "luogho vecchio" of the Compagnia di San Giovanni Battista dello Scalzo (Baccioni 1708, p. 48; Dow 2006, p. 118). The Baptist was said to have been modeled in *terracruda* (unfired clay) and presented to the Scalzo in 1584 by Valerio Cioli (O'Brien 2011, pp. 217, 221, docs. 1a, 1b). No mention is made of the artist of the Saint Paul. It is highly unlikely that these sculptures are the pair sold to Giovanni degli Alessandri in 1791, as the style of Valerio Cioli is far removed from Montorsoli's terracotta. The last indication of the works' presence in the Scalzo is an inventory of 1783, just before the Leopoldine suppression (Dow 2014, p. 86). These statues, together with an image of the Virgin, formed part of a cycle of twelve clay sculptures of the Apostles.

In addition to the statue by Cioli, another clay figure of the Baptist was in the Scalzo, modeled in 1590 by Carlo di Cesare Terra (O'Brien 2011, pp. 215, 256, doc. 42c), a little-known sculptor, very probably identifiable with Carlo di Cesare del Palagio, a Giambolognesque artist active in Bavaria, where he also made ephemeral decoration. Both names are associated with temporary decorative projects. Carlo di Cesare Terra is recorded in Florence in 1588 in connection with scenery decoration at the Teatro Mediceo (Testaverde Matteini 1991, pp. 63, 177–79, 185), and in 1590 is recorded at again at the Scalzo (O'Brien 2013, p. 415, note 430). Carlo di Cesare del Palagio was probably in Florence in 1589 to make decorations for the marriage of Ferdinando de' Medici and Christine of Lorraine (Diemer 2004, vol. 1, p. 43).

A third terracotta of John the Baptist (height 75 cm) remains above the door of the Scalzo. Dow 2014, pp. 85–86, fig. 3.9, claims that this is the work by Carlo Terra, but this cannot be the case as it was evidently made in the first quarter of the 16th century. In fact, the work can be connected with two similar glazed terracottas: one attributed to Master of the John Statuettes was with Alexandre Imbert and Seligmann, Rey and Co., New York (Riccetti 2014, pp. 50, 55, fig. 3); the other, dated 1504, is in the altarpiece by Benedetto Buglioni in the church of Santa Maria Assunta in Fabbrica di Peccioli (Gentilini 1992, vol. 2, pp. 396–97, 456).

22. Vasari 1966, vol. 5, p. 492; Casalini 1974, p. 301 note 38.

23. A letter from Sebastiano del Piombo in Rome to Michelangelo in Florence, on July 15, 1532, indicates that Montorsoli had already worked with Michelangelo but that he had not yet arrived in Rome (Poggi 1965, vol. 3, no. DCCCLXXXI).

24. Laschke 1993, p. 13. A papal brief from Clement VII dated July 12, 1533, to the superior general of the Servites, Girolamo da Lucca, excused Montorsoli from his monastic vows.

25. Sebastiano del Piombo, Rome, to Michelangelo, Florence; Poggi 1965, vol. 4, no. CMXIII: "in opera su la figura del Ducca Juliano." On July 17, Sebastiano had written that Montorsoli was already at work in the Medici Chapel; ibid., no. CMX. Vasari 1966, vol. 5, pp. 493–94, confirms Montorsoli's work on the figures of the dukes.

26. Sebastiano del Piombo to Michelangelo, Aug. 16, 1533; Poggi 1965, vol. 4, no. CMXXV.

27. Vasari 1966, vol. 5, p. 494.

28. Vasari 1966, vol. 5, pp. 494–95.

29. Vasari 1966, vol. 5, p. 495.

30. Laschke 1993, pp. 35, 159.

31. Vasari 1966, vol. 5, pp. 495–96. On the Annunziata sculptures, see Laschke 1993, pp. 34–35, 156, 159, nos. 2, 3.

32. Vasari 1966, vol. 5, p. 496. Laschke 1993, p. 16.

33. Vasari 1966, vol. 5, pp. 496–97. Laschke 1993, p. 52. In late July 1537, Khaireddin Barbarossa landed in Castro, south of Otranto, and news of this reached Rome on

August 2 (Setton 1976, vol. 3, pp. 431–32; vol. 4, p. 585).

34. Campori 1873, pp. 317, 332–33.

35. Saint Cosmas: Vasari 1966, vol. 5, p. 497; Laschke 1993, p. 16. Villa di Castello: Wright 1976, pp. 165–67, 626–31.

36. Alizeri 1870, vol. 5, pp. 327–28.

37. This can be deduced from a record of a lost document in the notes of Pietro Andrei (Archivio di stato di Massa): an act drawn up by Leonardo Bernoccio on Dec. 14, 1538: "MDXXXVIII Ind. XI. 14 Decembris Maestro Giovanni Maria Passallo, lapicida habitator Ianue, a nome del magnifico Gregorio Pallavicino, genovese, come da instrumento per mano et cetera riservata [rectius tamen] scriptura obligationis nuper facta inter magistrum Jacobum Mariam et dictum Antonio nomine magistri Fratris Angeli lapicide sculptoris et cetera."

38. The last reference to Montorsoli's presence in Genoa appears in a letter of June 17, 1547, written from Rome to Cosimo I, where Montorsoli states "ò dato fine all'opra del Signor principe d'Oria in Genova" (I have finished the work for Prince Doria in Genoa) (Archivio di Stato di Firenze, Mediceo del Principato, filza 383, c. 63r; published by Gaye 1839, vol. 2, p. 365, no. CCLV; Laschke 1993, p. 18).

39. Principi 2014, p. 116.

40. On the Sansovino-like quality of the Saint James in Naples, see Manara 1959, p. 25 note 17.

41. The starting date of the Maffei tomb is established by a contract of Jan. 21, 1529, between Mario Maffei, brother of Raffaele and a certain "Johannino da Firenze scarpellinus," identified by D'Amico 1987, pp. 479–82, as Montorsoli. However, this cannot be a reference to Montorsoli, since he assumed the name Giovan Angelo only on his ordination on Mar. 3, 1532. For example, he is called "Angelo dell'Ordine degli Iniesuati" when welcomed into the Servite order (Casalini 1974, p. 301 note 38). The "Johannino" mentioned in the Maffei contract is more likely to be Giovanni di Sandro de' Rossi da Fiesole, a collaborator of Cosini's (Dalli Regoli and Turchi 1991, p. 47; Campigli 2014, pp. 84–85). It is not possible to say when the commission passed from this Johannino to Silvio Cosini, but the latter was probably already at work on the tomb in the summer of 1529 (D'Amico 1987, p. 482 note 54), and in a letter of Nov. 11, 1531, Cosini is mentioned explicitly. Work must have been concluded shortly after Nov. 13, 1532, when Silvio was engaged

on the final phase of stuccoes for the tomb. Regarding Montorsoli's work on the Maffei tomb, Campigli 2005, p. 141 note 421, proposed an attribution to Montorsoli of the third pilaster on the left, a structure that is not attributable to Cosini, as earlier noted by Del Bravo 1992, p. 19 note 9.

42.   Ciardi et al. 1988: "Un sepolcro per un vescovo," note 12: Montorsoli seems to be identifiable with the "Agnolo" paid for twelve days of work at the rate of 16 soldi per day between Oct. 8 and 15, 1524 (Bardeschi Ciulich and Barocchi 1970, pp. 150–51, nos. CXLII–CXLIII). This identification is also suggested by the presence of Cosini and Francesco del Tadda in the same documents. On Montorsoli as one of the stonecutters for the workshop of San Lorenzo, see also Laschke 1993, pp. 12, 23–24; and Campigli 2006, pp. 101–2.

43.   Vasari 1966, vol. 5, p. 492. On Montorsoli's time with the Jesuates in Florence, see Laschke 1993, pp. 12–13.

44.   Vasari 1966, vol. 5, p. 492: "L'anno poi 1531, avendo in quel mentre apparato le cerimonie e uffici di quell'ordine, e studiato l'opere d'Andrea del Sarto che sono in quel luogo, fece, come dicono essi, professione; e l'anno seguente, con piena sodisfazione di quei padri e contentezza de' suoi parenti, cantò la sua prima messa con molta pompa et onore." On Montorsoli's interest in Sarto, see Cherubini 2005, p. 138.

45.   On the "gusto pittorico," see Bode 1892, text vol., pp. 165–66; Ciardi Dupré 1963, p. 30.

46.   Vasari 1966, vol. 4, p. 346; Cecchi 1986, pp. 47–50; Boucher 1991, vol. 1, pp. 3–23, 27–28.

47.   Vasari 1966, vol. 5, p. 494: "fece un modello grande di quella figura, che fu ritocco dal Buonarroto in molte parti: anzi fece di sua mano Michelagnolo la testa e le braccia di terra, che sono oggi in Arezzo tenute dal Vasari fra le sue più care cose, per memoria di tanto uomo." A letter from Vasari to Pietro Aretino of July 15, 1535 or 1538, testifies to the arrival in Venice of a "testa d'uno de gli avocati della gloriosa casa de i Medici" (Gottschewski 1909; Gilbert 1961, p. 19; Verellen 1979, p. 275), which Vasari had sent to Aretino. This is probably a copy of the model made by Michelangelo for one of the saints in the New Sacristy. Critics have debated whether this is related to Saint Cosmas or Saint Damian; it is recorded, according to Gilbert 1961, in a drawing in the Ringling Museum, Sarasota (SN705), which is attributed to Tintoretto or Palma il Giovane (Smith 1981; Marciari 2002, pp. 117, 120, figs. 9–10). This drawing would appear to be a copy of the Michelangelo model sent by Vasari to Aretino.

48.   Vasari 1966, vol. 5, p. 494: "E nel vero, o fusse lo studio e la diligenza di lui, o l'aiuto di Michelagnolo, ella riuscì poi ottima figura e la migliore che mai facesse il frate di quante ne lavorò in vita sua; onde fu veramente degna di essere, dove fu, collocata."

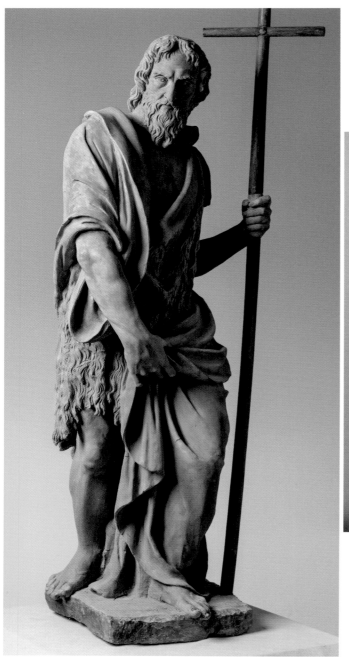

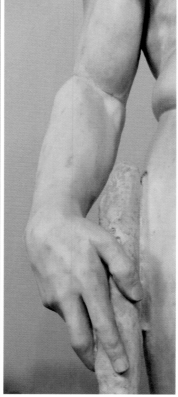

THE BAPTIST AND MARS

IDENTITY SHIFTS IN RENAISSANCE FLORENCE

Kurt Sundstrom

GIOVAN ANGELO MONTORSOLI'S SCULPTURE OF JOHN THE BAPTIST (FIG. I), now in the Currier Museum of Art, compels our attention both for its invention and its close connection with life in Florence. We know nothing about its original location or who commissioned it, but the energetic style of the terracotta allows us to date it to the 1530s, when the artist spent most of his time in Florence. Montorsoli likely made *John the Baptist* during one of two extended stays in the city, either between 1530 and 1532, or 1533 and 1539. Montorsoli entered the Order of the Servites on October 7, 1530, and took up residence in the church of Santissima Annunziata. He remained in Florence until September 1532, when he departed for Rome on Michelangelo's recommendation and at Pope Clement VII's request. At the Vatican, Montorsoli restored celebrated ancient statues. At the same time, he assisted Michelangelo on the Tomb of Julius II. In July 1533, Montorsoli returned to Florence, again at the pope's request, so that he could work with Michelangelo on the New Sacristy. Montorsoli was assigned the task of carving the marble sculpture of Saint Cosmas. Clement VII's death on September 25, 1534, led to Michelangelo's permanent departure from Florence at the end of the year, and work on the New Sacristy was left to assistants.[1] At the end of 1537 or beginning of 1538, Montorsoli completed the *Saint Cosmas*.[2] After an extended stay in Genoa, and following a conflict with the sculptor Baccio Bandinelli in 1547, Montorsoli left Florence for Messina, not returning for any length of time until after Bandinelli died in 1560.

The stylistic similarities between *John the Baptist* and Montorsoli's additions to the ancient sculptures in the Vatican suggest that they were done in the same period. On the *Hercules and Telephos*, the restored section of Hercules's right arm begins above the elbow, where the seam is clearly visible (FIG. 2). The articulation of the veins from the right forearm to the hand in both the Baptist and Hercules has a similar soft and smooth, fleshy quality. It may be coincidental that the arms fall in similar positions, but the definition of the musculature and the anatomical precision in the sculptures are nearly identical.

A tantalizing detail occurs in Montorsoli's replacement of the left arm of *Apollo Belvedere* (FIG. 3). Here Montorsoli rendered the grip of the bow as materially integrated with Apollo's hand. This is also his design for the raised arm of *John the Baptist*, where the closed fist encircles an equivalent length of the cross shaft, rendered together seamlessly in clay. As far as I am aware, there is no precedent for this assembly in a sculpture of John the Baptist. In all sculptures that include a cross, the hand or crux of the arm is not engaged materially with the shaft, but fashioned separately.

Montorsoli's formulation may have been based on the work of Antico, the court sculptor in Mantua, who created a bronze statuette of *Apollo Belvedere* around 1498 (FIG. 4). Even though Antico created his *Apollo* for the Mantua court, his design probably circulated in Rome before Montorsoli began his restoration of the marble. It may be significant that Antico and Montorsoli made their Apollo and John the Baptist figures by modeling wax or clay, rather than carving stone, and in both cases formed tubular openings within integrated grips to receive separate objects (a bow for the Apollo and a cross for the Baptist).[3]

While Montorsoli is not known for working in clay, his *John the Baptist* is an important example created during a resurgence of terracotta that began in the middle of the fifteenth century. Terracotta works were cheaper to produce, which allowed the middle class to adorn their homes with works of art. Terracotta was also used to produce veristic portraits, theatrical religious tableaux, and preparatory studies for larger

FIG. 4
Antico, *Apollo Belvedere*, ca. 1498. Bronze, partly gilded and silvered, height 41.3 cm. Liebieghaus Skulpturensammlung, Frankfurt. 1286.

FIG. 5
Michelozzo, *John the Baptist*,
1452. Terracotta, height
213 cm. Santissima
Annunziata, Florence.

works or works in bronze or marble.[4] The costlier media of marble and bronze were still preferred for large sculptures and prestigious public commissions. There were exceptions, of course, one of the most important being the life-size terracotta of *John the Baptist* made by Michelozzo around 1452 for the church of the Annunziata in Florence (FIG. 5). Michelozzo's figure was an extraordinary technical achievement, unprecedented at the time, which made clear that terracotta was a viable medium for monumental, three-dimensional sculptures. This work elevated the medium's popularity in Florence.

Although Montorsoli must have walked past Michelozzo's sculpture daily, it had little influence on his own image of John the Baptist, aside from the choice of medium. In fact, the numerous public representations of the Baptist in Florence have little in common with Montorsoli's sculpture. Since depictions of the Baptist are often closely tied to that city's social and civic institutions, it is natural that his visage was adapted according to location, function, and the political climate at the time a given. Modifications of standard forms often signal a shift in meaning that is tied to contemporaneous events.

At the time Montorsoli began shaping his *Baptist*, the Florentine Republican government had been under assault by supporters of the Medici family for more than two decades. After a long period as Florence's dominant family, the Medici consolidated their power in 1512, but the Republic was briefly restored beginning in 1527. Troops of the Holy Roman Empire sacked Rome that year and imprisoned Pope Clement VII. However, as leader of the Medici family, Clement quickly formed an alliance with Emperor Charles V to secure the help of the imperial army to restore Medici control of Florence.

It is likely that Montorsoli conceived his sculpture of John the Baptist in response to these fast-moving political events. The war between Republican Florence and the Holy Roman Empire from 1527 to 1530 proved disastrous for the city's economy. Florence was besieged by the imperial army, which made obtaining sustenance difficult. City finances were so strained that in the early months of 1530, the governing body, the Signoria, passed a resolution that all silver and gold in private hands were to be given to the mint to pay mercenaries and purchase weapons.[5] These dire conditions continued for several years, even after the city's capitulation in August 1530. The possibility of acquiring costly materials like marble and bronze was inconceivable, but clay was readily available, and the expediency of creating a work in terracotta must have appealed to Montorsoli. Clay allowed the artist to model and fire a sculpture within weeks, thereby responding to the quickly changing social and political conditions in Florence.[6]

CIVIC PATRONS: JOHN THE BAPTIST AND MARS

It is revealing that Montorsoli chose this particular moment to depict John the Baptist, the city's patron saint, who was traditionally regarded as the protector of the Florentine Republic. As hope for the restoration of the Republic began to fade with the appointment of Alessandro de' Medici as duke of Florence in 1532, images of John the Baptist became less common. The process of moving from a republic to a hereditary monarchy was slow but inevitable. Later in 1532, the Signoria was abolished. This body had governed the city since the late thirteenth century and had been the heart of Florentine life. Its demise represented the end of the Florentine Republic, which had existed in varying forms since 1115. The most conspicuous declaration of Medici supremacy occurred on the city's coin, the florin (FIG. 6). According to the Republican Galeotto Giugni, Duke Alessandro "changed the shape of the coins, and removed the people's sign, and in place of it in one part put up his family arms . . . and in the other where there had been carved the image of the precursor to Christ, Saint John the Baptist, there he had stamped the image of Saints

FIG. 6
Gold florin of the Florentine Republic, ca. 1252–1303. Obverse: John the Baptist; reverse: lily of Florence. Gold, diameter 1.95 cm. British Museum, London. 1885,0405.20.

Cosmas and Damian, the patron saints of the House of Medici, so that no memory remains of the ancient republic or of freedom."[7] With the removal of John the Baptist from the florin in 1534, representations of the saint as the symbol of civic pride begin to wane. The last gasp from the Florentine Republic came in 1537, when the young Duke Cosimo I de' Medici defeated a rebellion hoping to restore the old republic at the Battle of Montemurlo.

If Montorsoli created his figure of John the Baptist around 1533, before the complete dismantling of the historic Florentine Republic the following year, it would be among the last depictions of the city's patron saint produced in Florence during the sixteenth century. While political turmoil may account for the disappearance of the Baptist as a civic symbol, it could also offer an explanation for the unusual rendering of the terracotta in the Currier Museum, which falls well outside long-established artistic traditions. To better understand the sculpture, it will be necessary to trace the iconographic development of John the Baptist and the reasons behind the saint's appeal to Florentines.

John the Baptist recognized Christ as the Messiah and baptized him, and therefore is often called the Precursor.[8] According to legend, Florence adopted John the Baptist as its patron saint in the fourth century, when the city converted to Christianity.[9] However, his symbolic role in civic and religious life was not cemented until centuries later. Florence initially also relied on the protection of local saints, such as the early Christian martyrs Saint Zenobius, the first bishop of Florence, whose relics were housed in its first cathedral, and Saint Reparata, to whom the cathedral was dedicated. Early Florentine Christians believed that invoking an indigenous saint would be more efficacious. As Florence rose to economic and artistic prominence in the thirteenth century, John the Baptist became a more recognizable symbol; regional saints like Reparata were no longer regarded as appropriate personifications of a mighty city.[10]

Mars had been the protector of Florence in antiquity, and the selection of John the Baptist to succeed Mars as the city's patron saint was logical. Just as Mars was second only to Jupiter, the Baptist was considered the right hand of Christ – the saint and savior often appeared together in depictions of the Holy Family. John was invoked as the protector of agriculture, as Mars had been, with his feast occurring on the northern solstice, like the Mars-linked festival that called for a fruitful harvest.[11] Both John the Baptist and Mars were revered for their courage and warlike character. As humanist thought spread through Italy, such connections between pagan and Christian figures became acceptable.

At the same time, Florence claimed ancestry as an important ancient Roman colony. This assertion was buttressed by the belief that an ancient temple dedicated to Mars lay beneath the city's baptistery (in fact, it was probably built on a tower of the ancient city walls).[12] Giovanni Villani, a contemporary of Dante, wrote that Pope Sylvester reconsecrated the temple of Mars to John the Baptist in the early fourth century.[13] An ancient equestrian statue of Mars on a column was thought to have stood in the middle of the Baptistery. After it was moved to the Ponte Vecchio, it was swept away in the flood of 1333.[14] Dante, in the early fourteenth century, makes explicit reference to Florence's ancient bond to Mars:

> O hear them round my ruin! I was born
> in the city that tore down Mars and raised the Baptist.
> On that account the God of War has sworn
>
> Her sorrow shall not end. And were it not
> That something of his image still survives
> On the bridge across the Arno, some have thought
>
> Those citizens who of their love and pain
> Afterwards rebuilt it from the ashes
> Left by Attila, would have worked in vain.
>   Dante, *Inferno*, 13.142–50[15]

Giorgio Vasari memorialized this on the ceiling of the Salone dei Cinquecento in the Palazzo Vecchio by depicting the statue of Mars atop a column within the foundation of the Baptistery (FIG. 7).

The Baptistery and the statue of Mars on the Ponte Vecchio marked two of the city's boundaries in the Middle Ages, and the spirit of Mars as war god never disappeared from the Baptistery. The war carriages (*carracci*) that bore the city flags and an altar into battle in Dante's time were housed in the Baptistery, as were the standards of cities subject to Florence.[16] The city's militias gathered at the Baptistery and the statue of Mars in times of crisis, as Dante reminds us.

> Of men who could bear arms there were counted then,
> Between Mars and the Baptist, the fifth part
> Of what may be mustered there from living men.
>   Dante, *Paradiso*, 16.46-48[17]

Both the pagan god Mars and the biblical John the Baptist were used to champion not only Florence, but also its Republican government. The relationship between the figures is significant to our understanding of civic and spiritual life in Florence, and by extension to Montorsoli's sculpture.

FIG. 7
Giorgio Vasari and workshop, *Foundation of Florentia, a Roman Settlement* (detail), 1563–65. Oil on wood. Salone dei Cinquecento, Palazzo Vecchio, Florence.

DEPICTIONS OF JOHN THE BAPTIST IN FLORENCE

In the sixteenth century, perhaps no other figure, religious or secular, was laden with more inherent meaning for Florence than John the Baptist. So ubiquitous was his image that one could barely walk down a street without seeing the city's patron saint. Representations of the Baptist in Renaissance Florence varied greatly, ranging from his birth, childhood, adolescence, and adulthood to his imprisonment, death, and burial. From Ghiberti to Michelangelo, every major Florentine sculptor took up the subject. From 1252 to 1534, an image of the Baptist appeared on all Florentine coins (see FIG. 6), which circulated widely throughout Europe. John the Baptist featured prominently in the city's annual celebrations, and even today the most important holiday on the Florentine calendar remains June 24, the nativity of the saint. Occasionally, narrative images of the Baptist referenced the city's political, social, religious, economic, and civic life. Florentine citizens could easily decipher the particular meanings and nuances inflected by various artists.

Beginning in the thirteenth century, images of the young Baptist were commonly used for inspirational

FIG. 8
John the Baptist Enters the Wilderness, ca. 1275–1300. Mosaic. Ceiling of the Baptistery, Florence.

and spiritual instruction in homes, whether elite or modest. While bronze and marble were the preferred media of the aristocracy, the emerging merchant-class demand for affordable images helped revive the techniques of terracotta, stucco, and papier-mâché (*cartapesta*). Not only were these media less expensive, they could also be used in combination with molds to produce large numbers of images. Driving the demand for depictions of the young John the Baptist were the writings of Giovanni Dominici (ca. 1356–1419), who recommended that parents display images of the Christ Child and the young John the Baptist as religious and moral examples for their children (see CAT. 1). Born in Florence, Dominici knew well the importance of John the Baptist to the city. His *Regola del governo di cura familiar* of 1403 outlined five rules for the raising of children.[18]

In public settings, the young Baptist is most often shown at the age when he is about to enter the wilderness, or is already living there. One of the earliest depictions in Florence of this scene is on the mosaic ceiling of the Baptistery (FIG. 8), where the saint is shown wearing a camel shirt under a wool garment, holding in one hand a reed cross and in the other a banner. He strides into the landscape, leaving the comfort of an open countryside for rough, mountainous terrain spotted by trees. The landscape forecasts the difficulties he will soon endure. It was in this rugged environment that the Baptist adopted the austere life of a hermit. This vignette in a vast mosaic illustrating the Book of Genesis and the lives of innumerable Christian figures established the prototype for later Florentine images of the Baptist entering the wilderness (see CAT. 2). Influential fifteenth-century examples include a sculpture by Antonio Rossellino (see p. 97) and paintings by Filippo Lippi in the Palazzo Medici (1459) and Domenico Ghirlandaio in Santa Maria Novella (FIG. 9).

The most visually impressive and technically accomplished representations of the adult Baptist are the monumental sculptures commissioned to adorn the exteriors of important economic and ecclesiastical buildings in Florence. The greatest density of major Baptist imagery occurs, not surprisingly, on the Baptistery, then as now the center of religious life in Florence. Until 1874, all Catholic citizens of the city were baptized in the Baptistery. On its exterior, a set of doors and three groups of sculptures recount the life of John the Baptist, while inside a figure of the saint sits enthroned in the chancel.

Perhaps the most amazing feat of technical skill in the fourteenth century was the production of the Baptistery's doors by Andrea Pisano, who depicted scenes from the life of John the Baptist (FIG. 10).[19] When the massive bronze doors on the south portal were unveiled on the Baptist's feast day, June 24, 1336, it was the most expensive art project in Florence's history. Not only the patron saint of the city, John the Baptist was also the patron of the Cloth Guild, called the Calimala, which commissioned the work.[20]

In successive centuries, the Cloth Guild continued to fund images of the Baptist for Florence. Between 1412 and 1416, Lorenzo Ghiberti made an over-life-size statue of the saint for the exterior of Florence's economic hub, the Orsanmichele. More than eight feet tall and made in four pieces, the figure (FIG. 11) was the largest bronze cast since the fall of ancient Rome. It was also the first bronze since antiquity to be cast using the lost wax method. The work's strong ancient references, in style and in technique, reinforced the claim that Florence and its citizens were the equals of ancient Rome.

In the early sixteenth century, the Cloth Guild planned monumental sculptural groups to be placed above the doors of the Baptistery. Andrea Sansovino's *Baptism of Christ* was begun in 1505 (FIG. 12), and Giovanfrancesco Rustici's *Preaching of the Baptist* was executed between 1506 and 1511 (FIG. 13). Six decades passed before the third portal group was commissioned for the Baptistery – Vincenzo Danti's *Beheading of John the Baptist* (FIG. 14). By then, after the fall of the Republic and the establishment of Medici rule, public commissions of representations of John the Baptist were

FIG. 9
Domenico Ghirlandaio, *John the Baptist in the Wilderness*, 1485–90. Fresco. Cappella Tornabuoni, Santa Maria Novella, Florence.

FIG. 10
Andrea Pisano, *Histories of John the Baptist*, 1336. Bronze. Museo dell'Opera del Duomo, Florence. Door from the south portal of the Baptistery.

FIG. 11
Lorenzo Ghiberti. *John the Baptist*, 1412–16. Bronze, height 255 cm. Orsanmichele, Florence.

Andrea Sansovino, *Baptism of Christ*,
1505. Marble, height 282 cm and
260 cm. Above the east portal of the
Baptistery, Florence; now in the Museo
dell'Opera del Duomo, Florence.

Giovanfrancesco Rustici,
Preaching of John the Baptist, 1506–11.
Bronze, height 265 cm. Above the
north portal of the Baptistery, Florence;
now in the Museo dell'Opera del
Duomo, Florence.

Vincenzo Danti, *Beheading of John the
Baptist*, 1569–71. Bronze, height 243 cm.
Above the south portal of the Baptistery,
Florence; now in the Museo dell'Opera
del Duomo, Florence.

rare.[21] The precise motivation for this exceptional choice, made under the Medici government, is unknown, but Danti's sculptural group may allude to the death of the Florentine Republic, for which John the Baptist stood. In 1569, the very year in which Vincenzo Danti commenced the *Beheading of John the Baptist*, Cosimo de' Medici was created Grand Duke of Tuscany by Pope Pius V. He was no longer merely ruler of Florence, but a monarch who could claim dominion over a large portion of Italy. It is in this context that Danti's massive bronzes were unveiled on the evening prior to the vigil of the feast day of John the Baptist in 1571.[22]

Andrea del Sarto's *Holy Family with the Young John the Baptist*

In painting, the young Baptist most commonly appears in association with the Virgin and the Christ Child. He is shown about the same age as the Christ Child, with attributes such as his camel hair garment, banner, reed cross, and wool mantle. Typically, John gestures toward the cross or the Christ Child. Such images in public ecclesiastical spaces were intended for devotional purposes. On occasion, private commissions took liberties with traditional representations.

Artists sometimes employed the image of John the Baptist as an instrument of propaganda, but always in a pro-Florentine context. An extraordinary example of such artistic invention is Andrea del Sarto's painting of the Holy Family (FIG. 15), in which the artist and patron chose to use this standard subject to highlight political unrest and the social struggles of the day. Andrea del Sarto's composition was created shortly after the ouster of the Medici and restoration of the Florentine Republic in 1527. Commissioned by Giovanni Borgherini, an ardent supporter of the Republic, the painting echoes the political hopes and aspirations of his patron. In a highly unusual gesture, Christ passes the orb, the symbol of his power over the world, to John the Baptist – and by extension to the Florentine people.[23] The absence of any reference to an individual ruler or prince is marked. Unfortunately for Borgherini and other opponents of the Medici, the Republican movement ended not long after, when Florence was besieged by imperial troops from October 1529 to August 1530. With the capitulation of the city, Pope Clement VII installed his nephew Alessandro de' Medici as ruling duke of Florence. Borgherini was forced to beg for pardon in September 1530, which happened to be the month of the Andrea del Sarto's death.

FIG. 15
Andrea del Sarto, *The Holy Family with the Young John the Baptist*, ca. 1528–29. Oil on wood, 135.9 × 100.6 cm. The Metropolitan Museum of Art, New York. Maria DeWitt Jesup Fund, 1922, 22.75.

Montorsoli's *John the Baptist*

It was while the Florentine Republic was in the final stages of collapse that Montorsoli created his terracotta sculpture of John the Baptist (FIG. 16). Many elements of the work are commonly encountered in other depictions of the saint: he wears a camel skin, holds a staff with a cross, and gathers his wool overcoat with his right hand. The similarities end there. He is not baptizing, preaching, or waiting for the executioner's axe to drop. He is not an emaciated hermit living in the wilderness; rather, his muscular build and aggressive posture convey a sense of power. Florentine sculpture before 1530 rarely shows figures striding. The only time the Baptist ever appears striding is as a child, and in almost every case, whether painted or sculpted, he is shown moving laterally. Montorsoli's illusion of breaking into the viewer's space is unprecedented. And finally, nowhere in the cannon of John the Baptist imagery is the staff rendered so thickly.[24]

Montorsoli's sculpture, then, does not fall within the expansive parameters of John the Baptist iconography. The terracotta does not seem meant to inspire devotion. Is it possible that this determined figure was not intended for a religious context?

The striding deity

Montorsoli's *John the Baptist* stands apart from tradition most dramatically in his heroic, striding posture. The stance is not a classical contrapposto weight shift, but rather a variation upon the ancient Greek invention of *serpentinata* (serpentine form) and *rythmos*, as seen in the *Discobolus*. Instead of centering the figure's weight on a vertical axis, Montorsoli projects the statue's bulk beyond its core. This sense of

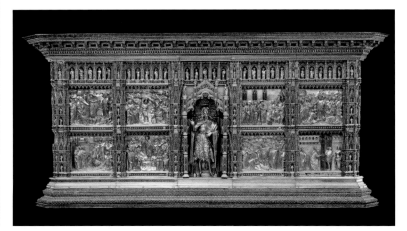

FIG. 16
Montorsoli, *John the Baptist*, 1530s.
Terracotta. Currier Museum
of Art.

FIG. 17
Mars Gradivus. Roman, 2nd century.
Marble, height 360 cm. Musei
Capitolini, Rome. From the Forum of
Nerva, Rome.

FIG. 18
Silver Altar from the Baptistery, Florence (1337–1483),
with the central figure of John the Baptist (1452) by
Michelozzo. Museo dell'Opera del Duomo, Florence.

FIG. 19
Detail of the left hand of FIG. 16.

unstable weight distribution creates the illusion of forward thrust. The bending of the knees and the staff supporting the body together enhance this sense of movement. Montorsoli's figure shares some features of Jacopo Sansovino's *Saint James* (see p. 19) in the activated torso of the upper body, with the left shoulder pushed forward and the right shoulder twisting back. By comparison, however, the legs of Montorsoli's Baptist bend more powerfully and demonstrably advance.

Montorsoli's striding Baptist derives from ancient representations of Mars Gradivus, or Mars the Strider, who was an important cult figure in ancient Roman art (FIG. 17). The Striding Mars protected Rome, its citizens, and its soldiers; and according to Livy was one of the gods by whom a general or soldier might swear an oath.[25] More specifically, the conjunction of civic protection and Mars was a well-established theme in ancient Roman propaganda. As previously noted, in Renaissance Florence the civic protector's evolution from Mars to the Baptist was well known, making it possible that Montorsoli deliberately adopted aspects of the war god's physique. Given the familiarity of the Baptist's predecessor, it is also likely that a Renaissance audience would have recognized the terracotta's Mars-like features.

During the final years of the Florentine Republic, the Baptist was invoked to propagate a message of civic unity just as Mars Gradivus had been in ancient Rome. Florence's militia was reinvigorated during the imperial siege of the city. The ceremony to induct new militia members took place between the Baptistery and the Duomo. There, young men swore allegiance to Florence and took up arms. In 1529, the ritual took place during the Feast of John the Baptist, and the Baptistery's Silver Altar (FIG. 18), with its central figure of the Baptist by Michelozzo, was moved outside for the oath ceremony.[26] The following year, the council of Florence codified this practice, which continued until 1534.[27]

Along with his striding posture, Montorsoli's *Baptist* further diverges from traditional Florentine depictions of the saint in the sculpting of the face. Rather than an emaciated hermit, the visage seems to be a deliberate evocation of a mature ancient warrior. Through the Baptist's martial expression, powerful stride, and muscular anatomy, Montorsoli has blended warrior and saint.

The most conspicuous departure from tradition and the strongest reference to Mars in the terracotta is Montorsoli's substitution of the simple reed cross with a thick, lance-like instrument. As far as I am aware there is no iconographic precedent for this. Although we cannot be certain of what the figure originally held

FIG. 20
Roman, *Mars and Rhea Silvia*, ca. 230–40 BC.
Marble, 125 × 245 cm. Palazzo Mattei, Rome.

FIG. 21
Silver denarius of Severus Alexander. Rome,
232–35. Reverse: "Mars Ultor." Silver,
diameter 1.9 cm. Currier Museum
of Art.

(the present cross is a replacement), the opening modeled into the terracotta hand of the figure (FIG. 19) makes clear that the shaft was thicker than tradition dictated. The gesture is even more important: Montorsoli's figure firmly grips the instrument as though he were holding a weapon such as a lance or a pike. This contrasts starkly with earlier representations of the Baptist where a thin reed cross might lean against his arm or be gently held.

The Baptist's gesture as crafted by Montorsoli directly recalls figures of Mars from ancient Rome.[28] The feature can be seen in the sculpture of *Mars Gradivus*, although it has lost both the top and lower part of the spear, and on a sarcophagus of Mars and Rhea Silvia from the third century (FIG. 20). The gesture can also be seen on Roman coins, which could be found everywhere in Italy. A denarius minted in the reign of Severus Alexander (222–35) shows Mars holding a spear in the same manner (FIG. 21). Andrea Mantegna included exactly this type of figure in his painting of *Parnassus* made for Isabella d'Este in 1497 (Musée du Louvre, Paris).

This blurring of past and present helped to make emphatic the relationship between Renaissance Florence and the ancient Roman Republic. It is very likely that Montorsoli's Baptist/Mars was intended to stir pro-Republican citizens toward reclaiming the city's glorious past. Montorsoli's contribution to the dual nature of John the Baptist by tapping ancient representations of Mars (which reminded viewers of the saint's ancient precursor as city patron) reflects the new historical insightfulness of Renaissance art.

The role of John the Baptist as symbol of the Florentine Republic was quickly suppressed by the new Medici regime under Duke Cosimo I as the Palazzo Vecchio was remade to celebrate the new regime. Before the Medici dukes came to power, the palazzo had celebrated the Florentine Republic, but the subsequent transformation of the building was so comprehensive that within a few decades, the only major wall painting to survive the Medici ascendancy was the fresco in the Sala dei Gigli by Domenico Ghirlandaio.[29] This room had been used to greet important dignitaries, and was the most suitable site to celebrate the virtues of Republican government. Donatello's marble *David* (now in the Bargello) was

FIG. 22
Benedetto da Maiano, *Doorway in the Sala dei
Gigli with John the Baptist*, ca. 1478–80. Palazzo
Vecchio, Florence.

FIG. 23
Giorgio Vasari, *Duke Alessandro de' Medici as Mars*, 1555–62. Fresco. Sala di Leone X, Palazzo Vecchio, Florence.

FIG. 24
Giorgio Vasari, *Duke Cosimo I de' Medici as Augustus*, 1555–62. Fresco. Sala di Leone X, Palazzo Vecchio, Florence.

FIG. 25
Francesco Salviati, *Mars*, 1543–45. Fresco. Sala delle Udienze, Palazzo Vecchio, Florence.

installed there in 1416. Sixty years later, the Signoria purchased Andrea del Verrocchio's bronze *David* from Lorenzo and Giuliano de' Medici, and installed it a few feet from Donatello's statue. In 1476, Benedetto da Maiano was asked to fashion a doorway between the Sala dei Gigli and the Sala delle Udienze (FIG. 22). Atop the portal facing the Sala dei Gigli, Benedetto placed his marble sculpture of John the Baptist.

When Duke Cosimo I took up residence in the Palazzo Vecchio, a new artistic program was devised to suppress Republican imagery and celebrate Medici rule.[30] Strikingly, a fresco by Giorgio Vasari begun in 1555 in the Sala di Leone X depicts Alessandro de' Medici, the first Medici duke of Florence, in the guise of Mars (FIG. 23). Like Montorsoli's sculpture of John the Baptist, Duke Alessandro grasps a lance in a commanding gesture. This image is adjacent to Vasari's full-length portrait of Duke Cosimo himself (FIG. 24), which also includes references to Mars. Depicted on the shield to Cosimo's right is the sign of Capricorn, long associated with Mars and the Emperor Augustus. Marzocco the lion, one of the oldest symbols of the Florentine Republic, can be seen literally bowing at the feet of the duke. In this audacious painting, the Medici usurped the traditional symbols of Florence to support the family's claims to hereditary rule in the manner of the ancient Roman emperors.

In the midst of all these changes undertaken in the mid-sixteenth century, Benedetto da Maiano's *John the Baptist* was left in place. But even this image did not survive unaltered, for its context had shifted. In a stunning effort to dilute John the Baptist's Republican connotations, the Medici commissioned Francesco Salviati to paint a large figure of Mars in the adjacent room (FIG. 25). The new work was positioned so that it could be clearly seen through the doorway under the statue of John the Baptist. Salviati's fresco co-opted an image of Republican government in exaltation of Duke Cosimo I. The Medici propagandists were also keen to draw parallels between the duke and Augustus, since both rulers took power from republican forms of government. Cosimo I claimed Florence by declaring himself the new Augustus, a claim literally embodied in Vincenzo Danti's marble portrait of the duke in the guise of Augustus, made around 1572 for the facade of the Uffizi (FIG. 26).[31]

FIG. 26
Vincenzo Danti, *Duke Cosimo I de' Medici as Augustus*, ca. 1572. Marble, height 280 cm. Museo Nazionale del Bargello, Florence.

FIG. 27
Michelangelo, *Apollo-David*, 1530–34. Marble, height 147 cm. Museo Nazionale del Bargello, Florence.

Ancient rulers had long appropriated characteristics of gods into their portraits to legitimize their authority. Danti's statue of Cosimo I as Emperor Augustus would have reminded Florentines of similar statues of Roman emperors, and even of Christlike depictions of religious figures such as Saint Francis, who was actively promoted as another Christ (*alter Christus*). These images remind us that Montorsoli's incorporation of pagan features into a sculpture of John the Baptist is not without precedent.

MICHELANGELO'S HYBRID FIGURE OF APOLLO/DAVID

While Montorsoli was making his terracotta Baptist/Mars, his teacher Michelangelo was creating his own fused figure. In 1530 and 1534, Michelangelo began work on a marble sculpture (FIG. 27) for Baccio Valori, but left it unfinished in 1534. Giorgio Vasari in 1550 identified it as "Apollo drawing an arrow from his quiver," while the 1553 inventory of the Medici collection called it an "incomplete David."[32]

Scholars have generally argued that the sculpture either represents David or Apollo.[33] A roughly defined rectangle on the figure's back resembles a quiver, while the mound beneath the right foot could be the head of Goliath (or the python killed by Apollo). The right hand reaching over the shoulder might be drawing an arrow, but it also resembles the pose of Michelangelo's earlier *David* who holds his slingshot in a similar way. Another suggestion is that the sculpture was in the process of being transformed from an Apollo into a David, and that the confusion has arisen only because the work was not finished.[34] These views seem at odds with the Renaissance's delight in hybridity – in adding ancient references to religious subjects – and Michelangelo's own interest in unfinished sculpture as worthy of appreciation. It is not unreasonable to consider that the multiplicity of the figure was intentional, especially since Apollo and David share many features, including their physical type.

Moreover, the sculpture might echo the opposing political views of the artist and patron. Michelangelo fervently supported the Republican cause, even designing fortifications for the defense of Florence against

FIG. 28
*Florentine Arch for the Triumphal Entry of
Prince Philip into Antwerp, 1549.* Print from
Grapheus 1550.

FIG. 29
Bartolomeo Ammannati, *Mars Gradivus*,
1559. Bronze, height 215 cm, Galleria
degli Uffizi, Florence.

Medici forces. On the other hand, Baccio Valori supported the Medici, who installed him as the city's governor in 1530. Valori's support wavered, however, and he later joined the Republican rebellion, which was soundly defeated in 1537 at the Battle of Montemurlo. Valori was executed and Duke Cosimo took possession of Michelangelo's unfinished sculpture. Even if we are uncertain of its precise identity, Michelangelo's figure certainly combines aspects of both David and Apollo, just as Montorsoli's *Baptist* blends its subject with references to Mars, and Andrea del Sarto's *John the Baptist* (CAT. 5) incorporates attributes of Bacchus.

THE BAPTIST VANQUISHES MARS

A triumphal decoration from 1549 is the only known instance in which Mars and John the Baptist appeared together in the same sculpture. Florentine citizens in Antwerp erected a temporary triumphal arch to celebrate the entry of Prince Philip, later King Philip II. Curiously, the arch made minimal reference to the Holy Roman Empire, the protector of both Florence and Antwerp. The figure on top of the arch is described as a carved golden statue of John the Baptist standing over Mars, "whom Florence once held as an idol, with a temple dedicated to him, and in the place of Mars they adopted St. John the Baptist as their patron."[35] The image of the patron saint of Florence subjugating their former pagan god is most unusual. The published illustration of the triumphal arch only shows the Baptist holding a lamb, while just to the right Marzocco holds the Florentine standard (FIG. 28). This image of John the Baptist triumphant was intended for non-Florentine audiences, who would have been most familiar with the saint as the symbol of Florence. Nonetheless, as the sixteenth century progressed under Medici rule, it was Mars who prevailed over John the Baptist in Florence.

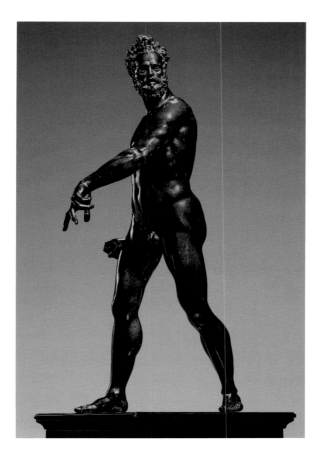

FIG. 30
Giambologna, *Mars Gradivus*, ca. 1580.
Bronze, height 39.5 cm. Staatliche
Kunstsammlungen Dresden.

The Medici dukes of Florence continued to commission major works representing Mars for political self-aggrandizement. Among the most celebrated are the monumental *Striding Mars* of 1583 by Bartolomeo Ammannati (FIG. 29) and Giambologna's bronze statuette of the same subject, known in several casts from around 1580 (FIG. 30). In these works, Mars, with his inherent references to ancient Rome, became a vehicle for celebrating the princely power of the Medici.

The evolving political landscape in sixteenth-century Florence, culminating in the overthrow of the Florentine Republic, profoundly influenced art of the time. Montorsoli's *John the Baptist* was made around 1533 at the moment when the Medici consolidated their authority. The image can be regarded as an assertion of the traditional power of the Republic, which could trace its descent from the ancient Roman Republic. In addition, the sculpture evoked the golden age of Florence, which gave rise to the sculptural decoration of important civic buildings like the Baptistery and Orsanmichele – fruits of the city's wealth and might. The fusing of two symbols of Florence – the pagan Mars and the Christian Baptist – into a single sculpture is a remarkable gesture brought about by political circumstances. Montorsoli's sculpture thus embodies a duality of identity that can often be found in Renaissance art. The quiet resolve of the Baptist is combined with the military might of Mars. The pagan god is no longer an idolatrous threat to the Christian faith, but a reminder of Florence's ancient glory. That Montorsoli's Republican advocacy was in the end unsuccessful gives the work its own pathos, especially as such heroic figures of John the Baptist had no successors.

1.   In a letter to Febo dated December 1534, Michelangelo says that he intends to leave Florence the following day. Parker 2014, p. 71.

2.   Laschke 1993, pp. 31–33, 149, 156.

3.   Antico's *Apollo Belvedere* is known in three versions. He also used the same method to attach a separately cast bow in his *Cupid* (Bargello), probably made by 1496 as a wedding gift to Isabella d'Este (Washington and New York 2011, pp. 7, 191). It is possible that Montorsoli saw Giovanni Battista Bregno's monument to Benedict Pesaro, for which Baccio da Montelupo provided the marble statues of Neptune and Mars (1503), located on the wall leading to the sacristy of the Basilica of the Frari. It had a similar type of tubular opening to attach an object. Mars's hand is fashioned to accommodate a shield or pike in the same manner as Antico's *Apollo* and *Cupid*. Montorsoli would again chose this method of attachment with his sculpture of the Apostle Paul (1558–62) in Santa Maria dei Servi, Bologna.

4.   Houston and London 2001, pp. 1–31.

5.   Cropper 1997, p. 40.

6.   X-ray fluorescence testing by Mary Kate Donais has detected traces of gesso, which suggests that the sculpture was originally painted white in imitation of marble, or possibly a color to mimic bronze. No traces of polychrome have been detected. Most polychromed sculptures do not have deeply incised pupils like Montorsoli's Baptist, but instead have flat surfaces that can be easily painted. See further under CAT. 8.

7.   Quoted in Robey 2013, p. 19 note 69.

8.   Voraigne 1993, vol. 1, pp. 331–32.

9.   It is likely the transformation occurred shortly after 313, when Emperor Constantine adopted Christianity as the Roman Empire's official religion.

10.   Chretien 1994, p. 23, believes that the waning of Zenobius and Reparata was because they were associated with feudal lords and thus not suitable for the emerging Republic.

11.   Chretien 1994, p. 21.

12.   The earliest octagonal baptistery, which predates the cathedral dedicated to Saint Reparata, dates from the late 4th to early 5th century (Villani, *Nuova cronica*, 1.60; Villani 1991). Both Villani and Dante relied on the *Chronica de origine civitatis florentiae* regarding the city's foundation (see Chellini 2009 and Pina 2014). Literary evidence suggests that Pope Nicholas II, a Florentine, consecrated the structure, which was dedicated to John the Baptist and known as the Chiesa di San Giovanni, on November 6, 1059; major construction ended in 1128. Modern excavations have shown that the Baptistery may have been built on the remains of a Roman guard tower or another Roman building (Toker 1976). Archaeological evidence suggests that there were two churches before the building of Santa Reparata, the earliest from around 780. Santa Reparata was replaced with the present Duomo in 1412 (see Verdon et al. 2000, p. 25).

13.   *Nuova cronica*, 2.23; Villani 1991.

14.   When Florence adopted Christianity, the equestrian statue of Mars was moved to a tower along the Arno. When Totila (Dante mistakenly writes Attila) destroyed Florence in 542, the tower and statue fell into the Arno. It was believed that the only way for Florence to rebuild was to retrieve and repair the statue. Once done, it was placed on the Ponte Vecchio.

15.   Translation by Ciardi 2003, p. 109. The original reads:

> raccoglietele al piè del tristo cesto.
> I' fui de la città che nel Batista
> mutò 'l primo padrone; ond' ei per questo
>
> sempre con l'arte sua la farà trista;
> e se non fosse che 'n sul passo d'Arno
> rimane ancor di lui alcuna vista,
>
> que' cittadin che poi la rifondarno
> sovra 'l cener che d'Attila rimase,
> avrebber fatto lavorare indarno.

16.   Trexler 1991, pp. 75–78.

17.   Ciardi 2003, p. 733.
> Tutti color ch'a quel tempo eran ivi
> da poter arme tra Marte e 'l Batista,
> eran il quinto di quei ch'or son vivi.

18.   Dominici 1860, p. 131.

19.   One set of doors and three groups of sculptures recount the life of John the Baptist on the exterior of the Baptistery. Inside, John sits enthroned in the chancel opposite the Virgin and Child, and below Christ.

20.   The Opera di San Giovanni, the entity appointed to maintain the Baptistery, came under the direction of the

Arte di Calimala, the guild of cloth finishers, sometime between 1157 and 1193. It was common practice to unveil major civic commissions on John the Baptist's feast day.

21.   Vasari tells us that the three 14th-century groups previously installed above the doors were removed from the Baptistery at the beginning of the 16th century (Vasari 1966, vol. 5, p. 477). Levin 2005, pp. 218–19, interprets this to mean that the refurbishment of all three portals was planned from the outset by the Cloth Guild.

22.   The Cloth Guild meeting on December 3, 1506, describes the original three statues that would be replaced by Rustici as "awkward and badly made . . . so abraded that in some parts they have begun to fall to ruin" (Levin 2005, p. 205). The sculptures by Andrea Sansovino and Rustici replaced Tino di Camaino's versions of the same subjects, and there is reason to believe that a comparable replacement was also intended for the sculptures representing the Theological Virtues over the third portal (ca. 1321–23). That plan was amended in the 1560s, when Danti was commissioned to represent the subject of the Beheading of John the Baptist instead.

23.   Gilbert 1977.

24.   Although the staff is not original to the sculpture, it conforms to the diameter of the terracotta section of the shaft in the Baptist's hand. The left hand has broken off just above the wrist; this clean break has been repaired. X-ray fluorescence testing by Mary Kate Donais shows that the clay composition of the hand is consistent with the rest of the sculpture. This indicates that the repair was made with original pieces of the hand, and it is therefore largely original in design. See CAT. 8.

25.   Livy, *History of Rome*, book 2, chapter 45: "He invoked the wrath of Father Jupiter and Mars Gradivus and other deities if he broke his oath. The whole army took the oath, man by man, after him." Also book 2, chapter 46. See Titus Livius, *History of Rome*, translation by Rev. Canon Roberts (New York, 1912); online: www.perseus.tufts.edu.

26.   See Cropper 1997, p. 44.

27.   Donato Giannotti suggests the following procedure: "I would like this ceremony to be one in the following way. In the feast days of John the Baptist, on a certain designated day, the Signoria should have a solemn mass sung in Santa Reparata, at which they should be present." (Questa cerimonia vorrei si facesse in questo modo. Ne' giorni della festa di San Giovanni, vorrei che la Signroia, in uno giorno deputato, faciessi cantare in Santa Reparata una solenne messa, alla quale elle si trovasse.) Donato Giannotti was secretary of the Council of Ten and leader of the short-lived Republic in 1527. For Giannotti's plea for the introduction of a city militia, see "Discorso di armare la città di Firenze, fatto dinanzi ai magnifici signori e Gonfaloniere di giustizia l'anno 1529" in Giannotti 1974, pp. 167–80.

28.   Kleiner 1981.

29.   Rubinstein 1987, p. 29.

30.   Sarah Dillon has questioned whether Benedetto da Maiano's *John the Baptist* was originally installed over the door in the Sala dei Gigli; it is documented in the Palazzo Vecchio in the 16th century (Dillon 2018). For a discussion of the Palazzo Vecchio before the fall of the Republican government, see Rubinstein 1995, pp. 47–79. For connections to antiquity: Rubinstein 1987. Around 1549, when the court moved to the Pitti Palace, the Palazzo della Signoria was renamed the Palazzo Vecchio.

31.   Dimitrios Zikos in Florence 2008, pp. 312–15.

32.   Vasari 1966, vol. 6, pp. 62, 63. Also Varchi 1564, pp. 28–29 [as Apollo].

33.   Surveyed in Bambach 2017, pp. 180–86.

34.   Bambach 2017, pp. 180, 183.

35.   Grapheus 1550.

FIG. I

Apollo Belvedere. Roman copy of a Hellenistic bronze.
Marble, height 224 cm. Musei Vaticani. Photograph by
James Anderson, 1850s.

COPIES, RESTORATIONS, AND CARICATURES
MONTORSOLI AT THE VATICAN

Alan Chong

THE DISCOVERY OF SEVERAL NEARLY COMPLETE ANCIENT SCULPTURES around 1500 created a sensation in the art world. Giorgio Vasari credited them with changing the course of art history by inspiring the so-called "modern manner," that is, the High Renaissance of Michelangelo, Raphael, and Titian. The *Laocoon, Apollo Belvedere, Hercules, Belvedere Torso, Venus*, and *Cleopatra*, "through their sweetness and roughness, with their corporality drawn from the greatest beauties of nature," banished the earlier "dry, crude, and harsh manner."[1]

In 1532, Pope Clement VII asked Michelangelo to recommend a young artist who could restore the ancient sculptures gathered in the Vatican's Belvedere Court. Michelangelo suggested Giovan Angelo Montorsoli, his assistant on the not-yet-complete Medici Tombs in the church of San Lorenzo, Florence, and the tomb of Julius II. Between September 1532 and July 1533 Montorsoli restored the most celebrated of the ancient discoveries – the *Apollo Belvedere* (FIG. 1) and the *Laocoon* – and "in addition gave directions for restoring the Hercules."[2] Because Montorsoli's reconstructions were in place until the mid-twentieth century, these gestures exerted great influence on artists and connoisseurs for more than four hundred years. Since the critical histories of these sculptures have been comprehensively examined,[3] it might be useful to reconsider their early restorations, which have been confused by a number of false connections. We will also consider the process of copying, emulating, and parodying ancient art.

APOLLO BELVEDERE

A Roman copy of a Hellenistic bronze, the *Apollo Belvedere* was discovered in 1489 and acquired by Cardinal Giuliano della Rovere, the future Pope Julius II.[4] Engravings by Agostino Veneziano and Marcantonio Raimondi (FIGS. 2, 3) show that the statue as found was missing its left forearm as well as the right hand, which seems to hover above the stump around which the python coils.[5] In 1508, the statue was moved into the Vatican and three years later raised onto a plinth, as shown by Raimondi.[6]

The first three-dimensional reimagining of the *Apollo* is Antico's elegant bronze (see p. 27), the earliest Renaissance sculpture to recreate an ancient marble. Antico made his model when he was in Rome in 1497 and cast the bronze for the Mantua court. We know this because Antico's model was actually stolen the following year and there was fear that unauthorized bronzes would be made from it, testimony to the prestige of both the *Apollo* and the Renaissance court artist.[7] Antico's version generally anticipates Montorsoli's restoration of 1532 to 1533 (FIGS. 1, 4), especially the left hand holding the truncated bow.

FIG. 2
Agostino Veneziano, *Apollo Belvedere*,
ca. 1518. Engraving,
26.9 × 16.9 cm. British Museum,
London. 1840,0808.12.

FIG. 3
Marcantonio Raimondi, *Apollo Belvedere*,
1511–20. Engraving. CAT. 19.

FIG. 4
Hendrick Goltzius, *Apollo Belvedere*,
ca. 1593. Engraving. CAT. 20.

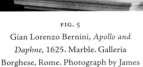

FIG. 5
Gian Lorenzo Bernini, *Apollo and
Daphne*, 1625. Marble. Galleria
Borghese, Rome. Photograph by James
Anderson, 1850s.

Montorsoli more freely interpreted the right hand of Apollo, where the outwardly flexed wrist and long fingers give the figure an exaggerated grace that would characterize it for the next four centuries.[8] With this addition, Montorsoli effeminized the *Apollo* by echoing the drapery and the god's frothy curls of hair. That no attempt was made to restore the entire bow reduced the figure's role as a hunter. Montorsoli's gesture would be almost directly copied by Gian Lorenzo Bernini in his *Apollo and Daphne* of 1625 (FIG. 5).

HERCULES

When the sculpture of Hercules holding his infant son Telephos (FIG. 6) was discovered in Rome in 1507, most of the right arm and club were missing, as can be seen in two sketches in a mid-sixteenth-century Netherlandish album based on an earlier source (FIG. 7).[9] Vasari says that Montorsoli only directed the restoration of the Hercules, but there seems no reason to doubt that Montorsoli carved the powerfully muscled arm that was attached to the figure. Strongly indebted to Michelangelo, the limb has also close affinities with the right arm of Montorsoli's *John the Baptist*, made shortly afterward. Montorsoli did not restore the full club and the left hands of father and son; these elements were added much later and have recently been removed.[10]

From its discovery through the eighteenth century, the statue was known as Emperor Commodus in the guise of Hercules. For example, Hendrick Goltzius's print (FIG. 8) identifies the subject as Hercules (in Greek) and additionally as the Commodus (Comodus Imperator). However, we now know that the sculpture has no connection with the famously megalomanical emperor, which has greatly diminished its fame. The identity of the infant also proved elusive to Renaissance viewers.[11] The lines by Theodor Schrevelius on Goltzius's engraving call him Telemon, and even J. J. Winkelmann in the eighteenth century thought the boy was Ajax.

Around the time Montorsoli was at work on the *Apollo* and *Laocoon*, a fragmentary river god was moved into the Belvedere (FIG. 9).[12] The missing head and arms were added to create a representation of the Arno River, in recognition of the reigning Medici pope, Clement VII. Carved into the vase is the lion Marzocco, a symbol of Florence. Although it has been suggested that Montorsoli restored the sculpture, the head of the figure is unlike Montorsoli's work, which suggests that another skilled sculptor, perhaps Baccio Bandinelli, was employed by the Vatican to restore antiquities.[13] The Vatican river god relates to the ephemeral figure of *Arno* that Montorsoli created for Charles V's triumphal entry into Florence in 1536. Placed on the Ponte Santa Trinità, the figure rested one arm on the lion of Florence.[14] Whether ancient or ephemeral, these river gods paved the way for Montorsoli's four river gods that ring the Fountain of Orion in Messina, begun in 1547 (FIG. 10).[15]

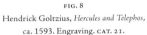

FIG. 8
Hendrick Goltzius, *Hercules and Telephos*,
ca. 1593. Engraving. CAT. 21.

FIG. 9
River God (Arno). Roman, 2nd
century; head: 16th century. Marble.
Musei Vaticani, Rome.

FIG. 10
Giovan Angelo Montorsoli, *River God
Tiber* (from the Fountain of Orion,
Messina), 1547–53. Print from
Hittorff 1835, pl. 26.

LAOCOON

On a visit to the Vatican in 1523, a Venetian ambassador compared the great ancient works on display, and wrote that the *Apollo* was praiseworthy, "but the excellence of the *Laocoon* makes one forget [the *Venus*] and the *Apollo*, which was once so much celebrated."[16] This surprising comment comes just fifteen years after the *Apollo* had been installed in the Belvedere, and while it commanded considerable attention from the Renaissance to the eighteenth century, its reputation inexorably declined. The elegant figure is now out of fashion, while the agony and anguish of the Laocoon group continues to fascinate modern observers, in the same way Munch's *Scream* does.[17] A recent suggestion that the almost-too-convenient discovery of the perfectly preserved *Laocoon* was an elaborate hoax by Michelangelo is another of the highly personal responses that have burdened the work's perception.[18] However, our taste for aggression, anxiety, and instability is not always historically appropriate, as John Shearman has reminded us.[19] While the discovery and critical reception of the *Laocoon* have been thoroughly explored, the immediate historical context of the restoration of the sculpture is worth reexamining.[20]

The ancient marble representing Laocoon and his sons was unearthed in Rome in 1506. Summoned to view the discovery, Michelangelo and the architect Giuliano da Sangallo instantly recognized it as the work Pliny the Elder had called "superior to all the pictures and bronzes in the world." The sculpture was acquired by Pope Julius II and installed in the Vatican Belvedere – an act which can be regarded as the foundation of one of the world's oldest museums.[21] The depiction of the Trojan priest Laocoon and his sons struggling in agony against the "wonderful clasping coil of snakes" (Pliny) is based on book two of Virgil's *Aeneid*, as Homer does not mention Laocoon.[22] A priest of Neptune, Laocoon attempted to expose the Trojan horse as a Greek trick but Minerva sent sea serpents to kill him and his sons to prevent his doing so.

More than providing a formal inspiration for Renaissance artists, the *Laocoon*'s emotional power suggested that art had a poetic force entirely independent of any text. The critic Ludovico Dolce, writing in 1557, found the ancient sculpture so compelling that he thought it might be considered the source of Virgil's moving description rather than the other way around: "Even Virgil in describing his Laocoon

FIG. 11

Giovanni Antonio da Brescia, *Laocoon*,
1506–11. Engraving, 28.3 × 25 cm.
British Museum, London.
1845,0825.707. Signed: IO AN BX.

FIG. 12

Marco Dente, *Laocoon*, ca. 1515–23.
Engraving, 47.7 × 32. 8 cm. Museum of
Fine Arts, Boston. P1331. See CAT. 22.

followed the way he had previously seen him depicted in the statue . . . which is still to be seen in Rome today. And it happens interchangeably that painters often take their inventions from poets, and poets from painters."[23] Dolce is not suggesting that the marble literally served as Virgil's source, but that it could stand equal to poetry.

When the *Laocoon* was originally discovered, each of the figures was missing an arm, as seen in a print by Giovanni Antonio da Brescia (FIG. 11), which also shows the sculpture on the ground before it was placed on a plinth in 1511 (FIG. 12).[24] Even at this early stage, the work was interpreted, since the three figures have been aligned as though on a picture plane, highlighted against a background – very likely at odds with its original concept as a pyramidal sculpture meant to be viewed from three sides, as Seymour Howard has argued.[25] The *Laocoon*, from the moment of its discovery, was viewed pictorially, a feature further emphasized by its placement in a niche and by later restorations. In short, an ancient sculpture was transformed into a Renaissance painting, which is all the more remarkable given the early role played by Michelangelo and Sangallo, a sculptor and an architect.

A COPYING CONTEST

According to Vasari, Giuliano da Sangallo (who was present at the work's excavation) invited the young sculptor Jacopo Sansovino to work at the Vatican, where his sketches and models after ancient sculpture were noticed by the celebrated architect Donato Bramante.[26] A kind of competition was arranged for four sculptors to make large wax copies of the *Laocoon*, with the winning version to be cast in bronze. Besides Sansovino, the participants were Zaccaria Zacchi da Volterra (see CAT. 26), Alonso Berruguete, and Domenico Aimo. Judged the winner by no less a personality than Raphael, Sansovino's wax was cast in bronze and presented to Cardinal Domenico Grimani of Venice. Vasari also states that Sansovino restored ancient sculptures, which greatly impressed Julius II. The contest probably took place in 1510, when all the participants were in Rome, that is, within a few years of the *Laocoon*'s discovery.[27] Like all good stories, Vasari's has a point beyond the specifics of the competition. It shows that Sansovino's precocious talent was endorsed by Sangallo, Bramante, Raphael, and the pope, while the bronze *Laocoon* introduces Sansovino to Venice, where he would spend the bulk of his career. Moreover, the test to produce accurate copies echoes ancient artistic contests – Pliny's humorous tales of Parrhasios painting a curtain so realistic that it fooled Zeuxis, or of Apelles besting Protogenes in a line-drawing contest, come to mind.

The desire to find Sansovino's copy of the *Laocoon* has proved fatally attractive.[28] A red chalk drawing of Laocoon has also been attributed to Sansovino (see FIG. 18), but there are no securely identifiable drawings by the artist nor does this sheet relate to his sculptures.

RAPHAEL AND HIS PRINTMAKERS

Raphael judged the contest among the four sculptors copying the *Laocoon*, but is not otherwise normally associated with the restoration of the ancient sculptures in the Vatican. Nonetheless, the *Apollo* and the *Laocoon* played significant roles in Raphael's circle.

Raphael operated a workshop of printmakers, including Marcantonio Raimondi, Marco Dente, and Agostino Veneziano, who produced engravings after his drawings.[29] Raphael even had a manager, Baviero de' Carrocci, who kept the engraved plates and controlled the printed output. The workings of this cottage industry seem to predict modern notions of originality, collaboration, copyright, and profit. In this view, Raphael emerges as a kind of Renaissance Warhol. The fact that the engravers sometimes produced almost identical replicas of some images suggests that unauthorized copies were sold surreptitiously.[30]

It has been more difficult to account for the prints after ancient sculpture, since there are no drawings by Raphael connected with the engravings of Agostino, Raimondi, and Dente (FIGS. 2, 3, 12).[31] Were they independent works that afforded the printmakers some meager profit outside the Raphael workshop, or were they also ordered by the master? One strong indication that some of these prints were produced under Raphael or Baviera is the existence of a very precise replica by Raimondi of his own print of the *Apollo Belvedere* (FIG. 3), in the fashion of other replica prints after Raphael. None of the prints of the first plate show wear, nor are there any meaningful variations in the second image, but the inscription on the latter version begins with the initial letter of "Sic" in reverse, almost as a kind of inside joke. Agostino Veneziano also produced two closely related engravings of the *Apollo Belvedere* and Raimondi made two prints of the Apollo Kitharodos.[32]

The prints after ancient sculpture are not typical reproductive prints in that they do not diffuse the invention of another living artist; even if these prints were based on drawings, the role of the intermediary is completely obscure: the inscriptions only identify the ancient work and the modern printmaker. There has been a tendency to see the prints after the *Laocoon* and the *Apollo* as documents of their condition, restoration, and placement, but in fact the images are interpretive.[33] Marco Dente's print of the *Laocoon* (FIG. 12), for example, suggests some of the excitement of its discovery amidst the ruins of Rome. The location is clearly not the Vatican, where the sculpture had been since 1506. Set against a crumbling wall decorated with egg-and-dart molding, and overgrown with foliage, the *Laocoon* is seen unrestored, embellished only by the plinth's inscription, which never existed in reality. It is significant that Dente employed a similar setting for another episode from Virgil's *Aeneid*, the boxing match between Entellus and Dares (FIG. 13), which incorporates a view of the Colosseum.[34] Dares, a young Trojan, fought the Sicilian fighter Entellus during games commemorating the death of Aeneas's father, Anchises (*Aeneid*, 5). These images of Laocoon and Dares are reminders that the Trojans were the legendery founders of Rome.

Dente produced another remarkable print of Laocoon and his sons (FIG. 14), not a depiction of the sculpture but an imagining of the narrative in an extensive landscape. At the left, an altar is aflame in front of the temple of Minerva; a domed building is perched on the hill. Laocoon and his sons are already entangled by serpents sent by Minerva, as another pair advances from the sea. The triangle of figures on a stone altar echoes the ancient marble, but Laocoon's gesture more immediately derives from an illustration in a fifth-century manuscript of Virgil that belonged to the humanist Pietro Bembo.[35] The manuscript also shows temples on the left with an altar. The print's design is very likely by Raphael, because of the imaginative composition and the musculature of the bodies, which can be compared to drawings by Raphael and his circle.[36]

In contrast to Dente's print of the Laocoon sculpture, which shows ancient ruins in decay, the second print envisions a nearly untouched past. It has been suggested that the inscription "ossa" (bones) on the stone fragment directly in front of the figures is a metaphor for the revivification of the ancient world through the printer's art.[37]

FIG. 13
Marco Dente, *Entellus and
Dares Boxing*, ca. 1520.
Engraving, 31 × 26.3 cm.
Rijksmuseum, Amsterdam.
RP-P-OB-35.970.

FIG. 14
Marco Dente, *The Death of Laocoon
and His Sons*, ca. 1520. Engraving,
26.4 × 38.7 cm, Rijksmuseum,
Amsterdam. RP-P-OB-35.984.

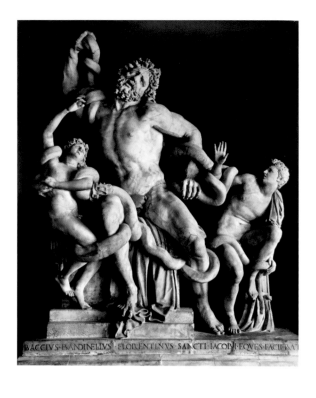

FIG. 15
Raphael, *Young John the Baptist in the Wilderness*, ca. 1516–17.
Oil on canvas, 165 × 147 cm.
Galleria degli Uffizi, Florence.

FIG. 16
Baccio Bandinelli, *Laocoon*, 1520–25. Marble. Galleria degli Uffizi, Florence.

LAOCOON AS THE BAPTIST

A painting by Raphael from around 1517 (FIG. 15) combines aspects of the *Laocoon* and the *Apollo Belvedere* in a representation of the young John the Baptist in the wilderness, wearing a leopard skin, an attribute of Bacchus that Leonardo da Vinci also depicted (see pp. 109–10).[38] The ancient sources have been significantly modified, but the diagonal gesture upward completes the missing arm of the ancient *Laocoon* – a restoration in paint. The figure reappears in a different setting in a chiaroscuro woodcut attributed to Niccolò Boldrini.[39]

BANDINELLI'S COPY AS RESTORATION

In early 1520, the sculptor Baccio Bandinelli recreated the missing arm of the *Laocoon*, as Vasari reports:

> Baccio made a large example in wax, which so resembled the muscles and the force and manner of the ancient work, and harmonized with it so well, that it showed how much Baccio understood art: and this model served him for making the whole arm of his own work.[40]

Although the wax arm was not attached to the original marble, Bandinelli was commissioned to produce a full-scale copy of the group for Leo X to present to King Francis I of France, who had initially requested the real sculpture.[41] The pope's death in late 1521 delayed the project, but Bandinelli's completed marble was sent to Florence in 1525. The arm as reconstructed by Bandinelli (FIG. 16) reaches up to grasp a tightly knotted snake that curls around the upper arm. In the end, the king of France received neither the original *Laocoon* nor Bandinelli's version, and only in 1540 did the French court manage to produce its own bronze copies of the Vatican antiquities.

When offered the commission to carve a *Laocoon*, Bandinelli claimed "that not only would he equal it, his spirit was sufficient to surpass it in perfection."[42] Such arrogance contrasts with Vasari's account of Sansovino's work, which was accompanied by no boasting and whose excellence was proven in competition and the judgment of senior artists. The Venetian ambassador to the Vatican had the chance to compare the *Laocoon* with parts of Bandinelli's copy, and offered a harsh assessment: "the master, even if he lived five hundred years and made a hundred versions, could never equal the original."[43] These sentiments were echoed by Michelangelo, who when asked about an artist who copied celebrated marble sculptures, "the imitator boasting that he had far surpassed the ancients, Michelangelo replied, 'One who follows behind others can never surpass them, and one who cannot do good work of his own cannot make good use of the work of others.'"[44] Everyone knew that Michelangelo was talking about Bandinelli, and Benvenuto Cellini also wrote that the jealous and greedy Bandinelli had "merely made a copy of the *Laocoon*."[45]

FIG. 17
Laocoon. Photograph by James
Anderson, ca. 1850s. The arm is based
on Montorsoli's restoration of 1532–33.

FIG. 18
Il Sodoma, *Laocoon.* Red chalk on paper,
33.5 × 22 cm. Gabinetto Disegni e
Stampe degli Uffizi, Florence. 14535F.

The idea of improving on antiquity recurs in another restoration project. Cellini was greatly taken by an ancient fragment that showed "beauty, strength of intelligence, and rare style." Duke Cosimo I allowed Cellini to transform this torso into a figure of Ganymede (now in the Bargello) with the addition of an elegant raised arm reminiscent of the *Laocoon.* Bandinelli, in contrast, saw the ancient torso as evidence that "these ancients knew nothing about anatomy and therefore all their works are full of errors," an opinion that accords with Bandinelli's claim to have improved the *Laocoon.*[46] With comments like these, Bandinelli emerges as the great villain of Renaissance art, at least according to sixteenth-century observers who report that he cut up Michelangelo's cartoon of the *Battle of Cascina* to prevent it from being seen by others, disfigured Michelangelo's sculptures, and conspired to destroy one of Montorsoli's most important works.

MONTORSOLI'S LAOCOON

Montorsoli's solution (FIG. 17) is significantly different from Bandinelli's arm, which bends upward, perpendicular to the ground. Montorsoli's arm stretches diagonally outward – a gesture more heroic, as though it were a last, desperate attempt to survive. This gesture echoes the angle of Laocoon's left leg, giving the figure a kind of symmetry. Montorsoli's hand turns toward the viewer so that the fingers are visible, while the snake runs parallel to the arm, but does not wrap around it. It almost functions as a piece of drapery in outlining and emphasizing the gesture. This, too, is a radically different concept from Bandinelli's, where the tightly knotted snake curls around Laocoon's bicep. Montorsoli's arm seems to be overcoming the serpent, where Bandinelli's entwined limb is being bent by the beast. In short, Montorsoli's Laocoon is winning, while Bandinelli's is losing.

A drawing of the figure of Laocoon (FIG. 18) shows the right arm complete, the gesture somewhere between the solutions of Bandinelli and Montorsoli. The position of the hand, with the palm facing the viewer, is identical to Montorsoli's solution, whereas Bandinelli carved the thumb pointing forward. The drawing's attribution is uncertain: it has sometimes been associated with Jacopo Sansovino, although there is no evidence that he reconstructed the arm. The drawing is more likely by Il Sodoma, who worked in the Vatican between 1508 and 1510 and returned to Rome in 1516.[47] Sodoma worked alongside Raphael at the Vatican and the Villa Farnesina, and the drawing, like Raphael's *John the Baptist,* demonstrates that reconstructions of the outstretched arm of Laocoon circulated well before Montorsoli began his own restoration.

Montorsoli's replacement arm in terracotta was remade in marble between 1725 and 1727. In 1905, Ludwig Pollak discovered the original ancient arm not far from where the *Laocoon* had originally been excavated. He presented the fragment to the Vatican, which waited more than a half century before reattaching it in 1959 (FIG. 19). The original arm bends behind Laocoon's head in an arrangement more compact

FIG. 19

Laocoon. Marble, height 242 cm. Musei
Vaticani, Rome. Present state of
the sculpture.

FIG. 20

The marble arm fitted to the *Laocoon*.
Photograph of 1959.

and less dramatic than the gestures imagined by Bandinelli and Montorsoli. Now somewhat forgotten, Pollak was a Czech dealer and connoisseur who settled in Rome and sold ancient sculpture to museums in Europe and the United States.[48] He also collected versions of the *Laocoon*, including two terracottas now in Princeton (CAT. 24). Tragically, he and his family were arrested by Nazi officials in 1943, and he died at Auschwitz.

Montorsoli's *Laocoon*, for that is what it was, exercised a tremendous hold on artists for four centuries, from 1533 when the exultant arm was added, until the original arm was reattached in the mid-twentieth century. It was Montorsoli's valiant gesture that so struck J. J. Winkelmann and Gottwald Lessing, as well as innumerable painters and sculptors. It is worth considering whether Montorsoli's arm was a vulgar misreading of the ancient work or a minor Renaissance inflection of the original.[49] For Kenneth Clark, Montorsoli "introduced a new kind of oratorical language" in his restoration of the ancient marble.[50]

The spirit of Michelangelo hovers over the restoration of the *Laocoon*, but his exact role has been clouded by later legends. Vasari simply reports that Michelangelo recommended that his assistant Montorsoli restore the Vatican antiquities. While the *Laocoon* played a major role in Michelangelo's work, the *Belvedere Torso* was perhaps even more influential. Giovan Paolo Lomazzo, writing in 1584 after the sculptor's death, commented that Michelangelo "had a belief that nothing could ever be added to the beauty of the *Belvedere Torso* . . . which he constantly followed."[51] This is sometimes interpreted as a reluctance on Michelangelo's part to restore ancient sculpture in any way, but this seems an exaggeration.[52] Michelangelo after all made a recommendation for the restoration of the *Apollo* and *Laocoon*, which were more or less complete sculptures compared with the *Belvedere Torso*. In the taste of the time, they seemed to demand full refurbishment.

The figure of Saint Cosmas (see p. 8) in the New Sacristy of San Lorenzo reflects the *Laocoon* in the aged anxiety and thrown-back position of the head. The marble was carved by Montorsoli soon after his work on the Vatican antiquities, but Michelangelo's supervision of the figure suggests that it was equally Michelangelo's interpretation of the *Laocoon*. Montorsoli made a full-scale model of the whole figure of the saint, which Michelangelo then retouched in many parts, according to Vasari.[53] And it is significant that Michelangelo himself made terracotta models of the head and the arms, which Vasari later acquired.

FALSE CONNECTIONS: A MYSTERIOUS ARM

In 1540, Primaticcio made molds of eight ancient sculptures in the Vatican in order to produce bronzes for Francis I. After having been promised antiquities by two earlier popes, this was the king's best chance of obtaining major works of ancient art, although in facsimile. Five of the bronzes survive at Fontainebleau, including copies of the three works restored by Montorsoli.[54] Primaticcio's replicas of the *Apollo Belvedere* and the *Hercules and Telephos* include Montorsoli's additions, but that of the *Laocoon* does not. Not only is Laocoon's right arm missing, but the arms of the two sons are also omitted. Perhaps these additions were temporarily removed in order to produce the mold, or Primaticcio decided not to include the restorations for aesthetic reasons.[55] However, it is unlikely that Montorsoli's arm was permanently removed in 1540.

Preserved in the Vatican is a roughly carved marble right arm with an L-shaped protrusion that slots into the shoulder of the *Laocoon*, as was demonstrated in 1957 (FIG. 20).[56] Jonathan Richardson the Younger first noted the arm in 1720, when he wrote that it had been left unfinished by Michelangelo,[57] a seductive attribution that survived for several centuries.[58] Over time, the arm has also been attributed to Montorsoli and Bandinelli.[59] However, aside from being unfinished, the arm bears no stylistic connection to Michelangelo nor does it resemble Montorsoli's restoration; and while the bend of the elbow and the coiled snakes are somewhat similar to Bandinelli's version in the Uffizi, there are also significant differences. In sum, the marble arm is so roughly finished that it is impossible to assign it to a particular artist or even to an approximate date. It would seem unwise to use this mysterious arm as evidence for Michelangelo's ideas about restoring antiquities.

Indeed the question arises whether the mysterious marble arm has any connection to the Renaissance whatsoever. It may well have been made in the early eighteenth century when the Vatican's antiquities were being rearranged and restored.[60] For example, in 1725, Agostino Cornacchini (1686–1754) was commissioned to make a new marble arm for the *Laocoon* to replace the old terracotta one, which Jonathan Richardson had found "not good Work, and moreover of a Colour Disagreeable."[61] Cornacchini's marble arm (see FIG. 17), which replicated Montorsoli's concept, remained on the *Laocoon* until 1959 (with a brief gap when the sculpture was taken to Paris). Therefore, it is possible that Cornacchini may also have been involved with the extra marble arm, perhaps made as an alternative to Montorsoli's limb. The slot in the *Laocoon* could have been cut at that time rather than in the sixteenth century. In the event, the new arm actually attached in 1725 reflected Montorsoli's concept of the 1530s.

FALSE CONNECTIONS: DRAWINGS INCORRECTLY ATTRIBUTED TO MONTORSOLI

Several drawings of the *Laocoon* have been assigned to Montorsoli, including a sketch of the head of Laocoon on the wall of a chamber under the New Sacristy (FIG. 21).[62] The mural drawings in this room have been attributed to Michelangelo, not without controversy. The head of Laocoon certainly provided inspiration to Michelangelo and Montorsoli for the head of Saint Cosmas, as we have seen. As a result, some experts who reject Michelangelo's authorship of the drawings in the New Sacristy basement have suggested Montorsoli as an alternative.[63] It is nearly impossible to attribute wall drawings on the basis of comparison to works on paper, which are made with different materials and on an entirely different scale. Nor are the basement drawings by a single artist. The one convincing wall drawing by Michelangelo (Villa Michelangiolo, Settignano) shows no more than a generic similarity with any of the New Sacristy works, and there are no secure mural drawings by Montorsoli.[64]

A two-sided drawing of the *Laocoon* (FIG. 22) has been interpreted as Montorsoli's preliminary studies for the restoration of the sculpture. The position of the father's right arm is somewhere between the solutions of Bandinelli and Montorsoli. The sheet appeared at auction in 1987 as by Montorsoli, an attribution then advocated by Arnold Nesselrath.[65] The inscriptions on the drawing were also believed to match the handwriting on a drawing by Montorsoli for the seal of the Accademia del disegno.[66] This theory has been refuted by Birgit Laschke and Ludovico Rebaudo, who pointed out that the proposed restoration of the son's arm would be impossible to achieve in reality.[67]

It may be helpful to ask what function the drawing might have served. Significantly, the *Laocoon* was not drawn as interlocking three-dimensional elements, but as isolated figural studies. The cautiously outlined and shaded figures lack the robust sense of a sculpture, and are unlike any of Montorsoli's drawings. The notations of breaks and of material are too vague for a sculptor, but may be useful reminders for a painter. In short, the rather tentative and inexpert drawings appear to date from later in the sixteenth century.[68]

FIG. 21
Italian, *Head of Laocoon*. Wall drawing. Basement of the New Sacristy, San Lorenzo, Florence.

FIG. 22
Italian, *Study of the Laocoon*, late 16th
century. Black chalk on paper,
40.4 × 29 cm. Musée Calvet, Avignon.
996-7-705.

BANDINELLI'S DESTRUCTION OF MONTORSOLI'S MARBLE

In 1538, Montorsoli prepared a model of Hercules wrestling Antaeus for the new gardens being planned at the Medici Villa di Castello.[69] With Duke Cosimo's approval, Montorsoli began work on the marble. But as he was completing the work, Montorsoli came into conflict with Baccio Bandinelli, who "used all possible effort against him" (con ogni sforzo pontava contro a colui), according to Vasari. Through gossip and intrigue, Bandinelli managed to seize Montorsoli's statue to cut up into decorative panels for Giovanni dalle Bande Nere's monument – perhaps out of jealousy that Montorsoli would achieve success in Florence.[70] Montorsoli was so angered by this that he refused to return to Florence, where he would have to encounter Bandinelli's "presumption, arrogance, and insolence."[71]

After Montorsoli's *Hercules and Antaeus* was destroyed, the project was assigned to Vincenzo Danti, who attempted three times to cast the group in bronze, without success. Finally, twenty years after Montorsoli's efforts, Bartolomeo Ammannati produced a monumental bronze that was installed in the garden (FIG. 23), which preserves the setting of Montorsoli's lost sculpture.[72] Another trace of the lost work of 1538 might survive in a small sketch attributed to Niccolò Tribolo, who was in change of the overall design of the gardens at Castello (FIG. 24).[73] It is difficult to judge how much of this concept can be credited to Montorsoli, but the arrangement of the figures differs significantly from Ammannati's. Hercules wears a draped lion skin, his attribute, and Antaeus lifts his right arm high in a last effort to survive. Antaeus's gesture is strikingly similar to Laocoon's arm, created by Montorsoli just a few years earlier. The arrangement of the lion skin and the compact arrangement of the two figures are appropriate for a monumental marble, which would require the additional support that a bronze would not. It is likely that the small pen sketch reflects Montorsoli's destroyed marble and its echoes of the *Laocoon*.

FIG. 23
Fountain at Villa di Castello, with
the bronze *Hercules and Antaeus* by
Bartolomeo Ammannati. Photograph
by Brogi, 1890s.

FIG. 24
Niccolò Tribolo (attributed to), *Hercules and
Antaeus*, ca. 1538. Pen and brown ink on paper,
6.4 × 4.4 cm. Museum of Fine Arts, Budapest.
1944.

Caricatures of the *Laocoon*

By the 1540s, the *Laocoon* had become a cultural obsession – a too-famous work that had been praised, copied, restored, and emulated. This naturally gave rise to caricatures and parodies. One, made in Venice around 1540, turns the exalted ancient *Laocoon* into three apes holding the same pose (FIG. 25). The woodcut is attributed to Niccolò Boldrini working from a design by Titian. H. W. Janson interpreted the print as a complex parody of ancient science.[74] The sixteenth-century scientist Andreas Vesalius had argued that the ancient surgeon Galen had based his treatise on dissected apes rather than dissected human bodies. David Rosand and Michelangelo Muraro rightly rejected this reading as unnecessarily obscure and suggested instead that the print compares art and nature.[75]

However, this woodcut seems to be about a specific work of art: the ancient *Laocoon*. Its figures have been replaced by apes, but the composition and even the emotional content remain completely recognizable. Indeed, Carlo Ridolfi in 1648 described the print as a frivolity (un gentil pensiero) "of three seated Barbary apes, entwined by snakes, in the guise of Laocoon and the sons, located in the Belvedere in Rome."[76] This fulfills the basic requirement of a caricature – the humorous exaggeration of the familiar, in this case, one of the most exalted and over-exposed cultural creations. Moreover, Ridolfi reminds us that the image must not be taken too seriously. Prints after the *Laocoon* circulated in Venice, while Jacopo Sansovino, the city's premiere sculptor and architect, had made one of the first copies of the sculpture, which was displayed in the city's Council of Ten.[77]

The setting is also critical to the understanding of the print, as it is nearly identical to the landscapes produced in Venice in the early sixteenth century, seen in the paintings of Giorgione and Titian, and the prints of Giulio Campagnola.[78] This pastoral setting must have been deliberately chosen to represent the art of Venice, which strongly suggests that modern Venetian art is being compared with ancient sculpture. Is it too much to imagine that the shaggy apes allude to the exuberant brushwork of Venetian painting? The apes could not be more different from the hard, smooth surfaces of the marble bodies of Laocoon and his sons. All good caricatures contain some element of self-parody, and Boldrini's woodcut technique might be seen as a contrast with the fine linear engravings of Dente and Raimondi in their copies of the *Laocoon*.

On the other hand, it is difficult to believe that Boldrini's woodcut represents Titian's mockery of Michelangelo, as has been suggested.[79] The *Laocoon* was not exclusively associated with Michelangelo, and there is no proof that Titian designed the woodcut, since the first attribution comes a century after it was made.[80]

FIG. 25

Niccolò Boldrini, *Caricature of the
Laocoon*, 1540s. Woodcut, 26.8 ×
40.3 cm. Rijksmuseum, Amsterdam.
RP-P-OB-30.979.

FIG. 26
Hans Schenck, *Antipapal Allegory*
(reverse of a portrait of Hans Klur),
1546. Stone, diameter 9.8 cm.
Bode-Museum, Berlin.

FIG. 27
Gian Jacopo Caraglio after Rosso Fiorentino, *Desiccated Anatomical
Figure Astride a Monster*, 1524. Engraving, 24.9 × 18.2 cm (image).
British Museum, London. H,7.32.

Dating from around the same time is a radically different appropriation of the *Laocoon*. A German medal design of 1546 uses the motif in a remarkable exercise in anti-papal propaganda (FIG. 26).[81] A Laocoonesque bearded old man bears the features of Pope Paul III; he rides on a serpent while a figure to the left defecates into the papal tiara. The inscription can be translated as "The son of corruption now reveals himself as beyond all godly things, whom Our Lord Jesus will kill by his breath." This strident Reformation image by Hans Schenck uses a familiar sculpture closely associated with the Vatican to attack the papacy, which had convened the Council of Trent the year before the medal was made.

ROSSO FIORENTINO: APOLLO AND LAOCOON, ANATOMY AND ART
A more distant but equally bizarre derivation of the *Laocoon* is Rosso Fiorentino's image of a screeching figure astride a roaring monster, his raised arm entwined with a snake (FIG. 27).[82] Significantly, the figure is just as dependent on the *Apollo Belvedere*, which has similarly positioned arms and even a stump to support the right hand. The original poem printed with Gian Jacopo Caraglio's engraving expresses the horror and anguish from the figure's point of view: "With fearful eyes I hide and withdraw."[83] Vasari calls this a "desiccated anatomical figure" (*figura di notomia secca*), which explicitly connects the image to the scientific study of cadavers.[84] Artists like Michelangelo, Montorsoli, and Cosini were reported to have dissected corpses in the name of art. Sixteenth-century anatomical prints show dissected bodies with contorted limbs and exaggerated gestures close to the pose of Rosso's figure, a parallel already seen in the artist's *Allegory of Death and Fame* of 1518.[85] Because the figure is hardly recognizable as derived from the *Laocoon* (unlike Boldrini's woodcut or Schenck's medal), it cannot be a parody or a caricature, which depend on a familiar reference.[86]

The helpless figure (he lacks a penis) might be a kind of self-portrait, since Rosso Fiorentino had just lost an important commission in 1524 and, even more career-damaging, had been accused of attacking Michelangelo's Sistine Ceiling. Rosso was forced to write an apology to Michelangelo in which he praised the ceiling as "divinely made."[87] Untraditional images, like self-portraits, are often self-reflexive, and the best interpretation of the print's tone and poetic gloss is that the figure is consumed by an obsessive passion for his art.[88] The subtle references to ancient sculpture are overwhelmed by the comic fear of the principal figure, a self-mocking tone that accords with Rosso's personal circumstances.

FIG. 28
Vincenzo de' Rossi, *Laocoon and His Sons*,
ca. 1570. Marble. W. Apolloni, Rome.

ADAPTING THE *LAOCOON*

Reverberations of the *Laocoon* were felt throughout the sixteenth century. Silvio Cosini borrowed the pose for Neptune's outstretched arm in a relief on the Jacopo Sannazaro monument in Naples, and for his *Flaying of Marsyas* (CAT. 27). Sculptural versions of the subject include Vincenzo de' Rossi's marble carved in the 1570s (FIG. 28), which gives the two sons greater prominence within a pyramidal composition.[89] The result, if somewhat awkward, is a work meant to be seen from multiple sides. Rossi has Laocoon grasp the serpent's head in his upraised arm – a gesture more defiant than Montorsoli's. In contrast to Rossi's expansive composition is the highly condensed rendering by Adriaen de Vries (Nationalmuseum, Stockholm). His bronze of 1623 positions the three figures at different heights to create a tightly spiraling composition.[90]

The composition of a father and son centered around an altar had an obvious parallel with depictions of the Sacrifice of Isaac. Artists borrowed freely from the *Laocoon* for this subject, as seen in a drawing by Il Sodoma and paintings by Andrea del Sarto and Titian.[91] A century later, Giuseppe Piamontini returned to a Laocoon-like composition for his bronze version of the Sacrifice of Isaac.[92]

Montorsoli's *John the Baptist* in the Currier Museum of Art taps into the artist's experience as restorer of ancient works. The unprecedented type of his *Baptist* is closer to the striding ancient warriors than to the gaunt hermit or delicate adolescent of earlier Renaissance representations. The musculature evident in the terracotta, especially the right arm and hand, resemble Michelangelo's work as well as the restored *Hercules and Telephos*. The head of the Baptist is older and more intense than earlier images of the saint: the anguished features of Laocoon may have been a critical influence. Finally, the pose of Montorsoli's Baptist resembles the *Apollo Belvedere*, although it has been given greater force and forward movement. The opposing types of the *Apollo* and the *Laocoon*, which played oversize roles in the Cinquecento, come together in Montorsoli's work. If they had not been discovered, they would have had to be invented. And in some very important ways – through their restorations, innumerable copies, and infinite variations – they were.

The quest to identify works described in the various sixteenth-century accounts of the *Laocoon* has often led to mistaken identities, as we have seen. Vasari reports that Clement VII went daily to the Belvedere courtyard for recreation and prayer, so Montorsoli, who was then restoring the *Laocoon* and the *Apollo*, was able to carve the pope's portrait in marble.[93] The result brought Montorsoli much praise and the pope conceived a "very great affection for him" because Montorsoli drew all night in order to have new things to show him each morning. In her admirable monograph on Montorsoli, Birgit Laschke suggested an identification of the lost bust of Clement VII on the basis of a nineteenth-century photograph (FIG. 29).[94] In fact, the bust had appeared at auction in 1988 as possibly a portrait of Cardinal Federico Cesi (1500–1565).[95] Around 1890, the bust had been photographed in the Palazzo Cesi, Rome, when it was called a bust of a Cardinal Cesi by Michelangelo.[96] If the attribution was wishful thinking, the identity of the sitter reflected family tradition, as confirmed by a medal of Federico Cesi made by Gianfederico Bonzagna in 1561 (FIG. 30), which shows the same profile.[97] The nineteenth-century photographs of the bust clearly show that this medal was affixed to the front of the base, which provides further proof for the identification. Close inspection of the marble bust (now in the Arp Museum, Remagen, on loan from the Rau Collection as Montorsoli's portrait of Clement VII), demonstrates that it is neither by Montorsoli nor a depiction of Clement VII, whose distinctive profile is absent in the marble.[98] Montorsoli's bust of the pope remains lost.

Charles Davis published a posthumous bust of Federico Cesi made in 1577 by Leonardo Sormano for the Cesi family pantheon in the family palace northeast of Rome.[99] Sormano's marble may have been based on the earlier bust.

The brothers Federico and Paolo Cesi owned one of the most magnificent Renaissance gardens adorned with ancient sculpture.[100] In 1537, Federico inherited the garden from his brother and expanded its holdings. Situated just southwest of Saint Peter's Basilica, it was depicted by Hendrik van Cleve (National Gallery, Prague) and described by Ulisse Aldrovandi in 1550. Federico Cesi was also a patron of Michelangelo, who designed a painting of the Annunciation for him (Santa Maria della Pace, Rome).

FIG. 29
Italian, *Portrait of Cardinal Federico Cesi*, ca. 1560. Marble, height 65.5 cm. Photograph by Romualdo Moscioni, ca. 1890. The bust is now in the Rau Collection, on loan to the Arp Museum, Remagen.

FIG. 30
Gianfederico Bonzagna, *Medal of Cardinal Federico Cesi*, 1561. Bronze, diameter 3.5 cm. Private collection.

1.   From the introduction to part three of the *Lives of the Artists*; Vasari 1966 (eds. 1550 and 1568), vol. 4, pp. 7, 8.

2.   Vasari 1966 (ed. 1568), vol. 5, p. 493: "e diede ordine di racconciare l'Hercole similmente." On Montorsoli's restorations, see Laschke 1993, pp. 25–30; Laschke 1998; Rebaudo 2007.

3.   Brummer 1970; Haskell and Penny 1981; Bober and Rubinstein 2010. The literature on the *Laocoon* is vast and varied, as seen below.

4.   Fusco and Corti 2006, pp. 52–56.

5.   Agostino's engraving: Illustrated Bartsch, vol. 27, no. 328; Mantua and Vienna 1999, p. 199.

6.   For the history of the sculpture in the early 16th century see: Brummer 1970, pp. 44–71; Bober and Rubinstein 2010, pp. 76–77; Winner 1998a; Bloemacher 2016, pp. 72–76.

7.   Washington and New York 2011, p. 7. In 1498, Ludovico Gonzaga complained that Antico's model of the *Apollo Belvedere* had been stolen to make unauthorized casts.

8.   The tree trunk needed to be raised slightly to support the new hand.

9.   From the so-called Marten de Vos sketchbook consisting of twelve drawings from around the 1560s based on various earlier sources. Brummer 1970, p. 133; Boon 1978, no. 615: folio 3 verso [perhaps by a Haarlem artist].

10.   See Haskell and Penny 1981, p. 188, repr.

11.   Brummer 1970, pp. 133–37; Haskell and Penny 1981, pp. 188–89; Bober and Rubinstein 2010, pp. 131–32.

12.   Rubinstein 1998, pp. 280–81.

13.   Möseneder 1979, p. 79, gives the restoration of the River God/Arno to Montorsoli. Collareta 1985 suggests that a model by Michelangelo might be the basis of the head. The Montorsoli attribution was argued by Rubinstein 1998. Laschke 1993, p. 30, rejected the attribution to Montorsoli, noting significant differences with the handling of the head of *Saint Cosmas*. Lorenzo Principi (conversation July 2018) suggests that the head may be by Baccio Bandinelli, based on comparison with the sculptor's work, including the papal monuments in Santa Maria sopra Minerva, Rome.

14.   Vasari 1966, vol. 5, p. 496. Additional details in Frey 1923, pp. 52–62, 70–72.

15.   ffolliott 1984, pp. 11–14. This remains the best analysis of the Messina fountains, with careful attention to the triumphal imagery: pp. 73–138, 163–78. See also Laschke 1993, p. 37.

16.   Albèri 1846, p. 116: "ma l' eccelenza del Laocoonte fa dimenticar questa [Venus] e l' Apollo, che per lo innanzi era tanto celebrato."

17.   For example, Richter 1992; Loh 2011. Kenneth Clark in his introduction to the television series *Civilisation* of 1969, used the *Apollo Belvedere* as an example of old-fashioned high-brow taste.

18.   Catterson 2005.

19.   Shearman 1967, p. 15.

20.   For the work's history in the Renaissance, see especially Rebaudo 2007; also Brummer 1970. On its critical history: Haskell and Penny 1981; Settis 1999; Rome 2006.

21.   See discussion in Rome 2006.

22.   The priest is named in Greek Λαοκόων or Laokoōn. Virgil's Latin is Laocoon.

23.   Roskill 2000, pp. 168–69.

24.   Print by Brescia: Illustrated Bartsch, vol. 24, no. 15; Zucker 1984, p. 352 [as ca. 1520]; Gramaccini and Meier 2009, p. 138. A drawing inscribed 1508 on the verso also shows the sculpture on the ground (Kunstmuseum, Dusseldorf); Winner 1974, pp. 100–102; Rome 2006, pp. 125–26. For the date of the plinth, see Rome 2006, p. 127, which correctly dismisses any close relationship between the Dusseldorf drawing and Brescia's print, since they are seen from slightly different angles.

25.   Howard 1959; Howard 1989; Brilliant 2000, pp. 64–66.

26.   Vasari 1966, vol. 6, p. 178.

27.   The evidence for the date is considered in detail by Mozzati 2007, pp. 569–70. Shearman 1977, pp. 136–37, had dated the competition to 1507 or 1508. We should

remember, of course, that all four participants may not have been together at the same time, and that Vasari may not have have been entirely accurate.

28.   The bronze belonging to Cardinal Domenico Grimani is independently documented; Boucher 1991, vol. 2, p. 361. Grimani seems to have been fascinated with the *Laocoon* as he commissioned Moderno's silver plaquette of the Flagellation of Christ (Kunsthistorisches Museum, Vienna), which is derived in part from Laocoon's pose (see p. 153). Another bronze attributed to Sansovino was in the collection of Cosimo I in 1553, and this is sometimes identified with a bronze in the Bargello (inv. 427), which lacks the right arm; Boucher 1991, vol. 2, pp. 314–15, fig. 21. See also Boucher 1991, vol. 1, pp. 9–10; vol. 2, pp. 361–62 [as tentatively attributed]. Another bronze, in the Victoria and Albert Museum, has also been attributed to Sansovino: Rome 2006, pp. 137–38, no. 24.

29.   Landau and Parshall 1994, pp. 120–46. Since then, a torrent of studies have considered the implications of the print workshop around Raphael: Viljoen 2001; Pon 2004; Witcombe 2008; Gramaccini and Meier 2009; Bloemacher 2016; and in a broader context, Mantua and Vienna 1999.

30.   Landau and Parshall 1994, p. 146. They note that there is no indication that the first plates were worn and needed to be replaced, especially since it would be easier to re-engrave the original plate; this refutes Shoemaker 1981, p. 11 (recently repeated without discussion in Chicago et al. 2005, p. 77).

31.   There is a drawing by Raphael or his circle of the *Apollo Belvedere* which is similar but not identical to the print by Agostino Veneziano: Mantua and Vienna 1999, nos. 29a, 132, 133.

32.   Agostino: In addition to FIG. 1, there is a version in reverse in a niche also signed "A.V."; Illustrated Bartsch, vol. 27, no. 329. Raimondi made two engravings, one in reverse, of Apollo Kitharodos (Bartsch nos. 332, 333); and Apollo with a harp from the *School of Athens* (Bartsch nos. 334, 335). See Bloemacher 2016, pp. 72–77, 268–83.

33.   This idea is developed by Norberto Gramaccini in Gramaccini and Meier 2009, pp. 22–31.

34.   Illustrated Bartsch, vol. 26, no. 195.

35.   Brummer 1970, pp. 115–17; Viljoen 2001. For the Virgil manuscript in the Biblioteca Apostolica Vaticano, Rome, see Wright 1993.

36.   A. Gnann in Mantua and Vienna 1999, p. 120.

37.   Viljoen 2001.

38.   Oberhuber 1999, p. 252, no. 153. The painting, which was in the Tribuna of the Uffizi by 1584, has also been attributed to the workshop of Raphael or to Giulio Romano; see Florence 1984, p. 222.

39.   The example of the woodcut in the British Museum, London (1874,0808.187) is exceptional for its careful highlighting in gold. The print is attributed to Niccolò Boldrini, from the middle of the 16th century, by: Gnann 2013, no. 182; Gnann 2014, pp. 164, 171, 216; N. Takahatake in Los Angeles 2018, p. 209 note 5. Attributed to Ugo da Carpi: Illustrated Bartsch, vol. 48, p. 108, no. 18; Carpi 2009, no. 17.

40.   Vasari 1966, vol. 5, p. 246: "Restaurò ancora l'antico Laoconte del braccio destro, il quale essendo tronco e non trovandosi, Baccio ne fece uno di cera grande che corrispondeva co' muscoli e con la fierezza e maniera all'antico, e con lui s'univa di sorte, che mostrò quanto Baccio intendeva dell'arte: e questo modello gli servì a fare l'intero braccio al suo."

41.   Vasari 1966, vol. 5, p. 246; Waldman 2004, pp. 55–57, 69. Bandinelli made a wax model and a full-scale drawing of his Laocoon.

42.   Vasari 1966, vol. 5, p. 246: "Baccio rispose che, nonché farne un pari, gli bastava l'animo di passare quello di perfezzione."

43.   Albèri 1846, p. 116; Waldman 2004, p. 69: "e già sono fatti li putti, che sono lì in una camera; ma il maestro, se anche vivesse cinquecento anni, e ne avesse fatti cento, non potria mai far cosa eguale."

44.   Vasari 1966, vol. 6, p. 118: "Domandato da uno amico suo quel che gli paresse d'uno che aveva contrafatto di marmo figure antiche delle più celebrate, vantandosi lo immitatore che di gran lunga aveva superato gli antichi, rispose: 'Chi va dietro a altri, mai non li passa innanzi; e chi non sa far bene da sé, non può servirsi bene delle cose d'altri.'" Lavin 1998, p. 198.

45.   Benedetto Varchi even mentioned the episode in his funeral oration for Michelangelo in 1564, when he specifically said that the copy was of the *Laocoon*; Varchi 1564, p. 39. For Cellini: Settis 1999, p. 224.

46.   Cellini 1901, p. 352: "bellezza, et di virtù di intelligientia, et di rara maniera"; and "Sapiate che questi antichi

non intendevano niente la notomia, et per questo le opere loro sono tutte piene di errori." On the disagreements between Cellini and Bandinelli, see Vossilla 1997.

47. Attributed to Sansovino by Middeldorf 1932, pp. 242–45, and Boucher 1991, vol. 1, pp. 9–10; vol. 2, p. 377 [who connected the sheet with a drawing of Laocoon's younger son in the Louvre, inv. 2712]. Charles Davis in *Kunstchronik* 46 (1993), pp. 360–61, attributed the Uffizi drawing to Sodoma. I. Leone in Rome 2006, no. 29 [as Sodoma but without citing Davis and with the wrong illustration]. Rebaudo 2007, p. 81, no. DS3 [as Florentine or Sienese, with incorrect inventory number and caption, and a summary of earlier attributions]. On Sodoma and Raphael, see Bartalini 2001.

48. Pollak's diaries and memoirs have been published: Guldan 1988; Pollak 1994. Mistakes about Pollak have crept into recent accounts: Bober and Rubinstein 2010, p. 165, attributed the discovery of the original arm to Adriano Prandi; Barkan 1999, p. 9, called him a German archaeologist.

49. Discussed by Brummer 1970, pp. 114–19; Brilliant 2000, pp. 1–10, 29–39.

50. Clark 1956, p. 220.

51. Lomazzo 1584, p. 437 (book 6): "Michel'Angelo ne fa fede ilquale non e mai potuto aggiungere alla bellezza del torso d'Hercole, Apollonia Ateniese che si trova in belvedere in Roma che fù da lui continouamente seguitato."

52. On the myths surrounding Michelangelo and antiquity see, for example, Barkan 1999, pp. 197–207.

53. Vasari 1966, vol. 5, p. 494.

54. Pressouyre 1969; Seelig-Teuwen 2003; Rome 2006, pp. 150–51. The other works copied at the Vatican were *Cleopatra* and *Venus*; the casts of the *Tiber* and two sphinxes do not survive.

55. Brummer 1970, p. 89, says that Montorsoli's restoration was not on the *Laocoon* in 1540. Rossi Pinelli 1986, pp. 186–87, suggests the cast is deliberately fragmentary.

56. Magi 1961, pp. 11–15, 46–47; Brummer 1970, pp. 88–89; Laschke 1998; Rebaudo 2007, pp. 30–42.
   Brummer 1970, p. 89, thought that Primaticcio's copy of the *Laocoon* of 1540 showed the edge of the right shoulder before it was cut down, supposedly to add the mystery marble arm. A drawing (ibid., fig. 76) purportedly shows a straight cut at the shoulder and a gap between it and the attached arm. Paolo Liverani in Rome 2006, p. 180, rightly questions the validity of this conclusion and suggests the cut and slots could have been made much later. Barkan 1999, p. 11, comments on Michelangelo's supposed mutilation of the *Laocoon*.

57. Richardson 1722, p. 277: "An Arm was begun for it by Mich. Angelo, but not Finish'd, as it Is it lies down by the Figures." The account of Roman monuments is by Jonathan Richardson the Younger (1694–1771), son of the painter Jonathan Richardson the Elder. Rebaudo 2007, p. 31 (repeated by Paolo Liverani in Rome 2006, p. 180), mistranslates the passage as a report that Michelangelo left the work unfinished "per modestia" and that the arm was behind the pedestal, but these elements are not in the original text.

58. Magi 1960, pp. 11, 46, as Michelangelo; Brummer 1970, p. 89. Barkan 1999, p. 11, maintains a connection with Michelangelo. On the critical reception of the arm, see Rebaudo 2007, pp. 30–42.

59. Rebaudo 2007, pp. 34–35, figs. 16–18, concludes that the arm is closer to Bandinelli than to any other artist. Visconti 1818, vol. 2, p. 243 note 1, attributed the arm to Montorsoli; the website catalogue of the Musei Vaticani (inv. 1067) listed the work as by Montorsoli in 2017 and 2018.

60. Daltrop 1982, pp. 18–19, 25, 27; Paolo Liverani in Rome 2006, pp. 180–81 [with earlier references].

61. Richardson 1722, p. 277. On Cornacchini's work of 1725–27, see Brummer 1970, p. 101; Rebaudo 2007, pp. 53–59.

62. Most of the wall drawings are assigned to Michelangelo by: Dal Poggetto 1979; Dal Poggetto 2012 (pp. 40–41 on the Laocoon drawing); and Hartt 1992. The attribution to Michelangelo is rejected by Elam 1981 and Collareta 1992. Other authoritative sources (Bambach 2017) have avoided discussion of the mural drawings.

63. Elam 1981, p. 601, fig. 24 [perhaps Montorsoli]. Elam attributed several drawings to Montorsoli. Collareta 1992, pp. 165–66, assigns some of wall drawings to Montorsoli, but calls the head of Laocoon anonymous 16th century (p. 172, fig. 15).

64. Bambach 2017, pp. 70, 72–73.

65. Auction of Michel Gaud, St. Tropez, at Sotheby's, Monaco, June 20, 1987 (lot 80). The assignment to Montorsoli: Nesselrath 1998a; Winner 1998, p. 125, figs.

8, 9; P. Liverani in Rome 2006, no. 39 [more hesitantly]; Viljoen 2007, p. 23 [who accepts the Montorsoli attribution without citing other views].

66. The inscriptions read: for drapery of one son: "questa c[on] panno" (this with cloth); "questo serpe fala no[n] rotta" (this serpent to render unbroken) and "e questo fala cosi" (and this is like that). Montorsoli's drawing for the seal: Laschke 1987; Laschke 1993, pp. 143, 165, figs. 177–79.

67. Laschke 1993, p. 27 note 23; Laschke 1998, p. 183 note 44. Rebaudo 2007, pp. 25–27, 87.

68. The Musée Calvet now more correctly calls the sheet Florentine ca. 1560.

69. Vasari 1966, vol. 5, p. 497.

70. ffolliott 1984, pp. 23–24. Vasari says that Bandinelli was angered by Montorsoli's taking over a commission in Genoa that Bandinelli had abandoned.

71. Vasari 1966, vol. 5, p. 501: "che per allora non volle altrimenti tornare a rivedere Fiorenza, parendogli che troppo fusse sopportata la prosonzione, arroganza et insolenza di quell'uomo."

72. Florence 2011, pp. 382–87.

73. Waldman 2006. The drawing has also been attributed to the Netherlandish artist Lambert Lombard (ibid., p. 99).

74. Janson 1946. See also Nadine Orenstein in McPhee and Orenstein 2011, no. 42.

75. Rosand and Muraro 1976, p. 190. They note that Titian's motto was "Art is more powerful than nature" (Natura potentior ars).

76. Ridolfi 1648, vol. 1, p. 183; Rosand and Muraro 1976, p. 188: Titian also designed images for prints, including "un gentil pensiero di tre Bertuccie sedenti, attorniate da serpi, nella guisa del Laocoonte, e de' figliuoli posti in Belvedere di Roma" (a nice idea of three seated Barbary apes, entwined by snakes, in the guise of Laocoon and the sons located in the Belvedere in Rome).

77. Cardinal Domenico Grimani owned the bronze cast of Sansovino's copy of the Laocoon made ca. 1508; it was bequeathed to the Republic in 1523 and kept in the guardaroba of the Council of Ten; then given to the Cardinal of Lorraine in 1534; Boucher 1991, vol. 2, p. 361.

78. Rosand and Muraro 1976, p. 188, identify specific comparisons, while suggesting that the weaker landscape of the caricature print reflects the absence of a drawn model by Titian.

79. Barkan 1999, pp. 11, 13–14, 16. Barkan's suggestion depends on several unlikely conjectures regarding Michelangelo's involvement with the Laocoon, including his making of the mysterious marble arm in the Vatican and the drawing of Laocoon's head in the New Sacristy basement.

80. Titian's authorship of the design is reported by Carlo Ridolfi (Ridolfi 1648, vol. 1, p. 183) and is usually accepted.

81. Wischermann 1979. The medal design is now attributed to Hans Schenck. The obverse is a portrait of Hans Klur, aged 47, accompanied by a figure of Death. The inscription on the reverse reads, "Nunc revelatur filius perditionis qui se extulit super omne quod deus est quem dominus nostr Iesus interficiet spiritu oris sui z thez."

82. Carroll 1987, pp. 24, 39, 73–74. Illustrated Bartsch, vol. 28: Commentary, pp. 192–94.

83. "Negliocchi spaventosi albergo e chiudo."

84. Vasari 1966, vol. 5, p. 16: "sua figura di notomia secca, che ha una testa di morte in mano e siede sopra un serpente, mentre un cigno canta" (his desiccated anatomical figure who has a death's head in his hand and sits upon a serpent, while a swan sings).

85. Kornell 1989, esp. p. 845.

86. Campbell 2002, p. 600, argues that this is an element of the print. Schmidt 2003, pp. 353, 369, goes further in titling the print "Laokoon-Parodie." The title conventionally given to the print beginning with Bartsch, "Fury," is inaccurate and historically unjustified.

87. Campbell 2002, p. 596.

88. Campbell 2002, pp. 600–602. Carroll 1987, p. 74, connects the print to Rosso's personal circumstances in 1524.

89. Heikamp 1990; Heikamp 2017.

90. Amsterdam et al. 1998, no. 41. Bronze, height 172 cm.

91. Il Sodoma: Uffizi, inv 1455F. Andrea de Sarto: Museo del Prado, Madrid; and Cleveland Museum of Art. Titian: Santa Maria della Salute, Venice.

92. Detroit and Florence 1974, no. 52, repr.; Wardropper 2011, p. 159, repr.

93. Vasari 1966, vol. 5, p. 493; echoed by Borghini 1584, pp. 495–96.

94. Laschke 1993, pp. 13, 61, 166, no. 6A, fig. 39.

95. Sotheby's, London, April 21, 1988 (lot 91, unsold); noting the traditional identification, and attributed to the late sixteenth or early seventeenth century.

96. *Catalogo delle fotografie esistenti nello stabilomento fotografico artistico commerciale di Romualdo Moscioni fondato fin dall'anno 1868 Roma* (Rome, 1893), p. 28, no. 2999: "Palazzo Cesi, Busto del Cardinale, di Michelangelo." Moscioni's negatives survive in the Fototeca of the Musei Vaticani and there are copies of the photographs in the Fototeca Zeri, Bologna, and the Kunsthistorisches Institut, Florence. I am grateful for the help of Katherine Bentz of Saint Anselm College and Alexander Kader of Sotheby's.

97. Attwood 2003, nos. 959; there is also a medal fom 1564: no. 1044. The reverse shows the church of Santa Caterina dei Funari, Rome, which was rebuilt with the support of Federico Cesi.

98. This opinion was developed with Kurt Sundstrom and Lorenzo Principi, and this text reflects their observations.

99. Davis 2014; Nocchi 2015.

100. Eiche 1995; Bentz 2013.

FIG. I

Giovan Angelo Montorsoli, *Charles V*, 1539–41.
Marble, height 78 cm. Museo Nazionale della Certosa di San
Martino, Naples. CAT. 11.

MONTORSOLI AND THE HAPSBURG COURT

Sergio Ramiro Ramírez

GIOVAN ANGELO MONTORSOLI'S REPUTATION AS A TALENTED FOLLOWER OF MICHELANGELO brought him to the attention of the court of Andrea Doria (1466–1560), the celebrated admiral and ruler of Genoa. For centuries Genoa had been the maritime connection between Italy and Spain, and the city also provided the conduit for Montorsoli's work to enter the circle of Holy Roman Emperor Charles V as part of the commercial and political dialogue between Genoa and the Hapsburg monarchy.[1]

Montorsoli's first commission in Genoa was a colossal portrait of Andrea Doria as an ancient commander, which he began in March 1539 and completed in July 1540.[2] After this project (of which only a fragment survives, in the Palazzo Ducale, Genoa), Montorsoli embarked on a series of works for the Doria family, as well as for Charles V's court, propelled by the Genoese family's efforts to cultivate the imperial court on its peripatetic journeys through Europe. Montorsoli spent two periods working in Genoa, from 1539 to 1541, and then from 1543 to 1547. Giorgio Vasari describes Montorsoli's work for Genoa and Spain, although his chronology is not clear. In conjunction with the Triton Fountain for the Villa del Principe in Genoa (see FIG. 16), Vasari says that Montorsoli made a similar "monster" – Tritons having human torsos and fish tails – that was sent to Nicolas Perrenot de Granvelle (1486–1550), the emperor's trusted advisor. Then Vasari writes: "He made a large Neptune in stucco, which was placed on a pedestal in the prince's garden. He made two portraits of the same prince and two of Charles V, which were taken by Cobos to Spain."[3] Montorsoli apparently made two portrait busts of Andrea Doria, and two of Charles V, the latter given to the imperial secretary, Francisco de los Cobos (ca. 1477–1547), who had them shipped to Spain.

In this period, Italian princes presented lavish gifts, often of works of art, to Hapburg officials to pave the way for their petitions to be heard by the emperor. Charles V had wisely delegated the processing of these requests to his senior courtiers, Cobos and Granvelle, who received and negotiated petitions before presenting them to the emperor. For example, in 1537, Duke Cosimo I of Florence gave Michelangelo's *Young John the Baptist* to Cobos. By amassing so many gifts of artworks, Cobos and Granvelle also played an important role in defining a new image of Charles V with strong classical references. These Italian works, which gradually supplanted the earlier Flemish style of representing the emperor, encouraged a wider shift in Charles V's image in alignment with the idea of a universal monarchy like that of ancient Rome, as had been advocated by Mercurino Gattinara (1465–1530), grand chancellor to Charles V. Although nearly all of the art objects were gifts to imperial courtiers rather than to the emperor himself, some of them made their way into his possession.

The image of Charles V as global ruler became especially prominent after his coronation as Holy Roman Emperor in Bologna on February 24, 1530. A determined propaganda campaign advanced the myth that Charles was the true successor to the Roman emperors.[4] The new imperial imagery combined references to antiquity with the Burgundian traditions associated with Charles V's dynastic lineage. The most successful purveyor of this new vision was Titian, who first painted Charles V in 1532 or 1533 after the defeat of the Ottoman army at Vienna.[5] Titian's portrait, now lost (see FIG. 4), showed the emperor wearing armor and holding a sword, its aggressive, authoritarian style eschewing humanistic or religious references. The image proved enormously influential for the development of military portraiture, not only of Charles V and his family, but also of Italian princes hoping to emulate the emperor.

By the time he made his bust of Charles V (FIG. 1), Montorsoli already had some experience portraying rulers in armor. In 1534, he was commissioned to make a wax portrait of the new duke of Florence, Alessandro de' Medici (1510–1537), for the church of Santissima Annunziata, Florence. Vasari states that the portrait "was executed in a way that was unusual from others and very beautiful," as the duke was portrayed "armed and kneeling over a helmet in the Burgundian style, and with one hand to his chest in the act of appealing to the Madonna there."[6]

Vasari emphasizes the distinctive nature of the portrait, which anticipates later developments, although the duke's posture still manifests the humility appropriate to the religious setting. The pointed reference to a Burgundian helmet, called a *burgonet*, connects the votive wax figure directly to Charles V, whose

FIG. 2
Montorsoli, *Charles V*, 1539–41.
Marble. Museo Nazionale della
Certosa di San Martino, Naples.
CAT. 11.

FIG. 3
Workshop of Montorsoli, *Charles V*,
1539–41. Marble, height 100 cm.
Museo Nacional del Prado, Madrid.
E288.

Burgundian court had developed a new style of helmet by drawing upon ancient examples.[7] Duke Alessandro owed his position to the emperor, who not only restored the Medici to power in 1530 but also arranged for his daughter Margaret to marry Alessandro. Around the same time, in 1532 or 1533, Montorsoli carved a marble bust of the duke's uncle, Pope Clement VII, which is now lost (see p. 56).

Two busts have usually been suggested as candidates for the portraits of Charles V mentioned by Vasari: one in the Certosa di San Martino, Naples, the other in the Museo Nacional del Prado, Madrid (FIGS. 2, 3).[8] Both show Charles V in his thirties, wearing a cuirass with two protective disks (besagews) decorated with fleurs-de-lis. The breastplate is almost identical to the armor made around 1525 to 1530 by Kolman Helmschmid of Augsburg (Real Armería, Madrid, inv. A.66).[9] In both busts, the emperor wears the chain of the Toisón de Oro, insignia of the grand master of the Order of the Golden Fleece.

In order to portray the emperor, Montorsoli probably used prints after Titian's portrait of 1532 to 1533, which circulated in an engraving by Agostino Veneziano dated 1535 (FIG. 4) and woodcuts by Giovanni Britto.[10] However, Montorsoli must have also seen the emperor in person during his triumphal entry into Florence on April 26, 1536, when the artist participated in making ephemeral decorations under the supervision of Vasari. Although the final likeness suggests that the emperor never actually posed for him, Montorsoli must have scrutinized his appearance as Charles V passed in procession.

Among the surviving portrait busts, the one in Naples is of the highest quality and appears to be the primary work from which the other busts derive. The face is finely delineated, with the iris and pupil carved

FIG. 4
Agostino Veneziano after Titian,
Charles V (1532), 1535. Engraving,
44.5 × 30.8 cm. Albertina, Vienna.

FIG. 5
Back of the bust in Naples (FIG. 2).

FIG. 6
Back of the bust in Madrid (FIG. 3).

FIG. 7
Montorsoli, *Bust of Jacopo Sannazaro*,
1540–41. Marble. Santa Maria del
Parto, Naples.

FIG. 8
Detail of the bust
in Naples (FIG. 2).

in the fashion of other portraits by the artist. The emperor seems to turn to engage the observer, as does Montorsoli's bust of Jacopo Sannazaro in Naples (FIG. 7), made around 1541 to 1542, roughly the moment when the bust of Charles V was being carved. The busts share expressive wrinkles around the cheeks and eyes, a feature also found in the Montorsoli's bust of Alfonso V of Aragón (see FIG. 15). The portrait of Charles V gains in naturalism through the teeth glimpsed within the half-open mouth, while the prominent veins at the temples soften the hardness of the marble (FIG. 8).

Each bust depicts a determined and formidable sitter. However, the somewhat lost look of a taciturn personality that Titian captured perfectly is missing in Montorsoli's rendering of Charles V. The sculptor tempers the emperor's famous extended lower jaw, described by Venetian ambassador Gaspare Contarini as "so wide and so long that is does not seem natural to the body."[11]

FIG. 9
Detail of the bust in Madrid
(FIG. 3).

FIG. 10
Detail of the bust in Naples.

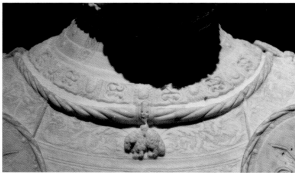

FIG. 11
Detail of the bust in Madrid.

FIG. 12
Workshop of Montorsoli, *Charles V*,
1539–41. Marble, height 51 cm.
Monastère royal de Brou,
Bourg-en-Bresse. 961.79.

FIG. 13
Detail of FIG. 12.

Close comparison of the two portraits of Charles V reveals that the carving of the face in the Prado version is less fine than that in Naples. For example, the treatment of the hair, which separates into fine strands along the cheek of the Naples bust, is more summary in the work in the Prado, where the hair is treated almost as a helmet (FIG. 9). Similarly, the ram signifying the Order of the Golden Fleece, which hangs from the end of the collar, has more convincing natural weight in the Naples bust (FIGS. 10, 11).

It is very likely that the Prado example was produced in a workshop in Genoa, reproducing the Naples original.[12] There are, however, other significant differences between the two busts in Naples and Madrid, which suggest that they might have had divergent roles. The delicate engraving found on Helmschmid's suit of armor is carefully rendered in the Prado marble, but almost entirely missing in the Naples portrait. Where one version emphasizes the convincing rendering of the face, the other presents an image of military authority, an approach that sets the stage for later sculptures of the Hapsburg rulers by Leone and Pompeo Leoni.

The marble bust in the Prado is documented in Spain by the end of the sixteenth century, as it appears in a 1602 inventory of the goods left by Philip II at his death in 1598. This supports its identification as one of the two portraits given to Spain, as reported by Vasari. At the beginning of the eighteenth century, the bust was located in the Galería del Poniente of the Alcázar Palace, Madrid, probably in an exterior niche, since the marble shows signs of wear (except on the back) as a consequence of exposure to the elements. Therefore, it is likely that the bust was in the Spanish royal collections from shortly after it was made until its entry into the Museo del Prado.

Another example of this model is found in the Brou monastery at Bourg-en-Bresse (FIG. 12).[13] Unfortunately, the work has suffered greatly from exposure, with the back, base, and parts of the armor and shoulders missing, and the surface heavily worn. The material appears identical to that of the Prado bust: a white marble with pyrite crystals and particles of mica, which could have been quarried in the Alps or at Carrara. The decoration still visible on the armor also shows close similarities with the bust in Madrid (FIG. 13). Although the foliage and flowers on the breastplate derive from the Naples portrait, the rest of the bas-relief carving on the Bourg armor matches that of the Madrid version. Consequently, it appears that the busts in Bourg and Madrid are workshop copies made in Genoa based on the original now in Naples. The most plausible hypothesis is that the two copies, being of equivalent quality, were sent to Spain in 1541, probably with Granvelle rather than with Cobos, who was not in Genoa at the time; Vasari's confusion of the two imperial courtiers is understandable.

These three portraits associated with Montorsoli belong to a concerted sculptural campaign to shape the imperial image. The Hapsburg palaces were adorned with portraits that connected Charles V with the great Roman emperors. This was also the case with the palaces and gardens dedicated to the imperial theme, such as the Alcázar in Madrid, where the Prado version of the bust was once installed. Relatives of the emperor and court officials requested similar sculptures. For example, a portrait that Margaret, Duchess of Parma, the natural daughter of Charles V, commissioned from Bartolomeo Cancellieri shows her seated near a bust of the emperor that bears a marked resemblance to Montorsoli's (FIG. 14).[14]

Another portrait by Montorsoli, depicting Alfonso V of Aragón, king of Naples (1396–1458), might be seen as furthering the connection between the emperor and the artist's Genoa patron, Andrea Doria. Alfonso's bust (FIG. 15), featuring a rounded breastplate, shares the general format of the portraits of Charles V. As the Spanish ruler of Naples, Alfonso was a precursor to Charles V and his hegemony over Italian states. It has therefore been suggested that Montorsoli's busts of Charles V, Andrea Doria (now lost), and Alfonso of Aragón formed a triptych celebrating Spain's connection with Italy, probably commissioned by the Doria court.[15] This theory is strengthened by the fact that all three busts would have shown the Order of the Golden Fleece. On the other hand, there is a lack of evidence surrounding the Alfonso portrait commission, whereas Vasari explicitly linked the portraits of Andrea Doria and Charles V. Nor, given the absence of documentation, is it absolutely certain that the bust in Vienna represents Alfonso of Aragón, rather than an ancestor of Charles V like the emperors Maximilian I or Frederick III. Finally,

FIG. 14
Bartolomeo Cancellieri, *Margaret, Duchess of Parma*, ca. 1550–55. Oil on canvas, 169.9 × 105.3 cm. Galleria Nazionale di Parma. 1466.

FIG. 15
Montorsoli, *Alfonso V of Aragón*, 1540s. Marble, height with base 96 cm. Kunsthistorisches Museum, Vienna. KK 5441.

FIG. 16

Montorsoli, *Triton*, ca. 1540–43.
Marble. Fountain at the Villa del
Principe, Genoa.

FIG. 17

Attributed to Montorsoli, *Study for the Fountain
of the Labyrinth in the Villa di Castello*, 1538. Pen
in brown ink on paper, 27.9 × 20.1 cm. Biblioteca
Nacional de España, Madrid. Dib/16/49/41/1.

FIG. 18

Félix Castello, *View of the Casa de Campo,
Madrid*, 1641. Oil on canvas. Museo
Arqueológico Nacional, on loan to the Museo
de Historia de Madrid.

there is the inconvenient fact that Alfonso of Aragón was a rival to Genoese power and was considering an attack on the city-state at the time of his death; however, this may have made no difference to Montorsoli's commission in the 1540s.

Fountains for Spain

Alongside the important clues Vasari provides about Montorsoli's Genoa portraits, he documents the sea monsters made for the Doria family and for Granvelle. The prototype described by Vasari is almost certainly the Fountain of the Triton at the Villa del Principe in Fassolo, just outside Genoa (FIG. 16). A muscular creature with a fish tail rests on a rock, holding open the mouth of a dolphin to allow water to cascade into a large basin. As an apprentice with the sculptor Andrea Ferrucci, Montorsoli had gained experience with marine imagery when he worked on a marble fountain for the king of Hungary. Fountains would become an extensive part of the sculptor's oeuvre. For a Servite monastery in Budrio near Bologna, Montorsoli designed an ephemeral fountain that included two clay figures of Faith and Charity painted to resemble marble.[16] The artist's river gods for the triumphal entry of Charles V into Florence in 1536 were enhanced by streams of water pumped from the Arno in a system developed by Niccolò Tribolo. Two years later, Montorsoli worked on fountains for the Villa di Castello under the direction of Tribolo. This included a marble *Hercules and Antaeus* that was destroyed through the machinations of Baccio Bandinelli. These projects acquainted Montorsoli with the practical and aesthetic demands of fountain design, especially the relationship with the surrounding landscape and the hydraulic engineering required by working fountains. A drawing attributable to Montorsoli represents a preliminary design for the Villa di Castello fountain (FIG. 17). The sketch is inscribed "invenzione del tribolo del duca Cosimo a Castello," indicating that the concept is by Tribolo.[17]

The so-called candelabra fountain, which had an elaborate column supporting several basins, was a form favored in Florence when Montorsoli began work on the Fountain of the Triton around 1540. Giovan Paolo Lomazzo coined the term in his *Trattato della pitture* of 1584, specifically for the description of Montorsoli's Orion Fountain in Messina (see FIG. 33), which was placed in front of the city's cathedral in an urban setting far different from the princely gardens of the Genoa and Madrid projects. "From the form of the candelabra are carved round, oval, and square fountains, at the bottom of which is a basin that receives water from above, emerging out of mouths of masks or from other similar things, and the top is made of some marine god or nymph who dominates the waters, as well as histories, sea gods, and putti."[18] Montorsoli's fountains of this type have a large, polygonal basin at the bottom, with a central column that supports basins of decreasing size as they ascend. Fanciful reliefs with masks and beasts are carved around the bottom basin, while larger marine deities adorn the column.

During his first stay in Genoa, before leaving for Naples in October or December 1541, Montorsoli made two large fountains. The first fountain was sent to Spain, as documented in a letter of September 22, 1540, written by Francisco de los Cobos to Charles V. This states that Andrea Doria had given Charles V a large marble fountain that had already been sent to the court in Madrid from Cartagena, a port in southeast Spain some 450 kilometers from Madrid. In his letter to the monarch, Cobos expresses astonishment at the magnificence of the gift, and offers his opinion that gratitude is due the donor. The document also explains the fate of the fountain. Cobos could not find a suitable place to install the fountain, since the Alcázar in Madrid was in the midst of an extensive remodeling campaign begun four years earlier, and because Charles V already possessed similar marble fountains at his palaces in Granada. For the time being, Cobos decided to keep the fountain.[19]

On April 18, Cobos ordered a certain Hernando del Corral to collect the fountain at Cartagena. Cobos paid Corral two hundred ducats for this, plus six to the *jurado* Tomás Garci for receiving the work at the port, and another five to the courier Pero Negro. On May 10, Garci acknowledged delivery of sixty-one boxes of marbles, and on May 28, 1540, the fountain arrived in Madrid on thirty-three carts pulled by two mules apiece.[20] Cobos did not inform the emperor of the fountain's arrival until September, probably because a proper location had yet to be found.

Fortunately, the fountain survived until Philip II extended the royal possessions in Madrid to the far bank of the Manzanares River, where he had acquired the villa of the Vargas family – a location that became known as the Casa de Campo (FIG. 18). Montorsoli's fountain can be identified with the so-called Fuente el Águila, or Eagle Fountain, in the "Ochavado," a private space in the royal garden. It was described in the eighteenth century by writers such as Antonio Conca and Antonio Ponz. The latter thought it dated from the time of Charles V because it was surmounted by the imperial double-headed eagle (now lost), with chains of the Golden Fleece and more imperial eagles decorating the large octagonal basin.[21] The fountain was removed from the Casa de Campo in the mid-nineteenth century, probably during the reign of Isabel II (1833–68) and is now stored in the Palacio Real, Madrid. In 2000, a modern copy of Montorsoli's fountain was installed in a courtyard of El Escorial, in the Real Colegio María Cristina (FIG. 19).[22]

The Eagle Fountain perfectly conveys imperial authority, based on the principles of Florentine fountain design that privileged architectural structure. The central shaft and the successive basins of decreasing size contain profuse sculptural decorations that project ideological and political ideas. The great double-headed eagle at the apex (FIG. 21) would have completed an imperial discourse full of allegorical elements, in the same way that the triumphal arches designed by Perino del Vaga did for Charles V's entries into Genoa of 1529 and 1533. The presence of the imperial eagle made the fountain unsuitable for public display during the reign of Philip II, since he did not succeed his father as Holy Roman Emperor. However, in the private royal gardens of the Casa de Campo it served as a reminder of the grandeur of the Hapsburg dynasty.[23] The fountain appears next to the equestrian sculpture of Philip III by Giambologna and Pietro Tacca (today in the Plaza Mayor, Madrid) in several seventeenth-century paintings that include depictions of the gardens of the Casa de Campo (FIG. 20).

The Eagle Fountain is one of the most successful creations to emerge from Montorsoli's workshop. The general scheme of the main basin resembles the so-called Dolphin Fountain at Villa del

FIG. 19
Copy of Montorsoli's Eagle Fountain of 1540, 2000.
Marble. Real Colegio María Cristina-UCM, San
Lorenzo de El Escorial.

FIG. 20

Spanish, *The Garden of the Casa de Campo with the Sculpture of Philip III and Montorsoli's Eagle Fountain*, ca. 1634. Oil on canvas, 149 × 181 cm. Museo de Historia de Madrid (on loan from Museo Nacional del Prado, P1288).

FIG. 21

Detail of FIG. 20 showing the double-headed eagle at the top of Montorsoli's Eagle Fountain.

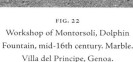

FIG. 22
Workshop of Montorsoli, Dolphin Fountain, mid-16th century. Marble. Villa del Principe, Genoa.

FIG. 23
Basin of the Eagle Fountain (FIG. 19).

Principe (FIG. 22).[24] The octagonal basin made for Spain is divided into three horizontal registers (FIG. 23), with the lowest frieze containing bas-reliefs depicting griffons, dolphins, masks of fauns, and shells. The convex intermediate section is carved with chains of the Golden Fleece strung like festoons. Above it, a concave register has geometric grooves. As in the fountain in Genoa, lion heads resting on single paws punctuate the design. In the Madrid fountain, these are placed at the vertices of the octagon, interspersed with paws supporting platforms with various objects.

Hybrid beings encircle the lowest section of the column, as if in some dance (FIG. 24). They link their limbs and flex their arms in different directions to balance the composition. The Tritons with their coiled tails resemble the Triton on the pulpit of San Matteo, Genoa, made by Montorsoli's workshop (FIG. 25).[25] Continuous lines of drill marks create a lively sense of shadow on these figures. This technique is also seen in the fantastic masks (FIG. 26), which are close to the work of Silvio Cosini, Montorsoli's collaborator in the period 1539 to 1541.[26] Montorsoli placed sirens in a similar arrangement in the Orion Fountain, Messina (see FIG. 33), but without reaching the quality of the powerful dancing figures in the Eagle Fountain.

FIG. 24
Figures around the lowest section
of the column in the Eagle
Fountain (FIG. 19).

FIG. 25
Workshop of Montorsoli, *Relief of a
Triton*. Marble, 73 × 46 cm.
San Matteo, Genoa.

FIG. 26
Attributed to Silvio Cosini, Mask on the
basin of the Eagle Fountain (FIG. 19).

FIG. 27
Middle section of the column of the
Eagle Fountain (FIG. 19).

Both Cosini and Montorsoli took up the monumental figural style of Michelangelo, which the work of Perino del Vaga in Genoa further encouraged. The flattened modeling in the larger figures contrasts strongly with the detailed treatment found in Montorsoli's portraits. On the other hand, the frowns, raised eyes, and half-open mouths seen in the figures on the Eagle Fountain are also seen in Montorsoli's *Saint Cosmas* in the New Sacristy at San Lorenzo in Florence.

In the middle section of the column are three nude figures: a faun with curly hair and pointed ears like the Triton of the Villa del Principe, a man wearing a turban, and a young man with curly hair (FIG. 27). Turbaned figures appear in other imperial monuments dedicated to the theme of maritime power in the Mediterranean, for example, at the base of the monument to Giovanni Andrea Doria, made by Taddeo Carlone in 1539 to 1540.[27]

In the upper section of the column, putti toy with a finely carved cloth that passes through rings carved onto the shaft – a playfulness that endows the work with great vitality (FIGS. 28, 29). The use of cloth reminds us of the children who flank the bas-relief with the Doria family's coat of arms in the church of San Matteo, although the latter are by the artist's workshop.[28] Putti of this type can also be seen in Montorsoli's presbytery of San Matteo and in the reliefs with trophies in the atrium of the Villa del Principe (FIG. 30), which are very similar to those of the Eagle Fountain in their curly hair, partly open mouths, and snub noses that give them a singular character. In the fountain, water flows from the uppermost basin through

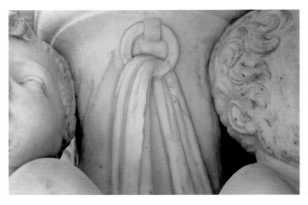

FIG. 28
Upper section of the column of
FIG. 19.

FIG. 29
Montorsoli, Putti in the upper
section of the original Eagle
Fountain, 1540. Marble.

FIG. 30
Montorsoli, *Trophies*. Marble.
Atrium of the Villa del Principe,
Genoa.

symmetrically arranged openings in putti mouths, and from similar holes in the lower basins, thus creating the sensation of rainfall.

ANOTHER SPANISH FOUNTAIN BY MONTORSOLI?

Documents allows us to recreate another monumental fountain sent to Spain, probably also sculpted in Montorsoli's workshop in 1540. On April 12, 1541, Abbot Filippo di Negro, an agent of the Doria family, wrote to Francisco de los Cobos to announce the delivery of a gift from Andrea Doria – a marble fountain contained in forty-four boxes.[29] Di Negro assured Cobos that the fountain was the most beautiful of all those that had been produced in Genoa, "both for the fineness of the marble, and for the fineness of sculpture."[30] He also recommended that Cobos use an accompanying drawing so that the fountain could be correctly installed. Antonio Doria himself had written earlier, on August 5, 1540, that the fountain had been completed in Genoa. Although Cobos tried to disguise some resistance to the gift, he finally agreed that the work could be sent to Cartagena where the *jurado* of the city would be responsible for forwarding it to the most appropriate place.

The fountain's disappearance makes a definitive attribution impossible. However, there is a strong possibility that it was designed by Montorsoli, since the artist was working for the Doria court in Genoa at this time and the design of the fountain shares many features with Montorsoli's work, including the Eagle

Fountain. Although we do not have the drawing that di Negro mentions in his letter, written instructions survive for assembling a novel type of fountain.[31] This memorandum clarifies certain parts of the design, especially the number of figures.

> First, the monsters, which the drawing shows as two but are actually three in number, are somewhat larger than life-size. The larger ones that are underneath the basin, which are shown as two, but are actually three, are life-size. The foundation is eight and a half feet wide, or slightly less, in the drawing of the work where only one figure is shown, there are actually two with the columns. They are somewhat less than life-size. The base at its largest dimension is 19 feet in diameter, the circumference is 57 feet with the first step next to the ground. The basin inside is 11 feet wide.

> Primeramente estos monstruos que en este designo se muestran ser dos son tres y de algo mayor grandeza que del natural. Las mayores que estan debaxo la basçia que paresce que son dos son tres y la grandeza del natural. La basçia es ancha de ocho pies y medio de ancho o poco menos en la altura donde se muestra sola una figura hay en la obra dos con las colonas como muestra el designo. Son grandes algo menos del natural. El pilon de baxo la mayor grandeza de su diametro es de dizenueve pies, la circumferencia de cincuenta y siete pies es a saber el primer escalon que esta junto a la tierra. El vaso de dentro es de anchura de once pies.[32]

The large size of the lowest basin (more than 16 meters, or 53 feet, in circumference) approaches the concept of the fishpond (*peschiera*) of the Triton Fountain in Genoa, made at about the same time, 1540 to 1543, and similar grand basins in the Orion and Neptune Fountains in Messina, made between 1547 and 1557. The reference in the document to the "first step next to the ground" implies the existence of several steps at the base, as is the case with the Eagle Fountain and the fountains in Messina. The arrangement of figures also resembles Montorsoli's Eagle Fountain, with three life-size figures in the first section, and two smaller figures in the upper level.[33]

The author of the document takes pains to detail the number of figures in the fountain, pointing out that only some of them can be seen in the drawing, but additional figures actually made up the work. The difficulty of images made from a single viewpoint is encountered in other drawings by Montorsoli, such as the one for the Neptune Fountain in Messina (FIG. 31).[34] The description of large sea monsters in the design suggests that Montorsoli is responsible for the lost second Spanish fountain, since the artist often used large hybrid figures at this time, as in the sculptures of Scylla and Charybdis in the Neptune Fountain.[35]

FIG. 31
Montorsoli, *Neptune Fountain in Messina*, ca. 1553. Pen in brown ink, and black chalk on paper, 42.8 × 57.2 cm. Biblioteca Nacional de España, Madrid. Dib/16/49/25.

FIG. 32
Montorsoli, *Sketch for a Fountain*,
ca. 1540. Black chalk and pen in brown ink
on paper. Harvard Art Museums/Fogg Art
Museum. CAT. 12.

A drawing by Montorsoli that shows Tritons holding up the basin of a fountain (FIG. 32) strengthens the case for Montorsoli's authorship. The figures' torsos, arms, and thighs exert great effort to hold up the basin as their long, coiled tails twist beneath them.[36] The combination of black chalk and brown ink suggests that the drawing is a preliminary study for a fountain, especially as the basin appears shaded and delineated in a slightly different manner from the figures. The project with three Tritons may have resembled the lost fountain sent from Genoa to Spain in 1541.

In elaborate fountains and imperial portrait busts produced through the patronage of Andrea Doria, the work of Montorsoli reached Spain in the early 1540s and was presented to the emperor and his powerful courtiers. By the end of the decade, Montorsoli would have the opportunity to show his work in Sicily, a possession of the Spanish monarchy. While his fountains in Genoa and Madrid were installed in highly restricted aristocratic settings (or not even installed at all), in Messina, Montorsoli successfully managed the creation and installation of two monumental public fountains. The Orion Fountain (FIG. 33), in particular, has strong connections to Charles V, and concludes Montorsoli's long and rich association with the emperor. Begun in 1547, a decade after Charles V's victory over the Ottomans at Tunis, the fountain perpetuates the emperor's triumph, which naturally recalled the ancient triumph of Scipio Africanus.[37] In 1535, the imperial fleet had gathered at the port of Messina to launch its attack on the Ottoman stronghold, and Charles V returned to Messina amid elaborate celebrations – making the city a fitting site for Montorsoli's public memorial to the victory. Meanwhile, Montorsoli's work in Spain provided more discreet delights for members of the imperial court, along with reminders of the generosity and allegiance of the Doria family.

FIG. 33
Montorsoli, *Orion Fountain*, Messina, 1553.
Print from Hittorff 1835, pl. 27.

1. For the relations between Spain and Genoa in the Renaissance, see Cadenas y Vicent 1977; Pacini 1999; Boccardo et al. 2004; and especially Marías 2004.

2. Laschke 1993, pp. 39–41, figs. 40–43.

3. Vasari 1966, vol. 5, p. 501: "simile al quale mostro ne fece un altro a que' signori, che fu mandato in Ispagna al Granvela. Fece un gran Nettunno di stucco, che sopra un piedistallo fu posto nel giardino del principe. Fece di marmo due ritratti del medesimo principe e due di Carlo Quinto, che furono portati da Coves in Ispagna."

4. On this issue, see: Yates 1975; Scolaro 1994; Sassu 2007.

5. Charles Hope in *Art Bulletin* 59 (1977), pp. 551–52. Rubens copied Titian's portrait around 1603 (private collection). See Wethey 1971, pp. 191–93; Falomir 2010; Bodart 2011.

6. Vasari 1966, vol. 5, p. 494: "la quale condusse fuor dell'uso dell'altre e bellissima, in quel modo che esso signore si vede armato e ginocchioni sopra un elmo alla borgognona e con una mano al petto in atto di raccomandarsi a quella Madonna."

7. Nickel et al. 1982, pp. 43–46; ffolliott 1984, p. 6.

8. For the bust in Naples, see CAT. 11. For the bust in Madrid: Blanco and Lorente 1969, p. 203; Coppel 1998, pp. 100–101; Lucía Varela in Granada 2000, p. 279; Madrid 2015, p. 187, no. 93.

9. Álvaro Soler del Campo in Madrid 2010, p. 132. Helmschmid's workshop produced another suit of armor for Charles in 1538 (Real Armería, Madrid, inv. A.129), which was also depicted in portraits (Fabio Speranza in Naples 2006, p. 266).

10. See under CAT. 11 for the woodcuts by Britto. On the prints after Titian's portraits, see Rosand and Muraro 1976, pp. 204–7, 314. Agostino Veneziano: Illustrated Bartsch vol. 27, no. 524.

11. Bodart 2011, pp. 93–114.

12. In Ramiro 2016, p. 287, I suggested that the artist could be someone close to Baccio Bandinelli, for example, Vincenzo de' Rossi. On reflection, I prefer the interpretation of Laschke 1993, p. 60.

13. The work was given to the museum by Wilhelmina Juritzka in 1961 (Malgouyres 2007, pp. 20–22). A letter of 1958 written by her husband, Prince Alfred Antonin Juritzky, states that he acquired the bust from a Parisian dealer in 1938. A letter from Princess Juritzka of 1970 reports the suspicion that the work may have been brought from Spain to France during the Spanish Civil War (1936–39).

14. Zeri 1978; Fadda 2013, pp. 133–34.

15. Laschke 1993, pp. 60–61.

16. Vasari 1966, vol. 5, p. 495. ffolliott 1984, p. 10.

17. Biblioteca Nacional de España, Madrid, B 16/49, no. 41. Ferretti 2016, p. 185, fig. 59. Traditionally attributed to Niccolò Tribolo: Bustamante and Marías 1991, p. 243, no. C.32.

18. Lomazzo 1584, p. 429: "Della forma ancora de' candelieri sopradetti ne sono cavate le fontane tonde, ovate & quadre, in fondo di cui si fa il vaso che riceve l'acqua che da di sopra esce fuori da bocche di maschere, ò d'altre simili cose, & in cima si fa un qualche Dio Marino, ò Ninfa che signoreggi le acque aggiungendovi anco historie, di Dei del mare & i suoi amori."

19. Archivo General de Simancas [AGS], Estado, Legajo 49, doc. 137: "El principe Andrea Doria ha embiado a Su Majestad una fuente de marmol muy buena [struck through: "cosa cierto digna de ¿consideracion?"]. La grandeza della se pesse en lo que ha costado de traer desde Cartagena aquí que no es poco. Paresçiome que porque en Granada hay muchas fuentes de mármol era mejor traerla aquí donde no havia ninguna. Y assi esta en la fortaleza. Su Majestad debe mandar cuando escriviere al principe Andrea Doria darle las graçias por ella que como digo cosa es por que se le debe dar." I am inclined to think that Cobos did not want to send it to another royal possession because of the high cost of moving it from Cartagena.

20. The first two registers of the central column were made in one piece. Therefore, six mules were required to draw one of the carts: "De la horden que ha de tener en el gasto de los dineros qe son para traer de Cartajena a Madrid una fuente de marmol": AGS, Contaduría Mayor de Cuentas, 1ª Época, Legajo 592, doc. 9.

21. Ponz 1776, vol. 6, pp. 161–62.

22. I am grateful for the assistance of María Jesús Herrero Sanz, curator of sculpture at the Patrimonio Nacional.

23. Tejero 1998, pp. 401–4, attributed the work to Montorsoli but was unaware of the document that dates

it with certainty, which led her to think that it could be one of the fountains in the Casa de Campo installed in the early 1570s, related to the arrival of fountains from Genoa for royal sites around Madrid. However, at that time the gift of a work to Philip II with Holy Roman Imperial iconography would have been indecorous. This allows us to identify with near certainty the arrival of the Eagle Fountain in 1540. As noted above, its installation in the Casa de Campo can be explained by the fact that it was stored in the Alcázar until it was placed in a less public location in the late 16th century.

24. Tejero 1998, pp. 412–13. This fountain has traditionally been assigned to Cosini, although the attribution has recently been rejected. Wiles 1933, p. 30, thought that the fountain might be connected with Montorsoli's circle, an idea supported by the formal analogies with the Eagle Fountain in Spain. The issue is deserving of further study.

25. Laschke 1993, p. 161, no. 12.

26. Principi 2014, pp. 117–18. See Cosini's work in San Lorenzo, Portovenere, and the wings of the angel in the Pisa Cathedral.

27. Manara 1959, pp. 28–29, figs. 17, 18; Stagno 2017, pp. 152–54.

28. Laschke 1993, p. 161, no. 12, fig. 79.

29. AGS, Estado, Legajo 1374, doc. 88 (cited by Urrea 1981, p. 161; and Gómez 2014, pp. 170–71). Finally, on July 17, 1541, Filippo di Negro wrote to Cobos with satisfaction that the fountain had reached Cartagena: AGS, Estado, Legajo 1374, doc. 86.

30. AGS, Estado, Legajo 1374, doc. 86: "sia per la finezza dei marmi et sia per la scultura."

31. Di Negro did not write the set of instructions, although he was close to Montorsoli in Genoa; Vasari 1966, vol. 5, p. 501. Di Negro was also closely involved in the shipment of Michelangelo's *Young Baptist*, a gift from Duke Cosimo I de' Medici to Cobos in 1537; Caglioti 2012, p. 36.

32. AGS, Estado, Legajo 1374, doc. 89, fol. 1r.

33. I have previously suggested (Ramiro 2016) that the original fountain was sent to Valladolid to the palace of Francisco de los Cobos, and from there to the Palace of Buen Retiro, Madrid, where it would have been copied as the Fountain of Tritons. This last work was at the Palacio Real de Aranjuez and is now in the gardens of the Palacio Real, Madrid. However, the fountain that was at the Buen Retiro is a different work, a *Glaucus* by Battista Lorenzi, based on a design by Giambologna (Loffredo 2012). The Fountain of Tritons is a mixture of different elements (Sancho 2000). While its column and basin can be associated with Genoa, the three marine deities appear to be by Giovan Giacomo Parraca da Valsoldo (ca. 1546–1597). Lorenzo Principi has shared convincing comparisons with a Triton in the Villa Pallavicino della Peschiere, Genoa. López 1997, p. 253, doc. 4, published a contract between Don Juan de Cardona and Giovan Giacomo Parraca for a fountain destined for Spain. If the Spanish crown also obtained work by Parraca, it might have been in shipments of the 1560s and 1570s under Philip II (Tejero 1998, pp. 410–11; Arciniega 2013, p. 96).

34. Bustamante and Marías 1991, p. 235, no. C.15.

35. See Laschke 1993, figs. 124, 125.

36. These figures closely resemble a bronze that belonged to Maurice de Rothschild at the beginning of the 20th century (Bode 1907, fig. CCLX).

37. ffolliott 1984, pp. 70–71, 134–37. On Charles V's triumph in Messina, see Jacquot 1975, pp. 430–31, 488 [with further references]; Mitchell 1986, pp. 152–54.

Michelangelo, Tomb of Lorenzo de' Medici in the New
Sacristy, San Lorenzo, Florence. Photograph, ca. 1880s.

Michelangelo, Tomb of Giuliano de' Medici in the New
Sacristy, San Lorenzo, Florence. Photograph, ca. 1880s.

Federico Zuccaro, *Artists in the New Sacristy*, late 17th century.
Black and red chalk on paper, 20 × 26.3 cm. Musée du Louvre,
Paris. 4554 recto.

THE IMPACT OF MICHELANGELO'S NEW SACRISTY

Lorenzo Principi and Alan Chong

IN 1519, GIULIO DE' MEDICI (LATER POPE CLEMENT VII) COMMISSIONED MICHELANGELO to design and decorate the New Sacristy (Sagrestia Nuova) at San Lorenzo in Florence, a church long patronized by the Medici family. The new structure was built off the right transept as a counterpart to the old sacristy designed by Filippo Brunelleschi, which contained on one wall the tombs of Piero and Giovanni de' Medici by Andrea del Verrocchio. The New Sacristy was also intended to house tombs of Medici family members, and is sometimes called the Medici Chapel. It was begun in 1519 and roofed over in 1524, as Michelangelo planned the sculptural program. Two monumental sarcophagi are surmounted by figures of the deceased, Lorenzo de' Medici, Duke of Urbino; and Giuliano de' Medici, Duke of Nemours (FIGS. 1, 2). Resting on the sarcophagi are figures of the four Times of Day. The two female figures of *Night* and *Dawn* are more highly finished than their male counterparts, *Day* and *Dusk*.

The completion of the New Sacristy was slow and difficult. The Republic of Florence, reestablished in 1527, exiled the Medici, with the result that the project was suspended until the defeat of the Republic in 1530. Michelangelo worked for the Republic against his former patrons, but his closeness to Clement VII gained him a pardon and he returned to work on the tombs. The four Times of Day were carved between 1524 and 1531, and the effigies of the two dukes were completed and installed by 1534.

The New Sacristy had a profound impact on art in Florence, most immediately on Michelangelo's assistants, who included Giovan Angelo Montorsoli, Raffaello da Montelupo, and Silvio Cosini. In 1533, Montorsoli accompanied Michelangelo from Rome to Florence to help with the project. Vasari reports that Montorsoli assisted with the two Medici dukes "in polishing them and in executing certain difficult undercuttings."[1] On an adjacent wall, the Virgin would be flanked by the two patron saints of the Medici family, Cosmas and Damian (see FIG. 9). Assigned the figure of Saint Cosmas, Montorsoli prepared a life-size terracotta model, which Michelangelo extensively retouched. Michelangelo himself made the terracotta models of the head and arms. Raffaello da Montelupo carved the Saint Damian.

The Times of Day were installed in the mid-1540s, and ten years later the New Sacristy was brought to its present arrangement under the direction of Giorgio Vasari and Bartolomeo Ammannati. The architecture and sculpture of the New Sacristy attracted enormous attention, as can be seen in the number of copies, and in Federico Zuccaro's entertaining drawing (FIG. 3) of draughtsmen clambering over the chapel and sitting on ledges to view the sculptures.

Michelangelo originally planned two pairs of reclining river gods in the ancient manner, to be placed at the foot of each tomb, but they were never completed. The arrangement appears in a drawing (FIG. 5), and another sketch gives measurements of one of the river gods, perhaps to instruct stonecutters.[2] A terracotta model of one of the river gods, probably made around 1525, also survives (FIG. 4).[3] These recumbent figures would have visually anchored each tomb ensemble. As presently arranged, the Times of Day on their roughly finished bases seem top heavy, as though about to slide off their sarcophagi. After Clement VII died in 1534, Michelangelo refused to transfer his loyalty to the succeeding Medici rulers of Florence, dukes Alessandro and Cosimo. He rejected their numerous invitations, and never again set foot in Florence.

FIG. 4

Michelangelo, *Model for a River God in the New Sacristy*, ca. 1525. Terracotta, length 147 cm. Casa Buonarroti, Florence.

SANDRO DI LORENZO'S *BACCHUS*

An early response to Michelangelo's river gods may be Sandro di Lorenzo's *Bacchus* (FIG. 6), a composition recorded in 1523, when Michelangelo was still working on the marble sculptures in the New Sacristy.[4] The reclining pose and intensely defined musculature have much in common with Michelangelo's river gods as sketched in figure 5. The turn of the head and the tucked-in leg are also similar. Sandro di Lorenzo (who is almost certainly the so-called Master of the Unruly Children) has transformed the river god into Bacchus – the large water vessels seen in the drawing have been replaced by a wine cask. If the *Bacchus* shows the influence of Michelangelo's river gods, then Sandro di Lorenzo must have encountered Michelangelo's models of the river gods at a very early stage, when the New Sacristy had not yet been roofed over.

COPIES OF MICHELANGELO'S *TIMES OF DAY*

The sculptures on the Medici tombs in the New Sacristy were among the most influential works of the Renaissance, and artists of all backgrounds and specializations copied them in drawings, paintings, prints, and sculptures. Around 1536, Battista Franco made two prints showing *Dawn* and *Dusk* lying on the ground with fanciful landscape or architectural backgrounds that have nothing to do with the New Sacristy.[5] These images had limited circulation, unlike Cornelis Cort's prints of 1570, which proved immensely popular. A Dutch artist who had settled in Italy, Cort went to Florence to make precise engravings of the three principal walls of the New Sacristy (FIGS. 7–9), plus a fourth print showing Andrea del Verrocchio's Medici monument from 1473 (FIG. 10). Inserted in a wall between the Old Sacristy and the transept of San Lorenzo, this tomb has no connection with Michelangelo's project, except that it entombs other members of the Medici family.[6] While commemorating the unveiling of Michelangelo's New Sacristy, Cort's print series thus also celebrates the Medici dynasty. The printmaker must have expected a commission from the

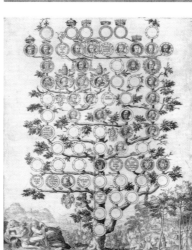

FIG. 7
Cornelis Cort, *Tomb of Lorenzo de' Medici in the New Sacristy*, 1570. Engraving. CAT. 14.

FIG. 8
Cornelis Cort, *Tomb of Giuliano de' Medici in the New Sacristy*, 1570. Engraving. CAT. 15.

FIG. 9
Cornelis Cort, *Virgin and Child with Saint Cosmas and Saint Damian in the New Sacristy*, 1570. Engraving. CAT. 13.

FIG. 10
Cornelis Cort, *Tomb of Piero and Giovanni de' Medici in San Lorenzo*, 1570. Engraving, 42.6 × 27.7 cm. The Metropolitan Museum of Art, New York. 57.572.30.

FIG. 11
Copy after Cornelis Cort, *Medici Family Tree*, 1569. Engraving, 55.5 × 42.7 cm.

family, as just a year before he had been generously remunerated for an engraving of the Medici family tree (FIG. 11).[7] For reasons unknown, however, Duke Cosimo failed to grant imprimatur to the prints of the New Sacristy.[8] Nonetheless, Cort's engravings were reprinted into the eighteenth century, and were the primary means by which Michelangelo's striking sculptures were known.

Small-scale sculptural reductions of the Times of Day were also in great demand. Jacopo Tintoretto owned several statuettes of Michelangelo's sculptures that he used in his compositions.[9] He reportedly commissioned models from Daniele da Volterra, Michelangelo's friend and collaborator, who had made gesso reductions of nearly all of Michelangelo's marble figures in the New Sacristy. Carlo Ridolfi writes that Tintoretto studied the Times of Day intensively, "making an infinite number of drawings by lantern light."[10] This is confirmed by the artist's many surviving sketches of the Times of Day, which show the works from unusual angles, often scattered with bright flickers of light (FIG. 12). These drawings appear to be studies of lightweight models that could be easily held and turned.

Marco Mantova Benavides, a connoisseur active in Padua in the mid-sixteenth century, owned a plaster reduction of *Dawn*, which is preserved in the university of Padua (FIG. 13).[11] The sculptor Alessandro

82

FIG. 12

Jacopo Tintoretto, *Study of Michelangelo's Day*, ca. 1550. Black and white chalk on paper, 35 × 50.5 cm. The Metropolitan Museum of Art, New York. 54.125 recto.

FIG. 13

Dawn, mid-16th century. Painted stucco, length 26 cm. Università degli Studi di Padova, Museo di Scienze Archeologiche e d'Arte. MB21.

Vittoria knew Benavides's collection, and in 1563 bought a model of a foot from *Day*, which he believed to be by Michelangelo.[12] Around this time, Johan Gregor van der Schardt made terracotta versions of the four Times of Day. The popularity of copies of this sort can be seen in the *Allegory of Sight* painted by Jan Brueghel the Elder and Peter Paul Rubens in 1617 (FIG. 14) where terracotta statuettes of Michelangelo's *Night* and the *Dawn* appear on a shelf in a collector's cabinet. They flank two copies of Michelangelo's *Slaves*, while ancient Roman busts fill the shelves below. Rubens placed his own *Tiger Hunt* of 1616 (now in the Musée des Beaux-Arts, Rennes) behind the terracottas, so that the foreground figure can be directly compared to the reclining poses of Michelangelo's sculptures. A seventeenth-century portrait of Michelangelo, attributed to Il Passignano, shows a terracotta model of *Day*.[13]

A cabinet belonging to Cardinal Ferdinando de' Medici in his villa in Rome, probably made by Pietro da Barga between 1572 and 1575, was decorated with bronze sculptures after Michelangelo's Times of Day.[14] A terracotta reduction of *Dusk* has recently been attributed to Barga (see FIG. 22). Pietro Tacca made bronze versions of the *Night* and *Dawn* around 1600.[15] There are also versions in other materials such as wax, alabaster, and ivory: a pair of ivories is recorded in the collection of Cardinal Leopoldo de' Medici in the mid-seventeenth century.[16] Life-size copies are also sometimes documented. In 1570, the sculptor Vincenzo Danti donated his full-scale copies of the Times of Day (attributed to Egnazio Danti and Timoteo Refati) to the new Accademia del Disegno in Perugia. The Florentine artist Rodolfo Sirigatti owned life-size copies of *Night* and *Dawn*, as noted in 1584.[17]

FIG. 14

Jan Brueghel the Elder and Peter Paul Rubens, *Allegory of Sight* (detail), 1617. Oil on wood, 65 × 109 cm. Museo Nacional del Prado, Madrid. 1394.

FIG. 15

Niccolò Tribolo, *Dusk*, ca. 1534–37.
Terracotta, height ca. 53 cm. Museo
Nazionale del Bargello, Florence.

FIG. 16

Niccolò Tribolo, *Dawn*, ca. 1534–37.
Terracotta, height ca. 53 cm. Museo
Nazionale del Bargello, Florence.

FIG. 17

Niccolò Tribolo, *Day*, ca. 1534–37.
Terracotta, height ca. 53 cm. Museo
Nazionale del Bargello, Florence.

NICCOLÒ TRIBOLO IN THE NEW SACRISTY

Niccolò Tribolo (1497–1550) had been commissioned to make sculptures of *Heaven* and *Earth* for the New Sacristy, but only finished the second in 1533, and it was destroyed in 1762 in a fire in the Uffizi.[18] When Michelangelo left Florence permanently in 1534, the New Sacristy was unfinished. Tribolo, appointed supervising architect of San Lorenzo in 1542, installed the Times of Day above the sarcophagi. Vasari reports that in the mid-1530s, Tribolo

> copied in clay all the figures in the Sacristy of San Lorenzo that Michelangelo had made in marble, namely Dawn, Dusk, Day, and Night. And they came out so well that Monsignor Giovan Battista Figiovanni, the prior of San Lorenzo, to whom he gave the Night because he had opened the sacristy for him, judging it a rare thing, presented it to Duke Alessandro, who then gave it to Giorgio Vasari who was staying with His Excellency, knowing that Giorgio gave his attention to such studies. This figure is now in his house at Arezzo, with other works of art.[19]

This event must have taken place before 1537 since Alessandro de' Medici was assassinated in January of that year. Vasari specifically characterized the quality of Tribolo's terracottas as inspired by Michelangelo. On another occasion, Tribolo made some terracottas in order to help the painter Giuliano Bugiardini complete a composition sketched by Michelangelo. Tribolo "made some sketch-models in clay, which were excellently executed, in that they were given that boldness and style which Michelangelo put into design, with a gradine, which is a toothed piece of iron, the gradine giving them some roughness so they might have greater force."[20] However, Tribolo's rough finish did not please Bugiardini, who used a wet brush to smooth away the marks of the scraper, which left the finished painting devoid of Michelangelo's influence.[21] This description of Tribolo's terracotta technique, along with the absence of a figure of *Night* in the series of statuettes that have been in the Bargello since 1879, suggests that these terracottas are the ones described by Vasari (FIGS. 15–17).[22] On the surface of the three terracottas are signs of the gradine that evoke the irregular surfaces of Michelangelo's marbles in the New Sacristy.

THE TERRACOTTA *DUSK* IN PITTSBURGH

Once Tribolo's authorship of the three terracottas in the Bargello has been established, it is easier to analyze the *Dusk* in the Carnegie Museum of Art (FIG. 18), which derives directly from the sculpture in the Bargello. The surface of the terracotta in Pittsburgh closely recalls Tribolo's work, and the figure shows the same departures from Michelangelo's original that Tribolo's terracotta does. For example, the curls of the hair and the presence of full, folded drapery that runs along the base are reminiscent of Tribolo but differ from Michelangelo's marble.

FIG. 18
Circle of Niccolò Tribolo, *Dusk*, 1540s.
Terracotta, length 52 cm. Carnegie
Museum of Art, Pittsburgh. CAT. 17.

The *Dusk* in Pittsburgh is not a slavish copy of Tribolo, however. The freshness of modeling and pliable sense of musculature suggest that a skilled artist close to Tribolo made the terracotta. The chiseled and defined volumes in the sculpture indicate that it was made in the middle of the sixteenth century. Portions of the left leg and the groin have been repaired more recently.[23]

The critical history of the Pittsburgh terracotta is somewhat confused. Ernst Steinmann in 1907 considered it a variant after Michelangelo, perhaps a model for a reduction in porcelain or bronze. Charles de Tolnay confused it with the work in Houston (FIG. 19), a sign that the copies of Michelangelo's Times of Day no longer held much interest for scholars in the twentieth century, who have been primarily interested in whether these versions were by Michelangelo and not in the wider reception of the New Sacristy. Some versions are rather eccentric in character, like those in the Chigi Saracini collection. These beautiful sculptures based on Michelangelo are fully deserving of study and appreciation in their own right, not least for the commentary they provide on the original sculptures and their setting. It is evident that the *Dusk* in Pittsburgh, although little known and almost never exhibited, is among the most important replicas of the Times of the Day.

Johan Gregor van der Schardt

In addition to the Tribolo statues, the most important clay copies of the Times of Day are those attributed to Johan Gregor van der Schardt (1530–ca. 1581), which were recorded in the massive collection of Paulus von Praun (1548–1616) of Nuremberg. The inventory drawn up in 1616 lists "The four images of day, night, midnight, and morning, one foot high, after Michelangelo."[24] The catalogue of 1719 is even more telegraphic: "The four times of day, lying."[25] No artist is given for these works or indeed for the majority of the terracottas in the collection, as has sometimes been assumed.[26] When Christophe de Murr compiled another catalogue of the Praun collection in 1797, he assigned the terracotta versions of the Times of Day optimistically to Michelangelo himself, while attributing copies after ancient works to Johan van der Schardt.

Despite the lack of documentation, circumstances suggest that van der Schardt might be the artist of Praun's Times of Day after Michelangelo, and of some of the other unattributed terracottas in the collection. In the 1560s, van der Schardt had been in Italy where, like many other artists, he had the opportunity to study Michelangelo's sculptures. The artist worked for the imperial court in Nuremberg beginning in 1570, and had close connections with collectors such as Willibald Imhoff and, after 1578, Paulus von Praun. A few works are identified as by van der Schardt in Praun's 1616 inventory.[27] Praun seems to have acquired a large number of objects from van der Schardt's estate after the artist's death in 1581, including some 170 terracottas.[28]

Three of the four Times of Day from the Praun collection survive, one in Houston and two in the Victoria and Albert Museum (FIGS. 19–21). The *Dusk* was probably destroyed, as in 1797 it was already described as broken.[29] From the seventeenth to the twentieth century, attributions of these terracottas alternated between Michelangelo and copies after him. Lars-Olof Larsson in 1984 attributed the works to van der Schardt, followed by Ursel Berger in 1994, and others.

The style of these terracottas is very different from those of Tribolo and other Florentine artists, which have more organically flowing musculature. Instead, the three works attributed to van der Schardt are sharply delineated with an almost choppy rendering of anatomy, familiar also from the work of another Netherlandish sculptor of the same period, Willem Tetrode (ca. 1525–after 1580). Nonetheless, it should be admitted that the Times of Day and the studies of body parts after Michelangelo (now in the Rijksmuseum and the Victoria and Albert Museum[30]) are very different

FIG. 19

Johan Gregor van der Schardt, *Day*,
1560s. Terracotta, length 30 cm.
Museum of Fine Arts, Houston. CAT. 18.

FIGS. 20, 21

Johan Gregor van der Schardt, *Dawn* and *Night*, 1560s. Terracotta,
length 23.3 and 26.4 cm. Victoria and Albert Museum, London.
A.5-1938 and A.6-1938.

Pietro da Barga, *Dusk*, ca. 1580.
Terracotta, length 28 cm. Tomasso
Brothers Fine Arts, UK.

in purpose and character from van der Schardt's signed or documented works. The artist's celebrated self-portrait is a hyper-realistic object, being highly finished and naturalistically painted, although only about half life-size. Carefully catalogued in the 1616 inventory as van der Schardt's self-portrait, the work is now in the Rijksmuseum. Praun also owned other documented portraits by van der Schardt, as well as a *Mercury* and a *Minerva* in bronze. Frits Scholten has made the appealingly modern suggestion that Praun's collection of works by van der Schardt, including his self-portrait, studies after other works, and independent statues, constituted a vast, virtual self-portrait of the artist.[31] We might resist this interpretation only because a fraction of the terracotta models in the Praun collection survive, and none of them is listed as by van der Schardt in Praun's inventory of 1616, which was started when the collector was still alive. Nor were the supposed works by van der Schardt grouped together. The strong and dynamic style of the Times of Day, especially the *Day* in Houston, leaves open the possibility that they are by another northern European artist active in the late sixteenth century.

FIG. 23
Day, 17th century? Terracotta, length
71.1 cm. The Metropolitan Museum of
Art, New York. 1971.206.35.

FIG. 24
Night, 2nd half of the 16th century.
Terracotta, length 31 cm. Museo di
Palazzo Venezia, Rome. 13441.

APPENDIX
Significant Renaissance terracotta sculptures based on Michelangelo's Times of Day in the
New Sacristy.

Dusk
1. Niccolò Tribolo, 1534–37. Bargello. FIG. 15.
2. Circle of Tribolo, 1540s. Pittsburgh. FIG. 18.
3. Attributed to Pietro da Barga, ca. 1580. Tomasso 2018, no. 5. FIG. 22.
4. Late 16th century. Ringling Museum of Art, Sarasota (SN5375). Height 34.3 cm.
5. Late 16th or early 17th century. State Hermitage, St. Petersburg (2500). Height 50 cm.
    Androsov 2008, no. 53.
6. 17th century? Metropolitan Museum of Art (1971.206.36). Length 78.7 cm.

Dawn
1. Niccolò Tribolo, 1534–37. Bargello. FIG. 16.
2. Johan van der Schardt, 1560s. V&A. FIG. 20.
3. Late 16th century. Ringling Museum of Art, Sarasota (SN5376). Length 61 cm.
4. 2nd half of the 16th century. Formerly Alejandro Pietri, Caracas. Length 63.5 cm.
    Goldscheider 1962, fig. 41.
5. 2nd half of the 16th century. V&A (4119-1854). Length 46 cm. Bonn 2015, no. 148.
6. Late 16th century (Prospero Bresciano or Marcello Sparzo?). Chigi-Saracini collection, Siena (293).
    Length 54 cm. Siena 1989, no. 35b.

Day
1. Niccolò Tribolo, 1534–37. Bargello. FIG. 17.
2. Johan van der Schardt, 1560s. Houston. FIG. 19.
3. Late 16th or early 17th century. State Hermitage, St. Petersburg (558). Length 59 cm.
    Androsov 2008, no. 51.
4. 17th century? Metropolitan Museum of Art. FIG. 23.
5. 17th century. State Hermitage, St. Petersburg (561). Length 39 cm. Androsov 2008, no. 52.

Night
1. Johan Gregor van der Schardt, 1560s. V&A. FIG. 21.
2. 2nd half of the 16th century. Palazzo Venezia, Rome. Giometti 2011, no. 9. FIG. 24.
3. 2nd half of the 16th century. Formerly Alejandro Pietri, Caracas. Length 63.5 cm.
    Goldscheider 1962, fig. 13.
4. Late 16th century (Prospero Bresciano or Marcello Sparzo?). Chigi-Saracini Collection,
    Siena (292). Length 54 cm. Siena 1989, no. 35a.

1. Vasari 1966, vol. 5, p. 493.

2. British Museum, London, 1859,0625.544.

3. Principi 2018, p. 113.

4. Charles Avery in *The Dictionary of Art* (London, 1996), vol. 20, p. 779, writes that some of the Master of the Unruly Children's terracottas are reworkings of Michelangelo's unrealized river gods.

5. Rosenberg 2003, pp. 115–18.

6. Sellink 2000, p. 145, incorrectly says that this tomb is in the Medici Chapel.

7. Meijer 1987. In November 1569, Cort was paid 15 ducats.

8. Barnes 2010, pp. 154, 157, suggests that the reason for Cosimo I's avoidance of the prints was because the

entombed Medici were not his direct ancestors, which is unconvincing, especially given the duke's desire to complete the New Sacristy.

9. Nichols 2015, pp. 67–72; Whitaker 1997; Rossi 1975, nos. 10–40. Borghini 1584, p. 551: "e poscia si prese per principal maestro l'opere del divino Michelagnolo, non riguardando à spesa alcuna per haver formate le sue figure della sagrestia di San Lorenzo."

10. Ridolfi 1648, vol. 2, p. 6: "si fece condur da Firenze i piccoli modelli di Daniele Volterrano, cavati dalle figure delle sepolture de' Medici, poste in San Lorenzo di quella Città, cioè l'Aurora, il Crepuscolo, la Notte, & il Giorno, sopra quali fece studio particolare, traendone infiniti disegni a lume di lucerna." Vasari 1966, vol. 5, p. 546: "là dove in detto tempo formò di gesso quasi tutte le figure di marmo che di mano di Michelagnolo sono nella Sagrestia nuova di San Lorenzo."

11. Recorded in the 1695 inventory of collection of Benavides (1498–1582); Favaretto 1972, p. 120. On the gesso in Padua, see L. Attardi in Favaretto and Menegazzi 2013, pp. 132–33.

12. Avery 1999, p. 54, no. 51.

13. Private collection. Exhibited in *Michelangelo and the Ideal Body* (National Museum of Western Art, Tokyo, 2018), no. 62 [as by Il Passignano].

14. Rome 1999, nos. 37–40. A *Dawn* by an artist close to Pietro da Barga is in the civic museums of Ferrara: Ferrara 1974, no. 152.

15. Volker Krahn in Bonn 2015, nos. 142a–b.

16. Red wax: Ashmolean Museum, Oxford (length 23.5 cm): Penny 1992, vol. 1, p. 79. Alabaster: Staatliche Kunstsammlungen, Dresden: Bonn 2015, nos. 140a–d. Ivory: Palazzo Pitti, Florence: Madrid 2007, p. 400.

17. Danti: Dimitrios Zikos in Florence 2008, pp. 324–25, as by Egnazio Danti and Timoteo Refati.
    Sirigatti: Borghini 1584, p. 20; Waźbiński 1987, pp. 94–95.

18. Krahn 2018.

19. Vasari 1966, vol. 5, p. 205: "Onde egli ripreso un poco d'animo, ritrasse di terra nella sagrestia di San Lorenzo, mentre s'andava pensando al bisogno suo, tutte le figure che aveva fatto Michelagnolo di marmo, cioè l'Aurora, il Crepuscolo, il Giorno e la Notte, e gli riusciron così ben fatte, che monsignor Giovanni Batista Figiovanni, priore di San Lorenzo, al quale donò la Notte perché gli faceva aprir la sagrestia, giudicandola cosa rara, la donò al duca Alessandro, che poi la diede al detto Giorgio che stava con Sua Eccellenza, sapendo che egli attendeva a cotali studi; la qual figura è oggi in Arezzo nelle sue case, con altre cose dell'arte."

20. Vasari 1966, vol. 5, p. 282: "fatti alcuni modelli in bozze di terra, i quali condusse eccellentemente, dando loro quella fierezza e maniera che aveva dato Michelagnolo al disegno, con la gradina, che è un ferro intaccato, le gradinò, acciò fussero crudette et avessino più forza."

21. Vasari 1966, vol. 5, p. 283: "il quale finalmente diede finita l'opera in modo che non si conosce che Michelagnolo la guardasse mai."

22. D. Lauri in Florence 2017, pp. 146–49.

23. Ultraviolet analysis by Michael Belman, objects conservator at the Carnegie Museum of Art, Pittsburgh.

24. Achilles-Syndram 1994, p. 145, no. 349: "Die vier bilder tag, nacht, mitternacht und morgen, eines schuchs hoch, nach Michel Angelo."

25. Achilles-Syndram 1994, p. 264, nos. 29–32: "Die vier tagzeiten, so liegen."

26. Achilles-Syndram 1994, pp. 144–50, 261–75. B. Boucher in Houston and London 2001, p. 170, erroneously states the 1616 inventory records that the Times of Day are by van der Schardt.

27. Achilles-Syndram 1994, pp. 124, 137, 138, 146–47.

28. Berger 1994, pp. 56–57; Scholten 2008, p. 201.

29. Murr 1797, p. 241, no. 32: "L'Aurore, le Jour, le Crepuscule et la Nuit. La quartiéme s'est cassé." Murr probably confused *Night* for *Dusk*.

30. Rijksmuseum: BK-2013-9-1 to 9-9; BK-2016-44-1 to 44-9. Victoria and Albert Museum: A.7-1938; A.8-1938.

31. Scholten 2008, p. 220.

Alan Chong is responsible for the sections on Sandro di Lorenzo and van der Schardt. Lorenzo Principi wrote the sections on copies, Tribolo, Dusk, and the Appendix.

CATALOGUE

CAT. 1
Florentine (close to Benedetto da Maiano and the
young Michelangelo)
Bust of the Young John the Baptist
ca. 1490s
marble, height 34.7 cm (13 ⅜ in.)
National Gallery of Art, Washington
Samuel H. Kress Collection, 1943.4.79

In fifteenth-century Florence, sculptors produced a significant number of marble busts depicting the Christ Child and the young John the Baptist, apparently in response to the recommendation of the Dominican friar Giovanni Dominici (ca. 1355–1419) that such images would be suitable models for children. In his *Regola del governo di cura familiare*, written between 1400 and 1405, Dominici suggested that a mother adorn her home with paintings or sculptures of young religious figures. "The child is mirrored in the holy Baptist wearing a camel skin – a young boy who enters the desert, plays with birds, sips nectar from leaves, and sleeps on the ground. It would not be amiss if Jesus and the Baptist, or Jesus and the Evangelist, as children, were depicted together."[1]

This marble bust has long been attributed to Antonio Rossellino (ca. 1427–1479).[2] A close comparison among Rossellino's works is a marble relief of the Virgin and Child, called the Altman Madonna (Metropolitan Museum of Art, New York), which dates about 1455 to 1460.[3] However, in contrast with that relief and most sculptures of the fifteenth century, which have a generalized sweet expression, the Washington bust has an emotional specificity. The boy's downward gaze and sense of

FIG. 1
Benedetto da Maiano, *Funerary Monument of Maria of Aragon* (detail), 1481–91. Marble. Sant'Anna dei Lombardi, Naples.

FIG. 2
Michelangelo, *Young John the Baptist*, 1495–96. Marble. Fundación Casa Ducal de Medinaceli-Sevilla. Photograph of 1930.

FIG. 3
Detail of FIG. 2.

interior absorption more closely resemble Florentine sculpture from the end of the fifteenth century. Charles Seymour in 1961 thought that the bust showed "a mystical withdrawal from this world to another realm of religious or poetical imagination."[4] As the palpable sense of sadness that comes from contemplating Christ's fate is unprecedented in the work of Antonio Rossellino from around 1460, the bust may have been made later, around the 1490s.

The drapery folds that resemble flattened tubes suggest that the bust was made in Florence under Rossellino's influence. On the other hand, the bust expresses a more modern style that has links with Benedetto da Maiano (1442–1497), the principal student of Rossellino. The fleshy lips, elongated eyes with subtly incised lids, and the thin, slightly raised eyebrows have parallels with the figure of the Virgin in the funerary monument of Maria of Aragón (Sant'Anna dei Lombardi, Naples), sculpted by Benedetto da Maiano between 1481 and 1491 (FIG. 1).

However, the flame-like forms of the hair on the Washington bust differ from both Rossellino's work, which has an edgier line in low-relief carving, and that of Benedetto da Maiano, who tends to arrange hair in tidy strands. The dynamic curls on the bust of the Baptist can be compared to early works by Michelangelo (1475–1564), who trained as a marble sculptor in the workshop of Benedetto da Maiano. Michelangelo's early sculptures of the 1490s show similar overlapping forms of hair, seen for example in his *Young John the Baptist* of Úbeda (FIG. 2) and the young faun accompanying *Bacchus* (Bargello).

The treatment of the eyes can also be compared with the *Archer* of 1496 to 1497 (on loan to the Metropolitan Museum of Art). The attribution of the bust of the young Baptist cannot yet be resolved, but its quality is confirmed by its affinity with the work of some of the most distinguished Florentine sculptors of the late fifteenth century – Antonio Rossellino, Benedetto da Maiano, and Michelangelo.

ATTRIBUTION

Since 1891, this bust has been consistently attributed to Antonio Rossellino, with only two exceptions. Adolfo Venturi (1935) thought that the softness of flesh and expression indicated that the bust was by Giovanfrancesco Rustici, perhaps interpreting a lost work by Leonardo da Vinci.[5] Charles Seymour (1961 and 1966), after suggesting that the bust shared qualities with the young Michelangelo's work, assigned it to Benedetto da Maiano.
Lorenzo Principi

PROVENANCE

This bust is first recorded in the church of San Francesco dei Vanchetoni, Florence, which was founded in 1602 by Ippolito Galantini (1565–1620) to teach Christian doctrine to children. The image of the young Baptist was thus wholly in keeping with the mission of the church. This bust was recorded in the church by 1756 as a pair to a marble bust of a boy (National Gallery of Art, Washington, as by Desiderio da Settignano).[6] Frequently described in early guidebooks as by Donatello, the two busts were placed over doors leading to the relic room.[7] The works cannot have been original to the church, since it dates from seventeenth century, nor did the two busts originate as pendants, being different in style and size.

Some time before 1914, the two busts had been moved to the local museum to avoid theft, and two plaster copies were placed in the church, where they remain. In March 1914, the church attempted to sell the two busts to the Italian state, but its offer of 15,000 lire was considered too low. Then, in September 1938, the church approved the sale of the busts for 500,000 lire to the Victoria and Albert Museum in London, but nothing came of this.[8]

Beginning in December 1938, the Austrian connoisseur Leo Planiscig negotiated the sale of the two marble busts to Duveen Brothers in New York.[9] In the summer of 1939, the confraternity of the Vanchettoni agreed to sell the busts with the following justification: "The two little children have no artistic interest and therefore they have no importance with respect to national artistic heritage."[10] The superintendent of Florentine museums Giovanni Poggi objected to the sale, but the ministry of education nonetheless consented to the sale in November 1939, just as World War II was beginning.[11] The church agreed to sell the two works to the dealer Eugenio Ventura for 350,000 lire, which would be used for the restoration of the building.[12]

In January 1940, Duveen purchased the two busts for $71,600.[13] This means that the Vanchettoni church received a mere $17,600, the equivalent of 350,000 lire, with the rest going to Ventura and Planiscig. The works were shipped from Genoa to New York in February 1940, shortly before Italian ports were closed to the United States. Correspondence within the Duveen firm as early as October 11, 1939, makes clear that the dealer intended to sell the busts to Samuel Kress. In February 1941, Duveen sold the Baptist alone to the Kress Foundation, New York, for $130,000, having first asked $280,000.[14] It was immediately sent to the National Gallery of Art in Washington for its grand opening, but the bust by Desiderio was not sold until a year later.

Leo Planiscig (1887–1952), who was the main contact with Duveen, had been director of sculpture and decorative arts at the Kunsthistorisches Museum in Vienna, but left for Florence after the German annexation of Austria in 1938. Planiscig attributed the busts to Desiderio (Christ Child) and Rossellino (Baptist). Planiscig's role as facilitator of this sale has been obscured, notably by Ulrich Middeldorf, perhaps in an attempt to protect Planiscig's reputation as a scholar.[15] Eugenio Ventura was a far more controversial personality, as he sold works of art to Nazi officials during the war; for example, in 1942 he met Hermann Göring to arrange for the purchase and the restoration of several paintings.[16]

REFERENCES

Richa 1754, vol. 4, p. 92 [Donatello]. Bode 1891, p. 89 [the two busts in the Vanchettoni church attributed to Rossellino]. Venturi 1935, part 1, pp. 79–80, fig. 66 [Rustici based on a model by Leonardo]. Washington 1941, p. 31 [Rossellino]. Seymour 1961, pp. 59–60 [Rossellino, connected with the young Michelangelo]. Seymour 1966, p. 245 note 27 [Benedetto da Maiano]. Middeldorf 1976, pp. 23–24 [thereafter as Rossellino, with earlier literature]. Gary Radke in Detroit and Fort Worth 1985, no. 56 [ca. 1460]. Coonin 1995, p. 61, fig. 3. Sénéchal 2007, pp. 82, 84, 217, no. SR 1.

1. Dominici 1860, p. 131: "Così si specchi nel Battista santo, vestito di pelle di cammello, fanciullino che entra nel diserto, scherza cogli uccelli, succhia le foglie melate, dorme in sulla terra. Non nocerebbe se vedessi dipinti Iesu e il Battista, Iesu e il Vangelista piccinini insieme coniunti." See Coonin 1995; also Lavin 1955 and Lavin 1961.

2. The earlier attribution history is summarized by Middeldorf 1976, pp. 23–24. The earliest assignment of the bust to Rossellino is by Bode 1891, p. 89, who attributed both busts in the church of Vanchettoni to the artist.

3. Gary Radke in Detroit and Fort Worth 1985, p. 178.

4. Seymour 1961, p. 59.

5. The assignment to Rustici is rejected by Sénéchal 2007, p. 217.

6. Inv. 1943.4.94. Middeldorf 1976, pp. 19–20. Bode 1883, p. 135, assigned both busts to Desiderio da Settignano; in 1891, he concluded that they were both by Rossellino (Bode 1891, p. 89).

7. Richa 1754, vol. 4 (1756), p. 92: "due busti di marmo del Donatello sono stati collocati sulle porte laterali, che mettono nella stanza detta della Reliquie" [two marble busts by Donatello have been placed over the side doors that lead into the room called that of the Relics].

8. Archivio della Congregazione dei Vanchetoni, 158/4. The mediator with the London museum in 1938 was Alfredo Ciolli.

9.   Duveen Records: Desiderio and Rossellino files. New York stock book 19 [1938], p. 136, no. 29833: "purchased from Mr. Planiscig Jan. 12/40," for a total cost of $82,340.

10. Pellegrini 2014, p. 247: "I due puttini non hanno alcun interesse artistico e quindi essi non hanno veruna importanza rispetto al patrimonio artistico nazionale."

11. Poggi's letter is dated Aug. 29, 1939. The ministry's letter is dated Nov. 25, 1939.

12. Archivio della Congregazione dei Vanchetoni, 158/4.

13. Duveen Records: Planiscig file: cable of Dec. 15, 1938 (image 166); also Desiderio file, letter of May 10, 1939. Rossellino file: letter of Jan. 12, 1940, to Ventura, is annotated with 15% commission paid to Duveen's Paris office for a total cost of $82,340.

14. Duveen Records: Kress file, 1941–43: invoice dated Feb. 27, 1941 (image 150). A price of $140,000 is shown in a letter of Feb. 21, 1941 (image 160). The Christ Child by Desiderio was sold to Kress in January 1942.

15. Middeldorf 1976, p. 19, giving Ventura as the owner. Duveen Records: New York stock book 19 [1938], p. 137: Planiscig received $4,680 in commission.

16. Hofacker 2004, p. 89; Pellegrini 2014. In December 1942, Ventura arranged the restoration of fifteen Impressionist and six early Italian paintings belonging to Hermann Goering.

CAT. 2
Benedetto da Rovezzano (1474–ca. 1552),
attributed to
John the Baptist ca. 1510
terracotta with polychromy, height 71.5 cm (28 ⅛ in.)
Cleveland Museum of Art
Bequest of John L. Severance, 1942.781

In the first decades of the sixteenth century, a number of painted terracotta statues of the young John the Baptist were produced in Florence. Approximately half life-size, they depict the figure sitting on or leaning against a rocky outcropping. Elegant and smoothly finished, with distinctively tousled hair, the works are based on earlier representations of the young John the Baptist entering the wilderness, a subject already found in the thirteenth-century mosaic in the dome of the Florence Baptistery (see p. 30) as well as in several sculptures. Around 1477, Antonio Rossellino carved a marble sculpture of the young Baptist striding into the desert holding a banner (FIG. 1). Installed over the door of the Opera di San Giovanni, directly opposite the Baptistery, the image was perhaps designed to be accessible to children receiving religious instruction.[1]

The Cleveland sculpture shows an older figure who neither moves through the landscape, nor is an emaciated hermit, as seen for example in the so-called *Martelli John the Baptist* by Donatello and Desiderio da Settignano (see p. 101).[2] Rather, the terracotta figures of the early sixteenth century represent a new type of the Baptist as a thoughtful young man, imbued with a sense of contemplation but not of sadness. It is no coincidence that the same physical and emotional type was used to depict the young David after the slaying of Goliath.

ATTRIBUTION

There is strong evidence that Benedetto da Rovezzano is the sculptor of the Cleveland *Baptist* and related terracottas, as can be seen by comparisons with the artist's *Saint John the Evangelist* carved in marble between 1513 and 1514 (FIG. 2), and a *Penitent Saint Jerome* in painted terracotta (FIG. 3). Rovezzano's bronze *Neptune*, made around 1537 to 1540 for Cowdray House in England (Victoria and Albert Museum), also offers strong points of comparison.[3] There are analogies in the angular and dynamic drapery with deep undercuts, the curly hair twisted into locks, and the eyes with very round irises and pupils.

Scholarly discussion has focused on the attribution of an extensive and mysterious group of terracottas, rather than on their meaning. The terracottas represent a wide variety of subjects: John the Baptist seated, standing, or in bust form,

FIG. 3
Benedetto da Rovezzano,
Saint Jerome, ca. 1510. Painted
terracotta, height 55 cm.
Bode-Museum, Berlin.

FIG. 4
Benedetto da Rovezzano?,
Seated John the Baptist, ca. 1510.
Terracotta with remains of paint,
height 68 cm. Museo Nazionale
del Bargello, Florence.

David, the penitent Saint Jerome, Saint Michael and the dragon, a knight trampling a victim, and the Spinario. Wilhelm Bode in 1901 discussed a few of these works in connection with a range of Florentine sculptors working in the first decade of the sixteenth century, but could not identify an artist and so applied the conventional name of "Master of John Statuettes."[4] Giancarlo Gentilini in 1980 and 1992 refined this group by noting the influence of Michelangelo's *David* and the strong connections with Jacopo Sansovino. A glazed example from the Duomo of Pescia can be dated to 1505, and Gentilini thought that the Cleveland work might follow shortly afterward.[5]

Bruce Boucher attributed the example in the Bargello (FIG. 4), the most highly finished of the group, to Jacopo Sansovino, but did not discuss the other works.[6] If the treatment of the face in the Bargello work seems close to Sansovino, the overall composition is actually quite stiff. The composition of another terracotta *Baptist* (FIG. 5) is more modern but its depiction of hair is extremely close to that of Benedetto da Rovezzano. Benedetto has sometimes been suggested as the maker of some of these terracottas, for example, by Carlo Gamba in 1920, who discussed a sculptural group showing a horseman trampling a soldier (FIG. 6).[7] Francesco Caglioti made a stronger argument for attributing the terracottas to Benedetto da Rovezzano in 1996 and 2012, followed by Giancarlo Gentilini in 2014.[8] It is likely that Benedetto da Rovezzano directed a

workshop that produced the terracotta figures, but several other artists, as yet unidentified, appear to have been involved and are deserving of further study.
Lorenzo Principi

PROVENANCE

This sculpture is first documented in 1889 in the collection of Emile Gavet (1830–1904), a French architect who also dealt in art, beginning with pastels commissioned from Jean-François Millet, followed by a wide variety of medieval and Renaissance decorative arts. Around 1892, he sold a large number of objects to Alva Vanderbilt to decorate her Newport mansion, Marble House, a collection later sold to John Ringling for his museum in Sarasota.[9] This terracotta was attributed to Andrea del Verrocchio in Gavet's catalogues of 1889 and 1894. It was auctioned with the same attribution at Petit, Paris, May 31–June 9, 1897 (lot 204, 12,500 francs to Gouin). Arnold Seligmann et cie of Paris sold the work around 1926 to John L. Severance (1863–1936), a Cleveland industrialist who amassed a fine collection that included masterpieces by J. M. W. Turner, Aelbert Cuyp, and others, installed in a mansion called Longwood.[10] To accompany this terracotta, still believed to be by Verrocchio, Severance also obtained a copy of the artist's bronze putto with a dolphin in the Palazzo Vecchio, Florence. Severance's collection was bequeathed to the Cleveland Museum of Art in 1936.

REFERENCES

Gavet 1889, no. 22, pl. VI [Verrocchio]. Gavet 1894, no. 203, pl. 50.[11] Cleveland 1942, no. 20, pl. XI [Verrocchio]. Pillsbury 1971, no. 30 [Master of the John Statuettes]. G. Gentilini in Impruneta 1980, p. 98 [Master of the John Statuettes, 1505–10]. Chong 2009, p. 12 [perhaps 19th century]. A. Bagnoli in Monte San Savino 2016, pp. 112–15.

TECHNICAL NOTE

Three samples from the sculpture analyzed by Oxford Authentication Ltd. in December 2010 show that the last firing of the work took place between 400 and 700 years ago (1310 to 1610).

---

1. See Paolozzi Strozzi 2013. A terracotta of the young Baptist (Bargello) has long been attributed to Michelozzo, but apparently dates from the 16th century; see Caglioti 2012, fig. 41, pp. 66–67 note 106.

2. Paolozzi Strozzi 2006.

3. *John the Evangelist*: Francesco Vossilla in Cinelli et al. 2002, pp. 62–66. *Neptune*: Caglioti 2012a.

4. Bode 1901. The group was expanded by others, including Fabriczy 1909, pp. 42, 43, 76, 134, 141, 145, 171; and Pope-Hennessy 1964, pp. 191–96.

5. Pescia: Gentilini 1992, p. 456, fig. p. 470 (p. 471 for another glazed terracotta of the Baptist); Schottmüller 1933, p. 146, also related it to the group of terracottas. On the group: Gentilini in Impruneta 1980, pp. 97–98, also pp. 85–86; Gentilini 1992, p. 456; Florence 1992, pp. 150–53. A. Bellandi in Fiesole 1998, pp. 372–73.

6. Boucher 1991, vol. 2, pp. 313–14. Sénéchal 2007, pp. 229–30, also accepts the Bargello terracotta as by Jacopo Sansovino, with the remainder by other hands. Warren 2016, vol. 1, pp. 60–66, attributed various terracottas to Sansovino.

7. Gamba 1920, p. 176.

8. Caglioti 1996, p. 101 note 76. F. Caglioti in Paris 2012, pp. 22–27. G. Gentilini in Brun 2014, pp. 6–13.

9. Chong 2009.

10. Paul Byk of Arnold Seligmann, Rey and Co., New York, to William Milliken, director of the Cleveland Museum of Art, Oct. 8, 1942 [museum file].

11. A photograph of this work appears in an album in the Clark Institute of Art, Williamstown, with catalogue headings taken from Gavet 1894.

FIG. 1
Donatello and Desiderio da Settignano, *John the Baptist (Martelli Baptist)*, ca. 1440 and 1457. Marble, height 173 cm. Museo Nazionale del Bargello, Florence.

FIG. 2
Benedetto da Maiano, *John the Baptist*, ca. 1478–80. Marble. Sala di Gigli, Palazzo Vecchio, Florence.

FIG. 3
Circle of Benedetto da Maiano, *John the Baptist*, 1480s. Painted terracotta, height ca. 49.5 cm. Art Institute of Chicago. 1977.917.

CAT. 3
Giovanfrancesco Rustici (1475–1554)
John the Baptist
ca. 1500–1515
marble, height 75.5 cm (29 ¾ in.)
Morgan Library and Museum, New York
Purchased by Pierpont Morgan, 1909, AZ031

Giovanfrancesco Rustici made a number of striking sculptures of John the Baptist, the most prominent being the *Preaching of John the Baptist* above the north door of the Baptistery in Florence (see p. 32). Commissioned in 1506, the group of three bronzes was completed in 1511, although Rustici was not paid fully until 1524.

Leonardo da Vinci assisted Rustici in modeling the waxes for the Baptistery bronzes, according to Giorgio Vasari.[1] Well known in his lifetime, Rustici is regarded as an eccentric figure. Pomponius Gauricus, in his 1504 treatise *De sculptura*, praised Rustici as one of the four best Tuscan carvers of marble, putting him in the company of Benedetto da Maiano, Michelangelo, and Andrea Sansovino.[2]

Based on his reputation as a close follower of both Leonardo and Michelangelo, Rustici was invited to France in 1528. Between 1531 and 1533, he was the highest paid artist at the French court after Rosso Fiorentino. He lived in Paris rather than at the court at Fontainebleau. A series of disappointments followed his prominent career, and he died, forgotten, in Tours in 1554.[3]

Rustici occupies a pivotal position in early sixteenth-century Florentine sculpture. While his work was strongly influenced by his friend Leonardo da Vinci, Rustici was also attentive to fifteenth-century sculpture. The marble figure of the adolescent Baptist in the Morgan Library recalls such important earlier models as the *Martelli Baptist* by Donatello and Desiderio da Settignano, and Benedetto da Maiano's sculpture in the Palazzo Vecchio (FIGS. 1, 2). The basic form, with the weight resting on the left leg, the left arm clutching a scroll, and the right dropped to the side, remains remarkably consistent over half a century. More specifically, the thinness of Rustici's ascetic figure is directly indebted to the *Martelli Baptist*, while the soft body and dreamy

No. 430—FIFTEENTH CENTURY MARBLE ST. JOHN
BY ANTONIO ROSSELLINO (1427-1490)

FIG. 4
John the Baptist, ca. 1900 (copy of
CAT. 3). Marble, height 76.2 cm.
Frontispiece to the Volpi auction
catalogue of December 17–19,
1917.

FIG. 5
Gianfrancesco Rustici?, *John the
Baptist*, 1500–1510. Marble, height
102 cm. Private collection.

gaze are derived from Maiano's work. In a departure from these earlier examples, Rustici leaves the shoulder uncovered, a feature which has a strong affinity with Michelangelo's *Young John the Baptist* (see p. 93), sculpted for Lorenzo di Pierfrancesco de' Medici (called il Popolano) between 1495 and 1496. However, the flaps of the garment in Rustici's sculpture are tied together with a rope, which is not seen in Michelangelo's work but may derive from Benedetto da Maiano, as shown in a terracotta probably based on a marble by Maiano (FIG. 3).[4] Since Michelangelo trained in Maiano's workshop, this terracotta bust may reflect a common source for these images of the young Baptist.

ATTRIBUTION AND DATING

J. P. Morgan purchased the marble figure of John the Baptist in 1909 as the work of Antonio Rossellino. He already owned Rossellino's sublime relief of the Virgin and Child, made between 1460 and 1475 (Morgan Library and Museum, New York).[5] In 1935, Ulrich Middeldorf attributed the *John the Baptist* to Giovanfrancesco Rustici with some hesitation. Shortly after, William Valentiner identified it as Michelangelo's lost statue of John the Baptist commissioned by Lorenzo di Pierfrancesco de' Medici, a theory that generated a certain amount of excitement among Michelangelo scholars.[6] However, in 1943, Charles de Tolnay, the leading Michelangelo expert of the twentieth century, attributed the marble to Silvio Cosini. Since then, Middeldorf's attribution of the marble to Rustici has been widely accepted, although its date remains in question: was it made before or after the great Baptistery bronze figures? Philippe Sénéchal (2007) dated the Morgan *Baptist* between 1495 and 1500, among Rustici's earliest works, while Tommaso Mozzati (2008) placed it around 1515, after the Baptistery bronzes, when the artist was adopting a new classicist style, as can be seen in his work at the Villa Salviati.[7] Both theories are plausible and it should be conceded that the eclectic range of Rustici's sources, as well as gaps in his career, makes dating this sculpture difficult. In any event, the marble *Baptist* shows the strong influence of Benedetto da Maiano, Rustici's teacher. Moreover, three years after Maiano's death in 1497, Rustici is recorded as occupying his master's workshop on the Via dei Servi.[8]

The statue apparently enjoyed some fame, as shown by the versions based on it. An almost identical composition, but more dryly carved, was sold in New York in 1917 by the notorious Elia Volpi (1858–1938), an antique dealer and forger, who formed the collection of the Palazzo Davanzati in Florence.[9] The auction consisted of a large quantity of Italian furniture and textiles. The *John the Baptist* (FIG. 4), attributed to Antonio Rossellino like Morgan's version, appeared as the frontispiece to the auction catalogue. Precisely duplicating Morgan's sculpture, Volpi's version is almost certainly a copy made in the early twentieth century. Another replica, in bronze, appeared on the art market in 1977 with an attribution to Benedetto da Maiano.[10]

ANOTHER *BAPTIST* BY RUSTICI

Rustici created several sculptures of John the Baptist. In addition to this marble and the monumental bronzes for the Baptistery, he made another *Baptist* in glazed terracotta (CAT. 4), as boldly modeled as the Baptistery figures. Rustici is also responsible for a terracotta bust of the infant Baptist (Bargello) and a marble relief of Christ and the Baptist as children (Louvre).[11] Another marble statue of the Baptist has recently come to light (FIG. 5).[12] The position of the right arm and the fleece that covers the right shoulder differ from the arrangement in CAT. 3, which shows that it is not a copy. Although the work is worn from exposure, and the head is a modern replacement, it is very likely by Rustici. The curls of the fleece are characteristic of the artist's style. In comparison with the work in the Morgan Library, the composition of the figure is more tightly closed and the distribution of weight on the legs less pronounced, factors that suggest the newly discovered work dates from just before the Morgan *Baptist*.

Lorenzo Principi

PROVENANCE

The sculpture is first recorded with Maurice de Rothschild (1881–1957), 47 rue de Monceau, Paris, who was a collector and part-time art dealer. In May 1909, he sold the statue as a work by Antonio Rossellino through Duveen Brothers in Paris to the famous American collector J. Pierpont Morgan (1837–1913). Morgan paid Duveen 450,000 francs, with 200,000 going to Rothschild.[13] J. P. Morgan Jr. (1867–1943), who inherited most of his father's collection, presented this work to the Pierpont Morgan Library, New York, when it was incorporated in 1924.

REFERENCES

Middeldorf 1935, p. 72, pl. 2a [Rustici]. Valentiner 1938 [Michelangelo]. Tolnay 1943, pp. 199–200 [Cosini]. M. Weinberger in *Art Bulletin* 27 (1945), p. 71 [Rustici]. Sénéchal 2007, pp. 31–33, 184–85 [Rustici, 1495–1500, with earlier literature]. Mozzati 2008, pp. 142–43 [ca. 1515]. Caglioti 2012, pp. 5, 7–8, 60–61 notes 48–51, figs. 25, 37 [ca. 1500].

1. Vasari 1966, vol. 5, pp. 477–78: "Non volle Giovanfrancesco, mentre conduceva di terra quest'opera, altri atorno che Lionardo da Vinci, il quale nel fare le forme, armarle di ferri, et insomma sempre, insino a che non furono gettate le statue, non l'abbandonò mai; onde credono alcuni, ma però non ne sanno altro, che Lionardo vi lavorasse di sua mano, o almeno aiutasse Giovanfrancesco col consiglio e buon giudizio suo."

2. Quoted in Sénéchal 2007, p. 12.

3. Mozzati and Sénéchal 2010, pp. 54, 58.

4. The work in Chicago is published by Wardropper 1991, p. 117, fig. 14, as the Master of the John Statuettes, ca. 1470.

5. Inv. AZ069. Bought in 1902.

6. Surveyed by Caglioti 2012, pp. 5, 7–8.

7. Tomasso Mozzati in Florence 2010, pp. 362–75 [with earlier references].

8. Mozzati 2008, pp. 65–66, 89 note 445, 141–42.

9. Volpi sale: American Art Galleries, New York, Dec. 17–19, 1917 (lot 430, height 30 in.). A photograph of the sculpture is in the Kunsthistorisches Institut, Florence; noted by Sénéchal 2007, p. 185; Mozzati 2008, p. 142 note 742, fig. 263.

10. With I.S.A.M.A. di Franco Vercelli, Turin; illustrated in *V Mostra mercato d'antiquariato: Assisi, 1 maggio–29 maggio 1977, Sacro convento di S. Francesco* (1977).

11. Bargello: P. Sénéchal in Florence 2010, pp. 308–9, no. 21. Louvre (the background is added later): Mozzati 2008, pp. 143–44, fig. 264.

12. Catalogued in an unpublished paper by Giancarlo Gentilini and Tommaso Mozzati (2013), who kindly brought the work to my attention.

13. Duveen Records: Paris stock book, 1908–11, fol. 74, stock no. 1357 (cost: 200,000 francs); Paris ledger 1, 1908–13, pp. 401, 427; and confirmed in Paris sales, 1908–17, fol. 22; client summary book, 1894–1918.

CAT. 4
Giovanfrancesco Rustici
John the Baptist
ca. 1505–15
glazed terracotta, height 100.3 cm (39 ½ in.)
Museum of Fine Arts, Boston
Gift of Mrs. Solomon R. Guggenheim, 50.2624

Giovanfrancesco Rustici's *John the Baptist* was modeled in clay, fired, covered in white glaze (with manganese glaze to outline the eyes, represent the pupils, and sketch in the eyebrows; see FIG. 2), and then fired again. The figure, about half life-size, slender, and elongated almost to the point of distortion, stands barefoot on rough terrain. He wears the goatskin tunic that identifies him as the Baptist, with the hooves tied over his right shoulder, emphasizing the forward twist of the upper body. His right arm crosses over his chest and he points with his right index finger, John's characteristic gesture.[1] The saint turns his head to his right, away from this gesture, creating torsion through the body. With an intensely expressive and focused gaze, he looks into the distance. His open mouth reveals teeth. Long curls reach his shoulders, and he has a beard and mustache. John's left arm and hand are held close to his body and his fingers, which seem never to have held a cross, press into his left leg. The artist eschews attributes beyond John's animal-skin garment.

The statue follows, in posture, gesture, setting, and clothing, three significant Florentine prototypes for the figure of John the Baptist: the first from the

FIG. I
John the Baptist and Christ (Behold the Lamb of God), 13th century. Mosaic. Ceiling of the Baptistery, Florence.

thirteenth-century mosaic scenes of the Life of the Baptist decorating the dome of the Baptistery of Florence; the second from Andrea Pisano's relief cycle for the bronze doors of the Baptistery (1330–36); and the third, Donatello's bronze *John the Baptist* of around 1457, now in the Baptistery of Siena. The two narrative cycles tell the story of John the Baptist's retreat into the wilderness and his mission, which culminated in the baptism of Christ, a moment of epiphany.[2] The same five scenes are represented in both cycles, though not in the same order. The first scene shows the young saint as a child heading out into the wilderness, an episode that became particularly popular in Florentine imagery and devotional literature (see p. 30).[3] He has already divested himself of his clothing and donned animal skins. For John it was a time of withdrawal from family and society: a period of reflection, repentance, and preparation for his mission as the precursor of Christ. He grew into manhood in this harsh setting, proclaiming and then preaching the coming of Christ as the "Voice of one calling in the wilderness," exhorting his listeners to "Make straight the way of the Lord" (John 1:23). In the mosaic of the Preaching of the Baptist, he holds a scroll citing that verse, and points upward. This is also the gesture of Rustici's bronze figure for the group of the *Preaching of John the Baptist* made for the north portal of the Baptistery (see p. 31). Rustici presents a powerful, heroic image of John as he addresses a Levite and a Pharisee, his pointing finger a rhetorical gesture of discourse.[4] Next in the narrative, John baptizes the

people who have gathered around him to hear him preach. The subsequent scene in the mosaic cycle presents the first likely source for the pose of the sculpture in Boston: John points over his left shoulder while speaking to a group to his right, holding a scroll citing the Gospel verse "Behold the Lamb of God, who takes away the sins of the world" (John 1:29). John points to Christ, who is represented as if just arriving at the scene (FIG. I). Andrea Pisano's relief of this scene shows the saint in a similar pose, also pointing to Christ.[5] Donatello's bronze *John the Baptist* evokes the episode by employing this pose and gesture, the isolated figure calling to mind the complete narrative.[6] All of John's preparations in the desert since childhood, followed by his preaching and baptizing, led to this moment, marking the arrival of Christ. It is a pivotal scene in the story of Christian salvation, marking the transition between John's mission as prophet and the fulfillment of that prophecy as Christ takes up his own public mission. It is in this broader narrative and sacred context that Rustici's terracotta *John the Baptist* should be considered.

In the sculpture, we see the extremely thin, barefooted figure, intensely focused on his message, telling his listeners that Christ is among them and calling for repentance. John's power comes from his message, his emaciated body a sign of the ascetic life he has lived. His beard and mustache indicate that he has reached manhood, in contrast, for example, to a group of terracotta sculptures of the younger, beardless John in the wilderness, such as

FIG. 2
Detail of CAT. 4.

that in Cleveland (CAT. 2). In Florence in the early sixteenth century, Rustici's terracotta *John the Baptist* would have expressed the need for spiritual if not physical asceticism in the devotee. Through his body and in his message, the figure modeled penitence for his Renaissance viewers, many of whom would have listened to preachers calling for repentance in sermons delivered in Florence in the decades around 1500.

The choice of glazed terracotta is particularly appropriate for the message, as the technique embodies both humility and transformation.[7] Shaped from the humble material of local clay, the sculpture supports the notion of the humility required for repentance. The choice of a white glaze asserts the power of repentance to transform the spirit. A popular devotional treatise, the *Monte delle Oratione*, describes the effects of contemplation and prayer in terms of the color white: "Up on this mountain of prayer our garments will become white like the snow and our faces will shine like the sun."[8] The white glaze confers to the humble clay figure the powerful transformative aspect of repentance, through color, radiance, and shine. The sculpture was metaphorically perfected twice, through its two firings in the kiln.

Another figure by Donatello helps clarify the significance of this *John the Baptist*, the sculpture of the *Penitent Mary Magdalene*, which is documented in 1500 in the Florence Baptistery, and may have been there earlier, or even made for the site. Rustici would have seen it in that setting. The

placement of the *Magdalene* in the Baptistery would have emphasized the ongoing need for repentance throughout the lives of all Florentines, who had undergone the cleansing ritual of baptism there. Donatello's *Magdalene* was made in wood – like clay, a humble material – painted and highlighted with gilding, which, like the white glaze, signaled the sinner's transformation.[9] Her thin but powerful body, shaped by acts of ascetic penitence, like the long hair that provided her only garment in the wilderness, is comparable to Rustici's *John the Baptist*. The Museum of Fine Arts' statue can be grouped with a number of sculptures of the Magdalene made in the decades around 1500, all in response to Donatello's powerful image.[10] By that time, it had become common to pair these saints in Florentine imagery, as in Sandro Botticelli's *Pala delle Convertite*, an altarpiece made for the convent church of Saint Elizabeth, which housed reformed prostitutes, as well as in Filippino Lippi's panels of John the Baptist and Mary Magdalene (Accademia, Florence), which would have flanked a central panel as part of an altarpiece.[11] Together, the Baptist and the Magdalene provided wide-ranging examples of repentance for all Florentines, and devotion to each of these saints crossed gender boundaries. They were both intimate companions of Jesus, and both experienced moments of epiphany and revelation: John at the moment of Christ's baptism, and the Magdalene as the first to see Christ after the resurrection.

Giovanfrancesco Rustici produced a glazed terracotta relief of the *Noli me tangere* for the altarpiece of the Augustinian convent of San Luca in Via San Gallo, which was, according to Vasari, glazed by Giovanni della Robbia. A white glaze even more brilliant than the creamy color of the *John the Baptist* was used to express the transcendence of this scene of revelation. That white was a choice in this image, as in the *John the Baptist*, is made clear by the contrast with Giovanni della Robbia's own multicolored *Noli me tangere*, made for another convent in Via San Gallo, and now in the cloister of Santa Maria Novella.[12] Set in a garden with Christ as gardener, the episode is common in both penitential literature and works of art associated with female devotional experience, where gardening became a metaphor for self-discipline.[13]

The original location of the Boston *John the Baptist* is unknown, but its humble material, transcendent white glaze, and stress on the ascetic body of John point to a setting that would have encouraged contemplation, prayer, and internal, penitential devotion. Placement in a convent church or the oratory of a confraternity would have provided fertile ground for the transformative repentance that John the Baptist represented in Renaissance Florence.

Marietta Cambareri

PROVENANCE

Irene Rothschild Guggenheim (1868–1954), New York, presented the work to the museum in 1950. Irene Rothschild attended public school in New York and then Hunter College. She set up nurseries and kindergartens for the children of working women.[14] In 1895, she married Solomon Guggenheim (1861–1949), the mining magnate and founder of the Guggenheim Museum in New York. She also presented the Boston museum with a sixteenth-century Flemish tapestry (50.2627).

REFERENCES

Marietta Cambareri in Ottawa 2005, no. 8. Hykin 2007. Sénéchal 2007, pp. 72–75, 197 [1510–20]. Mozzati 2008, pp. 75–77. Marietta Cambareri in Florence 2010, pp. 302–5 [with previous references].

1. This finger is a repair carried out in 2004, based on consideration of the position and anatomy of the hand.

2. Moskowitz 1986, pp. 7–30; Solum 2015, pp. 81–87, 109–17.

3. Lavin 1955; Lavin 1961; Solum 2015, pp. 119–32.

4. Tommaso Mozzati and Philippe Sénéchal in Florence 2010, pp. 256–67.

5. In the mosaic cycle, the scene is set between the Baptism of the Multitudes and the Baptism of Christ, while on the bronze doors, it precedes those scenes.

6. The right forearm may not be by Donatello, but likely reproduces his intention. Rustici would have known the figure in this form; the forearm, which had been missing when the statue was delivered, was attached by 1474. See Pope-Hennessy 1993, pp. 288, 348, fig. 287.

7. Cambareri 2016, pp. 41–45, 66–69.

8. Cited in Solum 2015, p. 193.

9. Dunkleman 2005.

10. Jansen 2000, p. 280.

11. Filippino Lippi's John has been suggested as a stylistic source for the Boston sculpture; Mozzati 2008, p. 76. See Jansen 2000, pp. 134–35, for the pairing of these saints.

12. Tommaso Mozzati in Florence 2010, pp. 322–27.

13. Solum 2015, pp. 186–95.

14. Davis 1989.

CAT. 5

Andrea del Sarto (1486–1530)
John the Baptist
ca. 1517
oil on wood, transferred to canvas,
71 × 50 cm (28 × 19 ⅝ in.)
Worcester Art Museum
Museum Purchase, Restricted Funds; Gifts from
Louise I. Doyle, Britta D. Jeppson,
The Reverend and Mrs. DeWolf Perry in memory of
Harriett Brooks Hawkins; the Worcester Art Museum
Members' Council, and Anonymous Donors, 1984.38

For Giovan Angelo Montorsoli, the idea of conflating a pagan god with John the Baptist may have come directly from the painter Andrea del Sarto, who depicted Florence's patron saint adorned with the attributes of the god of wine, Bacchus. Sarto died during an outbreak of the plague in September 1530, and was buried in the church of Santissima Annunziata, just weeks before Montorsoli entered the order of Servites in same church. Giorgio Vasari tells us that Montorsoli specifically studied the paintings of Andrea del Sarto at the Annunziata, which inspired him as he trained to sing his first mass (see p. 19).[1] Montorsoli would also have known Sarto's *John the Baptist* fresco cycle (painted between 1513 and 1536) located in the Chiostro dello Scalzo, very near the Annunziata.

Over the course of his career, Sarto's figures become more three dimensional and monumental, which must have appealed to sculptors. He shared a workshop with the sculptor Jacopo Sansovino, and Vasari reports that through "discussing together the problems (*dubbii*) of art, and Jacopo making models of figures for Andrea, they gave one another great assistance."[2]

Andrea del Sarto's figure of John the Baptist has the soft features of an adolescent. Beneath the red tunic is the saint's traditional camel-hair coat. In his left hand he gently holds a reed cross. A wreath made of a grape vine rests upon his full head of hair. Moreover, the cross is tied together by a section of vine. Grape vines were an attribute of Bacchus, the pagan of wine. Positioned before a blank background, the Baptist looks slightly down as his upper

FIG. 1
Leonardo da Vinci, *John the Baptist*,
ca. 1513–16. Oil on wood,
69 × 57 cm. Musée du Louvre,
Paris.

FIG. 2
Roman, *Patera of Rennes*, early 3rd century. Gold, diameter 25 cm. Bibliothèque nationale de France, Paris. Cabinet des médailles, 56.94.

torso twists, pushing his right shoulder forward. He points to the cross, the traditional gesture announcing the coming of Christ and his sacrifice.

Sarto's enigmatic combination of John the Baptist and Bacchus derives from Leonardo da Vinci's painting of the same subject (FIG. 1).[3] Leonardo's Baptist is a youth of about the same age as Sarto's. Both figures are rendered half-length before a blank background, with Leonardo's more androgynous figure smiling enigmatically at the viewer. Rather than wearing the traditional camel-hair coat, the saint in Leonardo's painting wears a leopard skin, another attribute of Bacchus. Around 1516 to 1517, Raphael also depicted John the Baptist wearing a leopard skin (see p. 48).

VINES AND WINE

The conflation of John the Baptist, precursor of Christ, with the pagan god of wine and ecstatic abandon seems incongruous at first glance. However, wine was essential to Christianity. At the Last Supper, Christ referred to wine as being his blood, and in the sacrament of the Eucharist worshippers consume bread and wine as the body and blood of Christ. Moreover, Christ identified himself with a grape vine, saying to the Apostles, "I am the true vine, and my father is the gardener," and "I am the vine; you are the branches" (John 15:1, 5).[4] One legend claimed that the Tree of Life was a grape vine. After it was removed from the Garden of Eden, Noah brought it back to life, and from that vine also came the wood of the true cross. Pierre Bersuire, in his *Ovidius moralizatus* (written 1340–42), directly compared Bacchus to Christ, claiming that because Bacchus wears a vine wreath, he carried on his head the symbol of the Passion of Christ.

There are also connections between the Baptist and Bacchus, because both figures are associated with redemptive ceremonial liquids. John baptized by pouring water over the supplicant, symbolically washing away original sin and promising eternal life. Roman priests of Bacchus poured wine from vessels to honor their god. This ceremony is shown in ancient Roman art, for example, on the third-century *Patera of Rennes* (FIG. 2), where Bacchus appears at the center wearing a crown of grape leaves, with a panther at his feet and a staff couched in his left arm. The similarity to depictions of the John the Baptist would have been obvious to Renaissance viewers. Moreover, Sarto's painting connects the transformative qualities of wine, both as an intoxicant and as the blood of Christ.

Leonardo da Vinci, Andrea del Sarto, and Montorsoli contributed to the duality of John the Baptist, where the saint takes on essential pagan attributes – whether of Bacchus or Mars (see essay by Sundstrom) – to expand the impact of the figure in ways that traditional attributes could not. These works can be compared to the so-called *portraits historié* where a recognizable individual adopts elements of a mythological or historical figure. This highly symbolic form of dress-up includes the Emperor Commodus in the guise of Hercules or Vincenzo Danti's portrait of Duke Cosimo I as Augustus (see p. 37), where the portrayed remains recognizable but the disguise enhances a characteristic. Similarly, the Florentine depictions of John the Baptist under discussion are not equal blends of pagan and Christian. Rather, the Baptist adopts a critical feature of an ancient type. Unlike Montorsoli's comingling of John the Baptist with Mars, which has political overtones, Sarto's innovative painting explores the intellectual parallels between pagan and Christian redemption.
Kurt Sundstrom

PROVENANCE

The painting is first recorded in 1863 when Peter Chardon Brooks (1798–1880), Boston, lent it to the Boston Athenaeum ("Sanitary Fair Exhibition," no. 168, as Andrea del Sarto).[5] Around this time, the painting was transferred from panel to canvas by George Howarth, who worked in Boston between 1839 and 1864. This is one of the first documented transfers, and is recorded on a stencil on the verso of the picture.[6] The painting descended to Brooks's cousin Phillips Brooks (1835–1893), the famed rector of Boston's Trinity Church, and then to his niece Harriet Brooks Hawkins. In 1959, the painting was given to All Saints Church, Worcester, which sold it to the museum in 1984.

REFERENCES

Freedberg 1982. Marilyn Aronberg Lavin in *Burlington Magazine* 125 (1983), p. 162.

1. Vasari 1966, vol. 5, p. 492.

2. Vasari 1966, vol. 6, p. 177: "conferendo insieme i dubbii dell'arte e facendo Iacopo per Andrea modelli di figure, s'aiutavano l'un l'altro sommamente."

3. For the opportunities Sarto had to study Leonardo's painting first hand, see Freedberg 1982, pp. 285–86.

4. Freedberg 1982, pp. 266, 281–88.

5. The provenance is documented in Freedberg 1982.

6. Freedberg 1982, p. 281.

CAT. 6

Marcantonio Raimondi (active 1504–27)
John the Baptist
ca. 1520
engraving, 8 × 4.7 cm (3 ⅛ × 1 ⅞ in.)
The Metropolitan Museum of Art, New York
The Elisha Whittelsey Collection,
The Elisha Whittelsey Fund, 1949, 49.97.52

Marcantonio Raimondi produced a series of fifty-three small prints, each measuring about eight by five centimeters, depicting Christ, the Apostles, and famous saints.[1] Nearly all the figures are framed by angular posts (FIG. 1), although a few have analogous natural features like the tree trunks that arch over John the Baptist in this print.

John the Baptist steps forward in the landscape and points toward a cross formed by the reeds to his staff, to indicate the advent of Christ. The pose has analogies to both the terracotta sculpture by Giovanfrancesco Rustici and the painting by Andrea de Sarto in the exhibition (CATS. 4, 5). The Baptist's gesture in this print is ambiguous since he points at the cross but apparently also beyond it. The full range of the saint's gestures, whether to a cross, to heaven, or to Christ, deserves further study

Raimondi made other prints of the Baptist, including a larger image of the standing saint (FIG. 2), and one of the Baptist seated on a rock in the wilderness (FIG. 3). The latter closely reflects the composition of terracottas made around 1510 (for example, CAT. 2).[2]

The series of small prints of saints (to which CAT. 6 belongs) has been almost completely ignored in the recent avalanche of writing on Raimondi, perhaps because they seem to be unambitious devotional images, with only vague connections with Raphael. In 1888, Henri Delaborde, probably the last scholar to give them serious consideration, thought he

could discern links to Raphael.[3] However, Giorgio Vasari in his biography of Raimondi regarded them as artistic models, perhaps because of the clarity of their attributes, and made the strange comment that they could be especially useful to unimaginative painters: "Marcantonio meanwhile, continuing to engrave, made some sheets with small figures of the twelve Apostles, in various styles, and many male and female saints, in order to help those poor painters who were weak in design, so these works would serve their needs."[4] Raimondi indeed put considerable imagination into these little images, which show intriguing connections with contemporary painting and sculpture. Saint James the Greater, for example, seems to turn to walk away from the viewer (FIG. 1).
Alan Chong

PROVENANCE
Sold by the Graphische Sammlung Albertina, Vienna.

REFERENCES
Delaborde 1888, no. 64. Illustrated Bartsch, vol. 26, no. 150.

---

1. Illustrated Bartsch, vol. 26, nos. 124–83, with the following exceptions, which are different in size and compositional type, or repeat the saint: nos. 151, 157, 162, 163, 165, 167, 175, 180.

2. Standing Baptist: Illustrated Bartsch, vol. 26, no. 99. Seated Baptist: ibid., no. 151.

3. Delaborde 1888, pp. 110–12.

4. Vasari 1966, vol. 5, p. 12: "Marcantonio intanto, seguitando d'intagliare, fece in alcune carte i dodici Apostoli piccoli, in diverse maniere, e molti Santi e Sante, acciò i poveri pittori, che non hanno molto disegno, se ne potessero ne' loro bisogni servire."

FIG. 1
Marcantonio Raimondi, *Apostle James the Greater*, ca. 1520. Engraving, 8.5 × 5.3 cm. Rijksmuseum, Amsterdam. RP-P-OB-11.804. Signed: MAF. Bartsch no. 127.

FIG. 2
Marcantonio Raimondi, *John the Baptist*, ca. 1510–20. Engraving, 10.7 × 6.3 cm. Rijksmuseum, Amsterdam. RP-P-OB-11.792. Bartsch no. 99.

FIG. 3
Marcantonio Raimondi, *John the Baptist Seated in the Wilderness*, ca. 1520. Engraving, 8.2 × 5.5 cm. Albertina, Vienna. DG1970/371. Bartsch no. 151.

CAT. 7
Francesco di Giuliano da Sangallo (1494–1576)
John the Baptist
1520s
marble, height 110 cm (43 ¼ in.)
Chrysler Museum of Art, Norfolk
Gift of Mrs. Cortlandt Field Bishop, 52.49.1

Donatello continued to play a critical role in Florentine sculpture for more than a half century after his death in 1466. For example, in 1515, as part of Pope Leo X's triumphal entrance into Florence, Donatello's last great work, the hallucinatory reliefs of the pulpit of San Lorenzo (1461–66), was cleaned and reinstalled.[1] This rekindled an interest in the great sculptor's work, not only on the part of Florentine artists such as Michelangelo, Giovanfrancesco Rustici, and Rosso Fiorentino, but also visionary and eccentric Spanish sculptors like Bartolomé Ordóñez, Alonso Berruguete, Diego de Siloé, and Pedro Machuca. Among the most refined of these Donatello revivalists is Francesco da Sangallo, who, as a twelve-year-old in 1506, had witnessed the discovery of the *Laocoon* in the company of his father, the architect Giuliano da Sangallo, and Michelangelo himself.[2]

One of the best indications of Francesco da Sangallo's passion for Donatello is the marble statue of John the Baptist in the Bargello (FIG. 1). Although the original setting of the work is unknown, it was in the Uffizi by 1704–14 and credited to Donatello by Jonathan Richardson the Younger in 1722. Hans Kauffmann in 1931 was the first to attribute the work to Francesco da Sangallo, an assignment generally accepted.[3] It can be confirmed through close similarities with the sculpture of Saint Paul on the tomb of Piero de' Medici (made between 1532 and 1558) at Montecassino.

The sculpture in the Chrysler Museum is undoubtedly also by Francesco da Sangallo. Less a figure of the wilderness than that seen in the Bargello, the work exhibits a technical virtuosity that ranges from the Donatello-like surface engraving (called *stiacciato*) to deep drill marks left visible in the hair. There are significant differences between the two marble figures of the Baptist that dispel any doubt of one being a copy of the other. In the Bargello work, the Baptist steps forward as he clutches a bundle of texts (the phylactery) close to his chest

FIG. 1

Francesco da Sangallo, *John the Baptist*,
1530s. Marble, height 170 cm.
Museo Nazionale del Bargello,
Florence.

FIG. 2

Francesco da Sangallo, *John the Baptist*,
ca. 1535–38. Bronze, height 53 cm.
Frick Collection, New York.
1916.2.41.

FIG. 3

Circle of Francesco da Sangallo,
Mary Magdalene, ca. 1520. Painted
terracotta, height 64.8 cm. Davis
Museum at Wellesley College,
Wellesley. 1967.15.

in a gesture of devotion, his eyes cast down to read it. The figure in the Chrysler Museum would have held a cross or staff in his left hand. The extensive use of the drill and gradine (toothed chisel) in the Bargello work indicates that it is later in date, while the Chrysler Museum's figure seems to have been made by an artist still somewhat tentative and less technically assured – the treatment of the hair and contours of the drapery are particularly telling in this respect. Moreover, the Bargello marble is life-size, which indicates that it was destined for an altar, while the considerably smaller marble now in the Chrysler Museum was probably meant to be placed over a baptismal font. Given this function, it was likely subject to refurbishments in the course of its history, perhaps involving coating with oil, which has partly yellowed its surface.[4]

Francesco da Sangallo also made a *John the Baptist* in bronze (FIG. 2), produced between 1535 and 1538 for the church of Santa Maria delle Carceri in Prato.[5] Although this example is different in medium, and separated from the two marbles by a number of years, the three works are linked by their response to Donatello; they echo the technique and form of the earlier artist, including his approach to anatomy and the treatment of faces.

Another indication of Francesco da Sangallo's close attention to the Quattrocento is the moving wooden statue of Mary Magdalene of 1519 in the church of Santo Stefano al Ponte, Florence, which interprets Donatello's famous sculpture made around 1455 (Museo dell'Opera del Duomo, Florence).[6] Related to the former work is a little-known *Mary Magdalene* in terracotta at Wellesley College (FIG. 3), which shares with the Bargello *Baptist* its physiognomy and the sinuous and winding strands of hair.

CRITICAL HISTORY

When the Chrysler Museum's sculpture first appeared at auction in 1950, it was attributed to the workshop of Donatello and already specifically connected with Francesco da Sangallo's *John the Baptist* in the Bargello.[7] However, scholars have long resisted the attribution to Sangallo. William Valentiner thought it was by Alceo Dossena, a famous forger of Italian marble sculpture.[8] Ulrich Middeldorf noted the similarities with the statue in the Bargello, but expressed doubts that it was by the same hand.[9] H. W. Janson suggested it was from Sangallo's workshop in the third quarter of the sixteenth century.[10] Darr and Roisman (1987) published the Chrysler marble as made under Sangallo's influence.[11] But Charles Avery in 1994 thought it was by Sangallo,[12] a view argued by Ortenzi (2006), who considered it a youthful work from the 1520s. Unfortunately, the sculpture has rarely been displayed by the Chrysler Museum.

Lorenzo Principi

PROVENANCE

The work was owned by N. M. Friberg, a railway executive in Stockholm; parts of his collection were deposited and exhibited at the Nationalmuseum, Stockholm, in the late 1940s. His collection was sold at auction at Kende Galleries, New York, May 18, 1950; this work, lot 19 (workshop of Donatello), failed to sell but was bought afterward by Shirley Falcke (1889–1957), president of Kende Galleries. Gift of Mrs. Cortlandt F. Bishop, née Amy Bend (1870–1957).

Captain Shirley Falcke, a British connoisseur, worked for the New York auction house American Art Association, which was owned by Cortlandt Bishop (an automobile and aviation enthusiast). At his death in 1935, Bishop left the bulk of his estate jointly to his wife (née Amy Bend) and to Mrs. Shirley Falcke (née Edith Nixon).[13] This explains the joint ownership of many works of art: Mrs. Bishop and Mrs. Falcke together gave William-Adolphe Bouguereau's portrait of Cortlandt Bishop as a boy to the New-York Historical Society, as well as books to the Morgan Library. Bishop's large French library was sold in 1938 as the property of Mr. and Mrs. Falcke. Francesco da Sangallo's *John the Baptist* was auctioned at Kende Galleries in New York; Falcke himself purchased it and presented it in Mrs. Bishop's name to the Chrysler Museum.[14]

Falcke led a dramatic life. He was the son of Douglas Falcke, an American stockbroker and antiques dealer based in London. According to newspaper accounts, in 1907, the eighteen-year-old Shirley Falcke shot himself in a cab because of his impending separation from an actress, Iris Hoey. He served with the Royal Horseguards and was promoted to captain. In 1924, Falcke won a £3,000 libel award against Melbourne newspapers for defamation of an exhibition of his paintings. He married Mary Kinder in 1914, Marjorie Wells in 1923, and later Edith Nixon.

REFERENCES

Darr and Roisman 1987, p. 789 note 17. Ortenzi 2006, pp. 73–75, figs. 84–87, 107. Ortenzi 2009, pp. 51, 53, 56.

1. Gentilini 2013, p. 82.

2. Francesco da Sangallo recounted the discovery a half century later in 1567. For the text, see Brummer 1970, p. 75.

3. Kauffmann 1931, p. 4. See Caglioti 2012, note 31, for the history of attributions.

4. Torraca 1986, pp. 35–36.

5. Morselli 1982, pp. 54–57.

6. Darr and Roisman 1987; F. Traversi in Florence 2016, no. 30.

7. Mentioned in the auction catalogue: Kende Galleries, New York, May 18, 1950 (lot 19).

8. Letter of Mar. 14, 1953, museum files.

9. Letter of Mar. 20, 1953, museum files.

10. Letter of Oct. 21, 1953; museum files.

11. Darr and Roisman 1987, p. 789 note 17.

12. Comment of Nov. 3, 1994; museum files.

13. *New York Times* (Oct. 12, 1939), p. 33; (July 3, 1949), p. 29. New York Supreme Court, 277 A.D. 108 (1950); June 13, 1950 [www.leagle.com /decision/1950385277ad1081353].

14. Letter from Herbert Kende to Falcke, June 17, 1953, stating that the work was in the Friberg collection and that Falcke purchased the work at auction. Falcke is listed in the catalogue as president of Kende Galleries, with Herbert Kende as vice president.

CAT. 8

Giovan Angelo Montorsoli
John the Baptist
1530s
terracotta, height 130 cm (51 ⅛ in.)
Currier Museum of Art, Manchester
The Ed and Mary Scheier Acquisition Fund and the
Kimon S. Zachos Acquisition Fund, 2017.7

The sculpture is in good condition, although along some of the drapery edges small areas of loss have been filled. The figure's left hand was repaired at the wrist, where it had previously broken, and there are scattered repairs in parts of the hand. However, the hand appears to be largely intact, with mostly original pieces. X-ray fluorescence spectrometry (XRF), conducted under the direction of Mary Kate Donais of Saint Anselm College in March 2018, indicates that the composition of the clay is generally consistent between the left hand, the right arm, and the left leg.[1] The base, which shows darker areas, is also generally consistent with the rest of the sculpture.[2] The darker patches are probably due to a flaw in firing.

The areas of white accretion in the crevices of the sculpture, suspected to be remnants of gesso, were analyzed by Fourier transform infrared microspectroscopy (FTIR) and scanning electron microscopy with an attached energy-dispersive X-ray spectrometer (SEM/EDS), under the direction of Richard Newman of the Museum of Fine Arts, Boston.[3] FTIR spectra indicated the presence of gypsum and lead white (specifically, hydrocerussite or basic lead carbonate). Gypsum (anhydrous calcium sulfate or calcium sulfate dehydrate) is the particle component of gesso that was typically used as a preparation layer in Italian painting and sculpture. Its presence here suggests that the sculpture's surface was at one time prepared for paint decoration. SEM analysis revealed gypsum grains, usually less than 15 μm, which make up most of the samples. Peppered throughout are small (sub-micron) particles and larger clumps of lead white. Lead white, a common pigment in European Renaissance painting, may be present as an additive to the gesso. Alternately, the lead white detected in these analyses may have been present as part of a paint layer.

Because of the difficulties involved in firing large terracotta sculptures, this work was very likely fired in at least five pieces that were assembled together. Besides the head, the sections comprise the upper-right torso from the shoulder to the waist, the left shoulder and arm, the lower torso from the waist to the knees, and the lower legs and base. Thermoluminescence testing indicates that there is a high probability that the terracotta was last fired in the sixteenth century.[4] The cross is not original to the work, but the tubular opening in the left hand was designed to hold poles inserted above and below the hand.

The back of the sculpture is less finely finished and is somewhat flattened, which suggests that it was not meant to be seen from all sides, but was designed to be installed near a wall or in a niche.
Valentine Talland

PROVENANCE

This terracotta probably belonged to the painter Tommaso Gherardini (1715–1796), Florence, who in January 1791 sold it and a terracotta of Saint Paul, both attributed to Montorsoli, to Giovanni degli Alessandri (1765–1828), Florence, for 35 lire (see essay by Principi). The two works are recorded in the Alessandri family's Villa del Petroio, Vinci, in an inventory of 1828. In 1879, the sculptures were described as in plaster, which may mean they had been replaced by copies. The *Baptist* is documented with Maud Margareta Blomqvist, Sweden; sold to a private collector; and purchased by the museum in 2017.

Back of CAT. 8
(see p. 12 for front view).

---

1. Elements identified are calcium, titanium, manganese, iron, nickel, zinc, lead, rubidium, strontium, and zirconium. There were higher levels of lead in the left hand and right shoulder than in the lower arm and leg areas. Donais conducted the analysis on Mar. 27, 2018, with assistance from Luke Douglass and Elizabeth Lomuscio.

2. One sample site on the base in the XRF analysis showed a higher presence of calcium, lower presence of iron, and no lead, in comparison with other sites. This may be an area of accretion or repair.

3. Newman conducted the FTIR and SEM/EDS analyses at the MFA's Research Analytical Lab in December 2017.

4. Art-Test, s.a.s., Florence, report dated Nov. 10, 2015.

CAT. 9
Jacopo Sansovino (1486–1570),
cast by Tiziano Minio (1511 or 1512–1552)
John the Baptist
1540s
bronze with gilding, height 53 cm
Liechtenstein The Princely Collections,
Vienna. SK20

Wearing an animal skin fastened by a belt high-lighted with gold, John the Baptist places his hand on his chest and turns his head to the right to reveal an anxious, worried expression. The figure is slightly bent over, as though from exhaustion. This is a very different Baptist from other representations of the sixteenth century: he is not the wide-eyed youth in the wilderness; nor the heroic preacher or baptizer of Christ, even less the striding athletic warrior. Indeed, the moment represented by the bronze is unclear. Is this the wasted figure after years in the desert? Or does his agony come from contemplating his own fate and that of Christ? While the gesture is related to representations of the Baptist pointing to a cross, it is closer to one of melancholic exhaustion.

The emphasis on the belt, which is gilded on this bronze, is not often encountered in Renaissance images of the Baptist, whose camel-skin garment is usually fastened with a rope or a strip of cloth, if at all. However, Matthew 3:4 states: "John's clothes were made of camel's hair, and he had a leather belt around his waist. His food was locusts and wild honey."

ATTRIBUTION

The attribution of this striking bronze is challenging. The subtle emotion and compact pose of the figure are recognizable as the work of Jacopo Sansovino of the 1540s, but the artist normally worked with other artists to cast bronzes, as would appear to be the case here.[1] Wilhelm Bode in 1904 and 1907 attributed this work with some caution: "The writer cannot say with absolute certainty Jacopo Sansovino is the artist, but its style bears the mark of Florentine workmanship." James Draper in 1980 wrote that the bronze was made in northern Italy

FIG. 2
Follower of Jacopo Sansovino, *John the Baptist Preaching*. Bronze, height 41 cm. Palazzo Grimani, Venice.

FIG. 3
Giuseppe de Levis, *John the Baptist*, late 16th century. Bronze, height 49.5 cm. Cleveland Museum of Art. John L. Severance Fund, 1952.276.

FIG. 1
Tiziano Minio, *John the Baptist*, ca. 1535. Limestone, height 175 cm. Nelson-Atkins Museum of Art, Kansas City. Purchase: William Rockhill Nelson Trust, 37-28.

in the late sixteenth or early seventeenth century. The auction catalogue of 2000 attributed the work to the circle of Sansovino. Bruce Boucher in his catalogue raisonné (1991) of Jacopo Sansovino's work does not mention the work. Luca Siracusano has recently attributed the bronze to Tiziano Minio (1517–1552).[2]

The figure's adjacency to a tree trunk suggests that it is related to a larger marble sculpture, since a bronze of this size would not require the additional support. Tiziano Minio's signed stone sculpture of John the Baptist (FIG. 1) has a similar gesture toward the chest and anxious turn of the head. The left arm, however, is treated differently, and the position of the head varies, with the result that the emotional engagement of the two works is quite distinct. This *John the Baptist* was most likely modeled by Sansovino and cast by Tiziano Minio, who was born in Padua and worked in Venice with Sansovino beginning in 1536. Between 1539 and 1541, he probably assisted Sansovino with the reliefs

on the exterior of the Loggetta under the Campanile in Venice.[3] Minio made the bronze cover of the baptismal font in Saint Mark's Basilica in 1545.[4]

Sansovino produced other depictions of the Baptist, including a signed marble statue of the seated Baptist, in the Frari church, Venice.[5] A bronze sculpture in the Palazzo Grimani of John the Baptist preaching (FIG. 2) also seems to reflect a design by Sansovino.[6]

The importance of the bronze in the Liechtenstein collection can be gauged by its reception in Venice and the Veneto in the later sixteenth century. Its gestures, anatomy, and treatment of the animal skin is echoed in a bronze by Giuseppe de Levis (1552–1611/1614) after a model by Angelo de Rossi (active ca. 1600), in the church of San Giorgio in Braida, Venice.[7] Another bronze of John the Baptist by these same artists has a similar composition (FIG. 3).[8]

Lorenzo Principi

PROVENANCE

The bronze is first recorded in 1904 in the collection of Alfred Beit (1853–1906), London, who made an immense fortune in gold and diamond mining in South Africa. He moved from his native Hamburg to London, where he built a grand mansion at 26 Park Lane in the late 1890s.[9] Wilhelm Bode advised Beit in his collecting, and in 1904 catalogued the entire collection. In 1891, Bode acquired a large group of bronzes from the dealer Isaac Falcke (1819–1909), and recommended that Beit purchase pieces that Bode did not want.[10]

Alfred Beit bequeathed most of his collection and estate to his brother Otto, but left this particular bronze to Julius Wernher (1850–1912), his German-born business partner in Wernher, Beit and Co., a leading force in the South African diamond and gold trade. The motivation for this gift is unrecorded, but it is somewhat surprising since Otto Beit was also an enthusiastic collector of bronze statuettes.[11] The Beit brothers and Julius Wernher were Germans who made prospered in South Africa and then settled in London. The sculpture by Sansovino was displayed in the Red Room of Bath House, Wernher's London residence on Piccadilly. Decorated in vaguely Renaissance style, the gallery featured an abundance of paintings, sculpture, and objects.[12] The collection descended to Sir Harold Wernher (1893–1973), Luton Hoo; and then to his grandson Nicholas Phillips (1947–1991); it was auctioned by heirs of the latter at Christie's, London, July 5, 2000 (lot 64, unsold), where it was catalogued as from the circle of Sansovino, around 1530 to 1550. Daniel Katz Ltd, London, sold it in 2001 to Prince Hans-Adam II von und zu Liechtenstein.

REFERENCES

Bode 1904, pp. 38–39, 64, repr. [Sansovino?]. Bode 1907, vol. 2, p. 23, pl. CLVI [Sansovino?]. James Draper in Bode 1980, p. 102 [North Italian, late 16th–early 17th century]. Katz 2001, no. 8 [Sansovino]. Manfred Leithe-Jasper in Vienna 2010, no. 29 [Sansovino, 1530–50]. Siracusano 2011, pp. 88–89, fig. 114 [Tiziano Minio?].

1. On bronze casting in Sansovino's workshop, see Boucher 1991, vol. 1, pp. 145–47.

2. Siracusano 2011, pp. 88–89.

3. Boucher 1991, vol. 1, pp. 151–52.

4. Boucher 1991, vol. 1, pp. 151, 165–66, figs. 422, 423.

5. Boucher 1991, vol. 2, pp. 323–24, figs. 93–95, as from the 1530s.

6. Boucher 1991, vol. 2, p. 355, fig, 350. The work was formerly in the Museo Archeologico and the Cà d'Oro.

7. Avery 2016, pp. 84–85, no. 40.

8. Avery 2016, pp. 85, no. 95. See also Wixom 1975, no. 133 [as Angelo de Rossi]. The work comes from the Trivulzio collection, Milan.

9. Bode 1904; Stevenson 1997, pp. 81–131.

10. Warren 1996, pp. 128–30, 140–42.

11. Bode 1913, esp. p. 51.

12. Charles Davis, "Inventory and valuation of works of art of artistic interest at Bath House Piccadilly, the property of Sir Julius Wernher" (April 1913); cited in Christie's, July 4, 2000 (lot 64). Photographs of Bath House taken by Bedford Lemare in 1911 can be seen in Stevenson 1997, figs. 1.2, 1.3, 1.4. Stevenson discusses South African collectors of old masters.

CAT. 10
Giovan Francesco Susini (1585-1653)
John the Baptist
ca. 1635
marble, height 102.9 cm (40 ½ in.)
National Gallery of Art, Washington
Patrons' Permanent Fund,
2005.109.1

The accession of Cosimo I as duke of Florence in 1537, followed by his coronation as grand duke of Tuscany in 1570, was accompanied by a decline in the representation of John the Baptist in public settings. The patron saint of Florence fell out of favor in comparison to symbols of the Medici family or of Tuscany as a whole. Vincenzo Danti's bronze group of the *Beheading of John the Baptist* for the Baptistery, completed in 1571, was the principal public representation of the saint in the period from 1540 to 1630. In the 1580s, Giambologna carved a *John the Baptist* in marble for the Salviati Chapel in San Marco, and a bronze version was made in 1588 (Santa Maria degli Angeli, Florence).[1] Images of the Baptist as a symbol of Florence could be encountered in foreign settings, as in a 1549 triumphal entry in Antwerp (see p. 38), since he was such a recognizable embodiment of the city. The late sixteenth-century interest in mythology and allegory seems to have further discouraged depictions of the Baptist.

After a long hiatus, Giovan Francesco Susini took up the subject of the young John the Baptist in the desert in a major work in marble completed in the 1630s. The depiction of the seated figure recalls representations of the young Baptist made in terracotta more than a century earlier (CAT. 2). However, Susini's figure has an elegantly spiraling pose: the head turns away from the gesturing arm while his legs pivot in opposite directions.

Susini's marriage of an early Cinquecento type with late Mannerist exaggeration has caused immense confusion among modern experts who have attributed this sculpture to Michelangelo, Andrea Sansovino, Pierino da Vinci, and Bernini, among others – attributions that span more than a century. Finally, Francesco Caglioti (2012) recognized the work as by Giovan Francesco Susini, more famed as the maker of fine small bronzes in the early seventeenth century. Indeed, the composition of a seated male nude very closely resembles Susini's *David*, which the artist modeled in terracotta (FIG. 1) and then cast in bronze.[2] One of the bronzes of the figure, signed by the artist, has been documented in the collection of the prince of Liechtenstein since 1658, and may have been acquired from the artist around 1635 to 1636. As with the Baptist, David looks away from his gesturing arm.

Susini was not alone in creating a graceful marble figure of the seated Baptist in the seventeenth century. At about the same time, another Florentine sculptor, Domenico Pieratti, also carved a young Baptist invested with elegance and a spiraling pose (FIG. 2). It has been argued that Pieratti's work represents a distinctly Roman style, in contrast to that of Susini and his circle. For example, Caravaggio's paintings of John the Baptist (Nelson Atkins Museum, Kansas City, and Galleria Doria Pamphilj, Rome) show a similar bent arm, but otherwise the poses are completely different.[3] The arm of Pieratti's Baptist more closely resembles that of Caravaggio's *Bacchus* in the Galleria Borghese, Rome, but significantly, Pieratti makes his figure turn away from his hand, here holding a honeycomb, a reference to the honey that nourished the saint in the wilderness.

The two marble figures by Pieratti and Susini are remarkably similar in type, format, and emotional impact, especially since no other marble sculptures of the young seated Baptist from the period are known.[4] Both sculptures revive the grace of early sixteenth-century Florentine sculpture..

ATTRIBUTION

In the early twentieth century, the marble sculpture in Washington was thought to be by Andrea Sansovino. It came to wider attention in 1949 when it was shown at an exhibition on Leonardo da Vinci in Los Angeles with a cautious attribution to Leonardo's nephew Pierino da Vinci (1529–1553). Then, in 1964, a lavish volume of 112 plates was published to advocate an assignment to Michelangelo, an idea that met with widespread ridicule. However, no convincing alternative was put forward and the work was variously assigned to Pierino da Vinci, Pietro and Gian Lorenzo Bernini from around 1614 to 1615 (Parronchi 2003), and even a nineteenth-century imitator.

The *John the Baptist* can be compared with Susini's documented works in marble: a signed, if somewhat worn, marble sculpture of Bacchus with a young satyr in the Louvre (M.R. 2096) and a *Venus* dated 1637 in the Villa La Pietra (Caglioti 2012). In 2005, the National Gallery of Art acquired the sculpture with the attribution to Susini.
Alan Chong

PROVENANCE

The sculpture was reportedly purchased in 1900 near Bologna by Albitez for Daniel Noorian as a work by Andrea Sansovino. Daniel Z. Noorian (d. 1929), New York and Newark; auction: American Art Association, New York, March 12–14, 1931 (lot 643, as Sansovino), unsold; by descent to Belle Ward Noorian. Piero Tozzi (d. 1974), New York (by 1964). Purchased by the museum in 2005 through Robert Simon Fine Art, New York.

REFERENCES

Los Angeles 1949, no. 101, repr. [attributed to Pierino da Vinci]. De' Maffei 1964 [Michelangelo]. Parronchi 2003, pp. 71–78 [Pietro and Gian Lorenzo Bernini]. Caglioti 2012, pp. 6, 58–60 notes 34–39 [Susini ca. 1635, with earlier literature]. Freddolini 2016, pp. 417–18 note 30, repr.

1. Charles Avery in Edinburgh et al. 1978, p. 136, no. 91.

2. Dimitrios Zikos in Florence 2013, p. 234.

3. Wardropper 2011, p. 119, citing James Draper. *The John the Baptist* by Susini in Washington is not mentioned in relationship to Pieratti's work, a comparison made by Freddolini 2016, p. 417.

4. Similar to the marbles by Susini and Pieratti is a terracotta of the seated Baptist, sold at Sotheby's, New York, June 10–11, 1983 (lot 62), height 29 cm, the head perhaps a replacement. Lorenzo Principi kindly brought this to my attention.

5. Caglioti 2012, p. 6.

6. De' Maffei 1964. The responses are recounted by Caglioti 2012, pp. 58–60.

7. Caglioti 2012, p. 6.

Montorsoli sculpted this portrait during his first stay in Genoa, from 1539 to 1541, around the time he also produced a bust of Jacopo Sannazaro in Santa Maria del Parto, Naples, and a portrait of Alfonso V of Aragón (see essay by Ramiro). The Holy Roman Emperor Charles V (1500–1558) is represented in the manner of ancient Roman busts, with short hair and an idealized face, which softens and somewhat conceals his famous jutting jaw. The likeness generally accords with the emperor's appearance

FIG. 1
Giovanni Britto after Titian,
Charles V, ca. 1535–40. Woodcut,
50 × 35.3 cm. British Museum,
London. 1846,0509.26.

FIG. 2
Giovanni Britto after Titian,
Charles V, 1540s. Woodcut,
40.5 × 28.2 cm. British Museum,
London. 1866,0714.51.

FIG. 3
Charles V, late 16th century. Marble,
height 72 cm. Private collection.

FIG. 4
Charles V, 18th century?
Marble, height 62.5 cm. Lady Lever
Gallery, Port Sunlight. LL 158.

after his coronation as emperor in Bologna in 1530. Montorsoli's bust strikes a balance between ancient and Burgundian traditions. For example, the state portrait in armor was adopted by some of Charles's Burgundian predecessors, such as Charles the Bold (1433–1477), and by Charles V himself as a boy in a painting that depicts him wearing armor and holding a sword (Kunsthistorisches Museum, Vienna, inv. 5618). The son of Philip the Fair of Burgundy, Charles was brought up in the culture of the Netherlands before his election as emperor in 1519.

Images of Charles V combine his roles of Christian knight and new Roman emperor. Such an expression of power through portraiture had considerable impact on the contemporaneous portraits of Italian princes striving to mimic imperial authority, including Andrea Doria in Genoa; Alfonso d'Este,

duke of Ferrara; and Cosimo I de' Medici, duke of Florence and later grand duke of Tuscany. This phenomenon is demonstrated by the numerous painted and sculpted portraits in armor commissioned from artists associated with the imperial court such as Titian, Bronzino, Cellini, Alfonso Lombardi, and Montorsoli. Montorsoli creates a forceful and determined image that asserts imperial dignity. The vitality of the portrait may have been derived from Titian's portrait of Charles V in armor made in 1533, known through prints by Agostino Veneziano and Giovanni Britto. Britto produced two woodcuts, one showing the emperor with a sword (FIG. 1), the other a close-up view with an attached sonnet in praise of the emperor's rule (FIG. 2).[1]

Despite the militaristic accouterments of the portrait, Montorsoli gives Charles V a depth of character through the expression of the face and treatment of the hair. The sitter turns slightly to his left, softening the rigid frontality of the image and giving it dynamism. The intensity of the gaze, with the iris and pupil sharply delineated, and the half-open mouth, which reveals some teeth, further humanize the marble. The gravitas of the character is accentuated through the wrinkles around the eyes, temple, and forehead, as well as the eyebrows, which are typical of Montorsoli, seen for example in the bust of Tommaso Cavalcanti (Santo Spirito, Florence). The rest of the face has a hardness and specificity of modeling that is different from Montorsoli's portraits of Sannazaro and Alfonso V. The beard achieves remarkable pictorial effects through the subtlety in which it blends with the skin. The marble is drilled to create a sense of shadow as it breaks up the strands of the beard.

According to Vasari, Montorsoli carved two portraits of Charles V, in addition to two others of Andrea Doria. The busts of the emperor were said to have been taken to Spain by the imperial secretary, Francisco de los Cobos. Charles V was in Genoa in 1541 and 1543, but Cobos did not accompany the emperor on those occasions because he was in Spain with the crown prince, the future Philip II. Therefore, it is more likely that the portraits by Montorsoli were entrusted to another courtier, Nicolas Perrenot de Granvelle, who took a large number of works of art back from Italy. The busts sent to Spain in the 1540s are most likely the works now in the Prado and the Brou Monastery (see pp. 64, 66). This bust, Montorsoli's protoype, was undocumented until it appeared in Naples in 1933.

Attribution

This bust was first attributed to Montorsoli by Martin Weinberger (1963), although with some hesitation, as he did not regard the portrait of Jacopo Sannazaro as by the artist. Marina Causa Picone in 1964 thought the bust was made in Naples, perhaps by the local sculptor Giovanni da Nola, with reflections of Montorsoli's work.[2] R. Middione (2001) failed to cite Weinberger and incorrectly credited Causa Picone with the attribution to Montorsoli. Karl Möseneder (1979) and Birgit Laschke (1993) in their monographs on Montorsoli attribute the bust to him.

Versions

Close copies of this bust by Montorsoli's workshop are in Madrid and Bourg-en-Bresse (see pp. 64, 66). In another version based on one of these examples, the features have been schematized and the face has lost the vitality of the Montorsoli's model (FIG. 3).[3]

A later copy, perhaps of the eighteenth century, is in the Lady Lever Gallery, Port Sunlight (FIG. 4).[4]

More distantly related works include a bust in the Palazzo Ajutamicristo, Palermo, where the sitter wears a laurel wreath and armor close to sculptures by Leoni. This bust is similar to one in the Palacio Mirabel, Plasencia. Both are probably from the 1540s. The bust of Charles V in the courtyard of the Casa de Pilatos, Seville, seems to have no connection to Montorsoli or his workshop.[5]
Sergio Ramiro Ramírez

Provenance

The work was deposited in the Certosa di San Martino, Naples, in 1933, presumably from an official or religious institution in Naples.

References

Weinberger 1963, p. 43, fig. 2. M. Causa Picone in Naples 1964, p. 9, no. 1. Möseneder 1979, p. 139 [Montorsoli]. Laschke 1993, pp. 59–60, no. 8 [Montorsoli]. Middione 2001, p. 65. Malgouyres 2007, pp. 20–22. L. Finocchi Ghersi in Trento 2009, p. 234, no. 38. Ramiro 2016, pp. 285–91.

1. Rosand and Muraro 1976, pp. 204–7, 314.

2. Naples 1964, p. 9: "certamente in ambito di Giovanni da Nola ma anche marcatamente in direzione montorsoliana," and states that it is unpublished.

3. *López de Aragón: 20 Years in Maastricht* (2015), pp. 110–11.

4. Liverpool 1983 [as Italian 16th century]. Edward Charles Baring, 1st Baron Revelstoke, sold at Christie's, London, June 28, 1893 (lot 139); to William Lever by 1914.

5. Despite the views of Trunk 2002, no. 70, fig. 80; and Estella 2008, pp. 22–23.

CAT. 12
Giovan Angelo Montorsoli
Sketch for a Fountain
ca. 1540
black chalk and pen in brown ink on paper,
11.9 × 17.4 cm (4 ⅝ × 6 ⅞ in.)
Harvard Art Museums, Cambridge
Charles A. Loeser, Florence,
Bequest to Fogg Art Museum, 1932.349

CAT. 12 verso.

The ancient figure of Laocoon had considerable impact on Montorsoli's fountains made in Genoa around 1540 to 1543, for example, the Dolphin Fountain and the sculpture of Triton (see essay by Ramiro). The artist's typical Triton, a hybrid beast that combines a human torso with a fish tail, taps into the muscular athleticism of Laocoon. The raised, outstretched arms of the sea creatures mimic Montorsoli's reconstructed arm of the ancient sculpture. This drawing appears to be a working sketch for a fountain consisting of a basin supported by Tritons. The project differs from Montorsoli's known fountains in that the Tritons are not freestanding or encircling a column, but support a large basin along the edges. Probably made in Genoa around 1540, the drawing may represent a preparatory stage of a fountain shipped to Spain, but now lost.

In addition, there exist two bronzes that appear to have been based on the sea monsters in Montorsoli's fountains, one in the Fitzwilliam Museum, Cambridge, the other formerly with Maurice de Rothschild, Paris.[1]

The drawing was evidently made in successive stages, first in black chalk, and then in pen with brown ink. The somewhat flattened basin seems to have been added later by the artist, who also sketched another figure at the right. The verso also has several sketches: a penis drawn in red chalk and a faint image, perhaps of a figure or a hand, in black chalk.

The assignment of drawings to Giovan Angelo Montorsoli starts from an album assembled by his pupil Giovanni Vincenzo Casale (1539–1593). Many of the sheets in the album, in the Biblioteca Nacional de España (see pp. 68, 73), bear sixteenth-century attributions and annotations.[2] The sheets directly related to Montorsoli's projects in Messina and Genoa show a stylistic similarity to the *Sketch for a Fountain* in the use of pen and carefully applied washes, sometimes with the addition of black chalk. On the basis of the Casale album, similar drawings of fountains can be attributed with confidence to Montorsoli.[3] Annamaria Petrioli Tofani judiciously added to Montorsoli's oeuvre a few other sheets in the Uffizi with old attributions to the artist.[4] Scholars of Montorsoli have otherwise avoided extensive discussion of the artist's drawings. The discovery of drawings in an underground room beneath the New Sacristy led to the attribution of some of the sketches to Montorsoli, a theory that has no firm basis given the vast difference in scale and medium between these sketches and the previously attributed drawings.[5] Finally, Montorsoli was instrumental in founding the Accademia del disegno at the end of his life. He provided support and funds for the organization, and designed its seal, as shown in a drawing.[6] Montorsoli carved the design into a marble plaque set into the floor of the painters' chapel, the Cappella dei pittori, at Santissima Annunziata, Florence (see p. 11).

Alan Chong

PROVENANCE

This drawing was part of a collection of some two hundred Italian drawings owned by Charles Loeser (1864–1928), son of the owner of a department store in Brooklyn. Charles was educated at Harvard and settled in Florence in 1890. He wrote articles on Renaissance art and furnished his Villa Gattaia with an impressive collection. Bernard Berenson, who had been his classmate at Harvard, also settled in Florence, but the two quarreled bitterly. Loeser bequeathed a group of objects to the Palazzo Vecchio in Florence, including two terracotta battle scenes by Gianfrancesco Rustici, an artist he wrote about.[7] Loeser also presented eight paintings by Cézanne to the White House, and the drawings to Harvard University. This sheet is recorded in the export inventory of 1928. The remainder of the collection remained with Loeser's family in the Villa Gattaia until the outbreak of World War II led to the confiscation of part of the collection. In 2011, a painting of Saint Catherine of Alexandra by Bernardo Strozzi, which had been seized by Nazi officials in 1943, was returned to Loeser's granddaughter Philippa Calnan, who gave the work to the Los Angeles County Museum of Art.

REFERENCES

Mongan and Sachs 1940, vol. 1, no. 95 [Florentine?, 16th century]. Vitzthum 1963, p. 57, pl. 41 [Montorsoli]. Möseneder 1979, p. 166. Laschke 1993, p. 169 [uncertain]. Francini 2000, p. 122 [cartella R, no. 3: "Scuola fiorentina (progetto di fontana)," 15 lire].

1. Cambridge: inv. M.15-1979, height 45 cm; Avery 2002, no. 65 [as perhaps after a lost 16th-century model]. Rothschild: Bode 1907, vol. 3, pp. 23, 35, pl. 260 [as Sansovino? or Montorsoli?].

2. Bustamante and Marías 1991 provides a comprehensive analysis of the album; there is an index of the drawings compiled by Alessandro Massai in the eighteenth century. Laschke 1993 makes the relevant connections with Montorsoli's major commissions. See also Vitzthum 1963; Kubler 1978; and Lanzarini 1998.

3. Uffizi, Florence (943E; Kubler 1978, fig. 10.7). Biblioteca Reale, Turin (15710). Staatliche Graphische Sammlung, Munich (12857). Musée Fabre, Montpellier (837.1.291; Vitzthum 1963, pl. 40). See Petrioli Tofani 2003, p. 151.

4. Petrioli Tofani 2003. Other assignments to Montorsoli include a drawing of a double tomb (Louvre, inv. 837); Wallace 1987. This has been refuted by Bambach 2017, p. 125, who attributed the drawing to Michelangelo's workshop (Stefano di Tommaso Lunetti?).

5. Elam 1981, p. 601, note 32; Collareta 1992.

6. Laschke 1987; Laschke 1993, figs. 177–80.

7. Loeser 1928.

CAT. 13
Cornelis Cort (ca. 1533–1578)
Virgin and Child with Saint Cosmas and
Saint Damian in the New Sacristy
1570
engraving,
41.9 × 29 cm (16 ½ × 11 ⅜ in.)
The Metropolitan Museum of Art, New York
Purchase, Anne and Carl Stern Gift, 1959
59.642.81

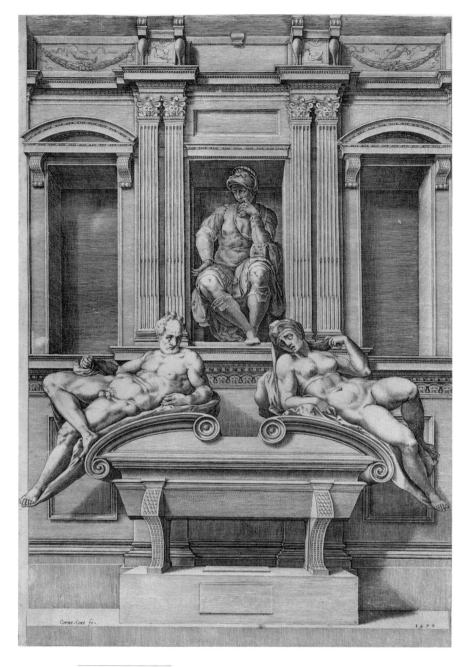

CAT. 14

Cornelis Cort

*Tomb of Lorenzo de' Medici
in the New Sacristy*

1570

engraving,

41.7 × 27.3 cm (trimmed; 16 ⅜ × 10 ¾ in.)

The Metropolitan Museum of Art, New York

Harris Brisbane Dick Fund, 1945

45.47.3(5)

Signed lower left: Corne. Cort fe.; dated lower right: 1570

Cornelis Cort
*Tomb of Giuliano de' Medici
in the New Sacristy*
1570
engraving,
42.2 × 27.2 cm (trimmed; 16 ⅝ × 10 ¾ in.)
The Metropolitan Museum of Art, New York
Harris Brisbane Dick Fund, 1945
45.47.3(6)

Dated lower left: 1570

See pp. 80–81 for further discussion.

REFERENCES
Sellink 2000, no. 219, 217, 218 [on CATS. 13–15; 1st states]. Rosenberg 2003, pp. 126–30 [Cort may have used drawings by Giovanni Battista Naldini for these prints]. Barnes 2010, pp. 153–57.

CAT. 16

Sandro di Lorenzo (1483–ca. 1554)

Bacchus

mid-1520s

terracotta with remains of paint

height 27 cm, length 39.5 cm (10 ⅝ × 15 ⅝ in.)

John and Mable Ringling Museum of Art, Sarasota

Museum purchase, 1949

SN1402

Bacchus, the god of wine, reclines uneasily on a wine casket, his left leg tucked under him. He holds a shallow cup in one hand and a pitcher in the other. The figure is based on ancient sculptures of river gods, and may have been inspired by Michelangelo's river gods, which were planned but never carved for the Medici tombs (see p. 80).

This work belongs to an extensive group of expressively modeled terracottas that have long been attributed to the Master of the Unruly Children, an artist apparently based in Florence in the early sixteenth century.[1] This particular composition is described in documents from 1523 when the artist Sandro di Lorenzo di Smeraldo submitted four terracottas to be valued as payment to a notary.[2] The context of the valuation suggests that the works may have been made by Sandro, but the documents do not state this. The four sculptures are described first as terracottas, then in the valuation three are called "terra cruda" or "terra non cocta," that is, unfired clay. The sculptures are listed as: a *Laocoon* painted to simulate bronze; a male child after Desiderio da Settignano, also painted bronze; a *Judith* after Andrea del Verrocchio; and a *Bacchus*. The composition of the *Bacchus* is described in detail: "a Bacchus, also of unfired clay, reclines and rests on a wine cask, and on the left side holds in his hand a vase that pours forth water, which is 3/4 braccia [44 cm] high."[3]

This description closely matches four extant terracottas, including this example. No other figures of Bacchus with these specific features are known, whether ancient or Renaissance, making it almost certain that the 1523 document refers to this composition. The other terracottas are: formerly with Daniel Katz, London (which is missing the cup and has a modern replacement head); Princeton

FIG. 1
Sandro di Lorenzo, *River God*,
ca. 1523. Terracotta, length 31.5 cm.
Private collection.

University Art Museum; and Trinity Fine Art, London (these last two lack the left leg).[4] Similar in form but lacking the pitcher is a terracotta in Detroit Institute of Arts.[5] Some of Sandro di Lorenzo's figures of Bacchus seem to have been paired with river gods (FIG. 1).

SANDRO DI LORENZO AS MASTER OF THE UNRULY CHILDREN

The valuation of 1523 provides circumstantial evidence that Sandro di Lorenzo is the Master of the Unruly Children. In addition, it can now be documented that in 1521 Jacopo Guicciardini ordered from Sandro "a terracotta cast" (*uno getto di terracotta*) depicting Filippo Benizi (1233–1285), superior general of the Servites who had revitalized the order.[6] Benizi was beatified in 1516, which undoubtedly occasioned the making of this portrait, and canonized in 1671. In 1592, the Guicciardini family gave the terracotta portrait to the church of Santissima Annunziata, Florence, where it remains (FIG. 2).

Further evidence comes from the testimony of Antonfrancesco Grazzini, founder of the Accademia della Crusca and known as Lasca, who in the 1530s, described seeing a terracotta group depicting six riders and foot soldiers in combat, at a terracotta workshop (*terraiuolo*) in the Piazza San Giovanni, Florence.[7] Not only was this subject (with this number of figures) produced by the Master of the Unruly Children (FIG. 3), but Sandro di Lorenzo had his studio in the Piazza San Giovanni.[8]

As one of the less prominent artists in Florence in the early sixteenth century, Sandro di Lorenzo needed to diversify his offerings and respond quickly to market demand. He produced a wide array of terracotta objects – not just statuettes, but also death masks and household crockery – and even made perfume.[9] On one occasion, Sandro made 160 painted terracotta dolls of the infant Christ Child to be presented to nuns. The 1523 valuation demonstrates the artist's nimbleness: the works included two copies of fifteenth-century sculptures by Desiderio and Verrocchio, and one of the earliest recorded terracotta reductions of the famous *Laocoon* in the Vatican. The *Bacchus* itself is a very early variant of the river gods in the New Sacristy,

which demonstrates that Sandro di Lorenzo had somehow insinuated himself into Michelangelo's circle. Other aspects of Sandro's work show similarities with Michelangelo's workshop.[10]

The theory that the Master of the Unruly Children is indeed Sandro di Lorenzo solves a long mystery. The conventional name was first coined in 1890 by Wilhelm Bode, who put together a group of terracottas and assigned them to the late fifteenth century.[11] More recently, the terracottas have received a bewildering array of attributions, from Giovanfrancesco Rustici, Jacopo Sansovino, and Niccolò Tribolo to Pietro Torrigiani and Bartolomeo Ammannati.[12]

Lorenzo Principi

PROVENANCE

The work belonged to Oscar Bondy (1870–1944) of Vienna, who formed a major collection of more than two thousand paintings, musical instruments, and decorative arts, which were displayed in his house on the Schubertring in Vienna. When Nazi Germany absorbed Austria in the Anschluss of 1938, Bondy's collection was seized because he was Jewish. This work was catalogued at that time in the music room.[13] Bondy owned sugar refineries in Czechoslovakia and was a Czechoslovakian citizen, which allowed him to leave Austria, after which he made his way to New York, where he died in 1944. Toward the end of the war, Bondy's collection was stored in Germany, and in 1945 was processed at the Central Collecting Point in Munich, when this terracotta was again catalogued.[14] In February 1948, the terracotta, along with part of the collection, was returned to representatives of Elisabeth Bondy, Oscar's widow, who had it shipped to New York.[15] Elisabeth Bondy sold the sculpture through Blumka Gallery, New York [as a river god by Jacopo Sansovino], to the Ringling Museum in January 1949 for $500.[16]

REFERENCE

Principi 2018, p. 86, no. 33.

1. On the critical history of the group, see Principi 2018, pp. 31–57, 81–109; also Avery 1981, pp. 46–49; Principi 2016, pp. 19–38, 53–67.

2. Butterfield and Franklin 1998.

3. Butterfield and Franklin 1998, p. 824: "uno Bacho, pure di terra non cocta, che istà a diacere et posasi in sun una bocte et dal lato mancho ha in mano uno vaso che butta acqua, che è di grandezza di 3/4."

4. Principi 2018, pp. 21–27.

5. Reproduced in Butterfield and Franklin 1998, p. 819, as attributed to Sansovino.

6. Principi 2018, pp. 57–63.

FIG. 3
Sandro di Lorenzo, *Battle between Horsemen and Soldiers*, 1510–20. Terracotta with traces of paint, height 54 cm. Daniel Katz, London (2007).

7. Lasca, *Lezione di maestro Niccodemo dalla Pietra al Migliaio sopra il Capitolo della Salsiccia* (Florence, 1589). Principi 2018, pp. 184–87. Lasca saw another terracotta of the same subject with Giovambattista del Verrocchio, whose workshop had belonged to Sando di Lorenzo between 1519 and 1526.

8. There are four versions of this battle scene, two in the Palazzo Vecchio, Florence; one in the Pushkin Museum, Moscow; and the one illustrated here in FIG. 3. See Principi 2018, pp. 283–91.

9. Waldman 2005; Principi 2018.

10. Principi 2018, pp. 44, 47, 62.

11. Bode 1890, pp. 103–5.

12. Surveyed in Principi 2016 and Principi 2018.

13. Listed in the inventory of Bondy's collection seized in 1938: "Terracottagruppe. Liegender bärtiger Bacchus mit Krug, aus dem Wein quillt, und Trinkschale"; Lillie 2003, p. 244. On Bondy and his collection, see ibid.,

pp. 216–45; and Theodor Brückler, report on Karton 15, 15/1 [BDA-Archiv].

14. Central Collecting Point no. 2256/9. Online: http://www.dhm.de. The depot possessor is listed as Hitler, but the object does not occur in any of the lists for the Führermuseum, Linz. The object entered the Allied Central Collecting Point, Munich, on July 2, 1945, and was returned to Austria on Nov. 29, 1946.

15. The terracotta was turned over to Bondy's representatives, the shippers Kühner & Söhne, on Feb. 17, 1948; BDA-Archiv, RestMat, K. 15-1 M2, PM Bondy Oskar, fol. 54. I am grateful for the assistance of Anita Stelzl-Gallian of the Büro der Kommission für Provenienzforschung beim Bundeskanzleramt, Vienna.

16. Elisabeth Bondy's paintings were sold by Kende Galleries, New York, on March 3, 1949. Blumka Galleries, New York, seems to have sold the sculptures and objects: a bust by Sebastian Loscher was acquired by the Museum of Fine Arts, Boston (49.4); a sculpture by Nicolas Weckmann, among others, was sold to the Metropolitan Museum of Art (48.154.1).

Back of CAT. 17
(see p. 84 for front view).

CAT. 17
Circle of Niccolò Tribolo
Dusk
1540s
terracotta with traces of paint
height 46 cm, length 52 cm, depth 23 cm
(18 ⅛ × 20 ½ × 9 in.)
Carnegie Museum of Art, Pittsburgh
Decorative Arts Purchase Fund, 68.28

PROVENANCE

The work was owned by Carl Alexander, Grand Duke of Sachsen-Weimar-Eisenach (1818–1901), Weimar, who bequeathed it to privy councillor (Geheimer Hofrat) Carl Ruland (1834–1907).[1] An accomplished scholar of art and literature, Ruland served as private secretary and librarian to Prince Albert in London beginning in 1859, and remained in service to Queen Victoria after the prince's death in 1861. In 1870, Ruland became director of the Weimar museums and was later the founding director of the Goethe Museum.

Ruland's son reportedly sold the sculpture to the Count Pourtalès, Germany, and it was then owned by Benno de Terey (1903–1973), New York. Benno de Terey's father, Gábor Térey, was director of the Museum of Fine Arts in Budapest. Benno immigrated to the United States after his father's death in 1927 and became a reknowned interior designer in New York, where he created displays for the decorative art dealers French and Company. Sold by Benno de Terey to the museum in 1969.

REFERENCES

Steinmann 1907, pp. 82, 84 note 3, fig. 18. Thode 1908, vol. 1, p. 485. Tolnay 1948, p. 155, no. 8. D. T. Owsley in *Carnegie Magazine*, no. 44 (1970), pp. 25–26 [perhaps Pietro Francavilla]. Wixom 1975, under nos. 138–39 [attributed to Tribolo].

---

1. Steinmann 1907, pp. 82, 84 note 3; Thode 1908, vol. 1, p. 485.

Back of CAT. 18
(see p. 85 for front view).

CAT. 18

Johan Gregor van der Schardt (ca. 1530-1581)

Day

1560s

terracotta

height 21.3 cm, length 30 cm (8 ⅜ × 11 ¾ in.)

Museum of Fine Arts, Houston

The Edith A. and Percy S. Straus Collection, 44.584

PROVENANCE

This terracotta was one of four reductions of the Times of Day by Michelangelo that belonged to Paulus von Praun, Nuremberg. In 1801, the Praun heirs sold the collection to Johann Friedrich Frauenholz (1758–1822), an art dealer in Nuremberg; it was then acquired in 1803 by Oberstleutenant von Gemmingen, Nuremberg. In 1842, most of the terracottas in the Praun collection were sold to the sculptor Ernst Julius Hähnel (1811–1891), Dresden (by descent to his widow and daughter), and then owned by the South West African Trust Company, 1922.

Dr. A. B. Heyer, London, owned thirty-three of the Praun terracottas, which were sold in twenty-six lots as by Michelangelo or his school at Christie's, London, February 24, 1938. The work in Houston (lot 61) was sold for £105 to Smith, and was by far the most expensive object in the sale; the two other Times of Day now in the Victoria and Albert Museum (see p. 85) made £27 and £32. The other works were dispersed: a relief of Hercules and Atlas is in the AD&A Museum, University of California, Santa Barbara (1964.480); an arm and hand are in the Victoria and Albert Museum; and eighteen others are in the Rijksmuseum, Amsterdam.[1]

Arnold Seligmann, Rey and Co., Paris, sold *Day* in March 1939 to Percy S. Straus (1876–1944), New York. President of Macy's, Straus began collecting in 1921 and left his collection to the museum in Houston because his son had settled there.[2]

REFERENCES

Murr 1797, p. 241, nos. 29–32 [Michelangelo]. Houston 1945, no. 76 [Michelangelo]. LeBrooy 1972, pp. 52–61 [Michelangelo]. Honnens de Lichtenberg 1991, pp. 64, 65 [different in character from the two terracottas in the V&A]. Achilles-Syndram 1994, pp. 264–65 [van der Schardt, with earlier references]. Berger 1994 [van der Schardt]. O'Grody 1999, pp. 295–96.

On the *Dawn* and *Night* in the Victoria and Albert Museum: Larsson 1984, p. 25–27 [van der Schardt]; Houston and London 2001, no. 31 [van der Schardt].

---

1. Seventeen terracottas from the 1938 auction were acquired by Percival Wolff of Montreal (he acquired another separately). They were sold by his descendants to a consortium that gave them to the Museum of Vancouver. The museum placed nine at auction at Sotheby's, New York, Jan. 31, 2013 (lot 354, attributed to van der Schardt), but they failed to sell. All eighteen were later purchased by the Rijksmuseum, Amsterdam.

2. Invoice from Seligmann, Rey to Strauss, Mar. 30, 1939 (museum files), gives Dr. A. von Frey as owner after the auction in 1938. This is presumably Alexander von Frey (1881–1951), a Hungarian based in Lucerne and Paris (see www.lostart.de). Frey owned another of the Praun terracottas after Michelangelo.

Marcantonio Raimondi (active 1504–27)
Apollo Belvedere
ca. 1511–20
engraving, 29.2 × 16.3 cm (11 ½ × 6 ⅜ in.)
The Metropolitan Museum of Art, New York
The Elisha Whittelsey Collection,
The Elisha Whittelsey Fund, 1949, 49.97.114

See discussion on page 47. The *Apollo Belvedere* was raised onto a plinth in 1511, so this engraving must date from that year or after. This print is a later version by Raimondi of an almost identical image (Illustrated Bartsch, vol. 27, no. 330). The *S* in "sic" in the inscription is reversed in the second version.

REFERENCES
Illustrated Bartsch, vol. 27, no. 331. A. Gnann in Mantua and Vienna 1999, p. 90. Gramaccini and Meier 2009, pp. 151–52. Bloemacher 2016, pp. 72–76.

INSCRIPTIONS
Inscribed on plinth: Sic. Romae. Ex. Marmore. Sculpto (Carved in marble as in Rome).

CAT. 20
Hendrick Goltzius (1558–1617)
Apollo Belvedere
ca. 1593, published in 1617
engraving, 41.2 × 30.3 cm (16 ¼ × 11 ⅞ in.)
Harvard Art Museums / Fogg Museum, Cambridge
Gift of William Gray from
the collection of Francis Calley Gray, G1667

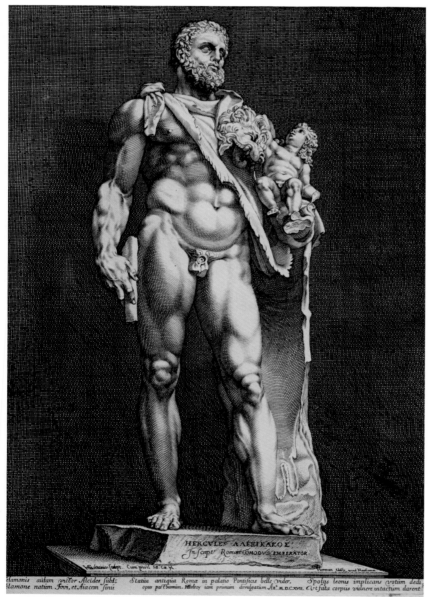

HERCVLES ΑΛΕΞΙΚΑΚΟΣ
Inscript: Romæ. COMODVS IMPERATOR.

clamonis aulam victor Alcides subſt: Statua antiqua Romæ in palatio Pontificis belle, vider.   Spolys leonis implicans protum dedi,
clamone natum Jovi, et Aiacem sinit   opus post Eximium. Hickey iam primum divulgatium An.º M.D.C.XVII. Et ſata corpus vulnere intactum darent!

CAT. 21

Hendrick Goltzius
Hercules and Telephos
ca. 1593, published in 1617
engraving, 41.1 × 29.8 cm (16 ⅛ × 11 ¾ in.)
Harvard Art Museums / Fogg Museum,
Cambridge, Mass. Gift of William Gray from the
collection of Francis Calley Gray, G1666

GOLTZIUS AND ANCIENT SCULPTURE

Hendrick Goltzius produced three remarkable engravings after the ancient Roman sculptures that he saw in Rome in 1591, two of them restored by Giovan Angelo Montorsoli. Before he went to Italy, Goltzius had made prints of mythological gods and Roman heroes, which are occasionally based on the bronzes of Willem van Tetrode, a collaborator of Benvenuto Cellini.[1] Goltzius's prints of the 1590s after ancient sculptures have a greater specificity, as they are obviously depictions of monumental marbles, sometimes accompanied by modern observers.

Despite the fame of the prints, especially the image of the *Farnese Hercules* (FIG. 1), questions linger about their status. They are based on drawings apparently made on the spot in Rome, but of the forty-three surviving drawings made after twenty-seven sculptures, Goltzius made only three engravings, and did not bother to publish them.[2] Instead, they were issued in 1617, immediately after the artist's death. No convincing explanation has yet been advanced for Goltzius's hesitation.

The prints of the two Hercules sculptures each have two related drawings of the same size, one in black chalk on blue paper, the other in red chalk (FIG. 2). There is only one black chalk preparatory drawing for the engraving of the *Apollo Belvedere* (FIG. 3). The two red chalk drawings of the *Hercules and Telephos* and the *Farnese Hercules* have been indented on the reverse to trace the design onto the plate, which suggests that the red chalk drawing for the *Apollo* print is lost.[3] Many of the other Roman subjects exist in two different drawings (all are preserved in the Teylers Museum, Haarlem). In general, when two drawings survive of the same subject, the black chalk drawing on blue paper is less finished than the red chalk drawing on white paper, although this is not always the case.[4] Twenty of the sheets are indented for transfer to a second drawing.

Goltzius made the prints after his return to the Netherlands, perhaps in 1592 or 1593, as the engraving style is comparable to works from those years, and certainly before 1600 when the artist abandoned printmaking.[5] Goltzius may have intended to make more engravings of ancient sculptures (or even of Michelangelo's *Moses*), but set the project aside: the naturalism and genre sensibility of the three engravings are quite different from the rest of Goltzius's prints. The black chalk drawing of one of the Dioscuri even contains two small observer figures like those found in the completed prints, suggesting that the artist was planning to engrave the image.[6] Jan Piet Filedt Kok (1993) has proposed that the three engravings were not completed by Goltzius. He believes that the *Hercules and Telephos* and the *Apollo Belvedere* were largely engraved by another artist, because of the mechanical-looking backgrounds.

Today, the *Farnese Hercules* (FIG. 1) is one of Goltzius's most famous prints, perhaps because it appeals to a modern sensibility: the muscle-bound giant comically dwarfs the observers, who gaze upward like the bored little putti in Raphael's *Sistine Madonna*. The figures in the completed prints do not appear in the preparatory drawings; those in the *Farnese Hercules* are derived from a separate metalpoint drawing. These observers are not added merely for scale but to enhance the sense of wonder on encountering marvels of ancient art, and perhaps to reinforce the idea that the sculptures need to be viewed from different angles, as Goltzius himself experienced. Dressed in sixteenth-century clothing, these proxy viewers remind us of the modern world, and thus of the distance between antiquity and the present day.

FIG. 1
Hendrick Goltzius, *Farnese Hercules*,
ca. 1593. Engraving, 41.9 × 30.3 cm.
Rijksmuseum, Amsterdam. RP-P-OB-10.348.

The print of the *Apollo Belvedere* includes a young artist hard at work sketching the statue. Amusingly diminutive and shy, the figure seems to echo Goltzius's own incognito presence in Rome in 1591. Karel van Mander in 1603–4 says that Goltzius shunned the attention of prominent Roman patrons and artists, but dressed like a German peasant and went by the name of Hendrick van Bracht.[7]
Alan Chong

PROVENANCE
Francis Calley Gray (1790–1856), bequest to his nephew, William Gray; gift to Harvard University, 1857.

REFERENCES
Reznicek 1961, vol. 1, pp. 325–26. Brummer 1970, pp. 50, 71. Filedt Kok 1993, p 182. Luijten 2003, pp. 119, 122. Leesberg 2012, nos. 380, 379.

INSCRIPTIONS
CAT. 20:
Inscribed on base: HG Sculp. Apollo Pythius. Cum privil. Sa. Cae M. Plinth: Herman Adolfz. excud. Haerlemens.
Margin: Status antiqua Romae in palatio Pontifis belle vider / opus posthumum, HGoltzij iam primum divulgat. Ano. M.D.C.XVII. Vix natus armis Deluis vulcanijs / Donatus infans, sacra Parnassi iuga / Petij. draconem matris hostem spiculis / Pythona fixi: nomen inde Pythij. Schrvel
Numbered: 3
CAT. 21:
Inscribed on base: HERCULES [ALEXIKAKOS. in Greek] / In Script. Roman. COMODUS IMPERATOR
Plinth: *H*Goltzius sculpt. Cum privil Sæ. Cæ. M. / Herman Adolfz. excud. Haerlemen
Margin: Statua antiqua Romae in palatio Pontificis belle vider. / opus posthumum. *H*Goltzy iam primum divulgatum An.o M.D.C.XVII. Telamonis aulam victor Alcides subt, / Telamone natum Jovi, et Aiacem sinu / Spolys leonis implicans votum dedi, / Ut fata corpus vulnere intactum darent. / Schreve

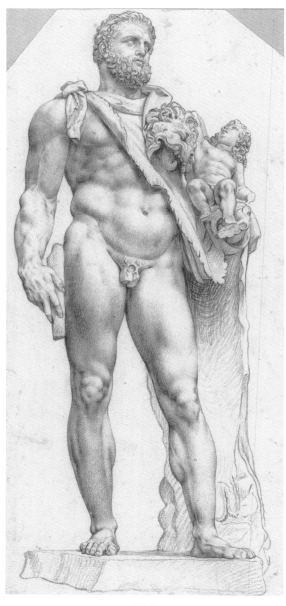

FIG. 2
Hendrick Goltzius, *Hercules and Telephos*, 1591. Red chalk on paper, 39.4 × 18.2 cm. Teylers Museum, Haarlem. N 27.

1.   Goddard and Ganz 2001.

2.   On the drawings, see Reznicek 1961, vol. 1, pp. 89–94, 201–2, nos. 200–253; Miedema 1969; Luijten 2003.

3.   Reznicek 1961, vol. 1, nos. 206, 207, 208, 226, 227.

4.   Brandt 2001.

5.   Reznicek 1961, vol. 1, p. 419, connected the prints to the series of the Nine Muses dated 1592. They seem even closer to the *Pygmalion and Galatea* dated 1593, as pointed out by Ackley 1981, p. 12. Leesberg 2012, p. 368, simply dates the prints to 1592 and adds, "They were probably left unfinished and were completed and posthumously published."

6.   Luijten 2003, p. 129, no. 40.2. Luijten says that the figures were included to indicate the immense scale of the sculpture.

7.   Miedema 1994, pp. 390, 391: "wat boerigh op zijn Hooghduytsch vercleedt, liet hem noemen Hendrick van Bracht" (dressed somewhat like a peasant in German clothing, and calling himself Hendrick van Bracht).

FIG. 3
Hendrick Goltzius, *Apollo Belvedere*,
1591. Black chalk on blue paper,
62 × 45.1 cm. Teylers Museum,
Haarlem. K III 23.

CAT. 22
Marco Dente (active 1515–27)
Laocoon
ca. 1515–23
engraving, 44.5 × 32.7 cm
(trimmed; 17 7/16 × 12 15/16 in.)
The Metropolitan Museum of Art, New York
The Elisha Whittelsey Collection,
The Elisha Whittelsey Fund, 1949, 49.97.122

Marco Dente, or Marco da Ravenna, arrived in Rome from his native Ravenna in 1515. He worked for the publisher Baviera (Baviero de' Carrocci) along with fellow engravers Marcantonio Raimondi and Agostino Veneziano. Dente was killed in the Sack of Rome in 1527. Rebaudo suggests that the print dates before the spring of 1523, when the arms of the two sons of Laocoon were partly restored. A printmaker in the workshop of Antonio Lafreri copied the main portions of Dente's image in 1552 for the *Speculum Romanae Magnificentiae* (p. 147).

PROVENANCE
Graphische Sammlung Albertina, Vienna.

REFERENCES
Illustrated Bartsch, vol. 27, no. 353 [originally as Raimondi]. Brummer 1970, p. 78. Mantua and Vienna 1999, no. 276. Rebaudo 2007, pp. 12–13, 82, no. DS 8. Gramaccini and Meier 2009, no. 91.

INSCRIPTIONS
Signed lower left: MRCUS. RAVENAS. Inscribed on plinth: LAOCHOON

The plinth carried the further inscription (see p. 46): ROMAE IN PALATIO PONT IN / LOCO QUI VULGO DICITUR / BELVIDERE. [In the palace of Rome in the place called the Belvedere.]

‧LAOCHOON‧

‧ROMAE‧IN‧PALATIO‧PONT‧IN‧
‧LOCO‧QVI‧VVLGO‧DICITVR‧
‧BELVEDERE‧

CAT. 23

Nicolas Béatrizet (active 1540–66)

Laocoon

1550s

engraving, 44.4 × 29.2 cm (17 ½ × 11 ½ in.)

Illustrated: British Museum, London.

1920,0420.41.

Exhibited: Harvard Art Museums / Fogg Museum.

John Witt Randall Fund, R835NA.

37.2 × 24.9 cm (sheet).

In the period from around 1510 to the Sack of Rome in 1527, printmakers in Raphael's circle in Rome occasionally made images of the famous ancient sculptures in the Vatican. The middle of the sixteenth century witnessed a surge in printmaking after the antique, primarily through the work of foreigners living in Rome, including the publishers Antonio Salamanca and Antoine Lafréry, or Lafreri (from Spain and France respectively), and engravers such as the Netherlanders Hieronymus Cock, Cornelis Cort, and Jacob Bos, as well as the Frenchmen Nicolas Béatrizet, Stefano Duchetti, and Étienne Dupérac. They produced a vast number of prints of ancient and Renaissance monuments, as well as maps and vistas of Rome, which were gathered into albums that could be easily marketed, most famously by Lafreri in the *Speculum Romanae Magnificentiae* (Mirror of Roman Magnificence). Although the title was created only in the mid-1570s, prints for the series were made beginning in the 1540s, some for other projects or as independent works.[1]

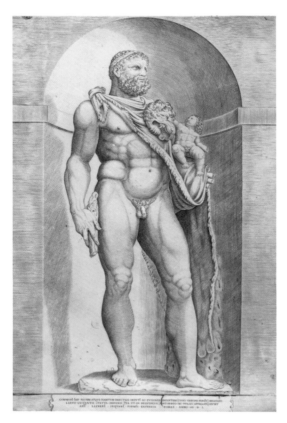

Hercules and Telephos, 1550. Engraving, 45.4 × 30 cm.
Rijksmuseum, Amsterdam. RP-P-1888-A-13798.
Made for *Speculum Romanae Magnificentiae*.

The Vatican's ancient sculptures were reproduced in differing ways. The *Apollo Belvedere* continued to be shown as it had been found in the late fifteenth century, without Giovan Angelo Montorsoli's restoration of 1532–33. For example, the engraving in the *Speculum Romanae Magnificentiae* is dated 1552, but copies Marcantonio Raimondi's *Apollo* made nearly forty years earlier (CAT. 19).[2] On the other hand, the ancient marble *Hercules and Telephos* appeared in print for the first time in 1550 with Montorsoli's added limbs (FIG. 1), in an engraving that may be by Jacob Bos.[3]

Montorsoli's restoration of the *Laocoon* was first depicted in a print in 1539, on the frontispiece for Euralio Morani's poems on the ancient statues of *Laocoon, Apollo Belvedere,* and *Venus*.[4] Although certain liberties have been taken, Montorsoli's reconstruction of Laocoon's right arm is faithfully reproduced. Another print of the restored sculpture was issued in 1544 as part of Bartolomeo Marliani's illustrated guidebook, *Urbis Romae Topographia*.[5]

Because the illustrations in *Speculum Romanae Magnificentiae* were produced over many decades by many different artists, Lafreri no doubt felt related images needed some consistency. Thus the statues in the Vatican Belvedere were often rendered with heavy shadows, with inscriptions presented as though carved on the marble plinths; the river gods were given a distinctive format for their inscriptions.

Two prints of the *Laocoon* were included in Lafreri's collection of Roman images, one showing the work in a niche, the other setting it against a plain wall (CAT. 23 and FIG. 2). Both have been attributed to Nicolas Béatrizet, although neither is signed and the images differ considerably in style.[6] They have been called copies of Marco Dente's print of the *Laocoon* (CAT. 22), but this is the case only for figure 2.[7] A portion of the egg-and-dart molding from Dente's engraving can be glimpsed under Laocoon's left armpit in figure 2, showing that the copyist did not fully understand the sculpture. This print also lacks a unifying sense of shadow, which leaves Laocoon's musculature disjointed and scaly in appearance. That Laocoon is shown with Montorsoli's restoration, but the sons are not, seems to suggest that the print is based on several different models.[8] CAT. 23 reflects Montorsoli's restoration of the arms of the three figures, while the print in figure 2 shows the arms of the sons unrestored. The shading of the body and the characterization of the sons in CAT. 23 are significantly different from Dente's print, to the extent that it cannot be considered a copy.

We suggest that the two engravings of the *Laocoon* in the *Speculum* are not by the same artist. While the print in figure 2 would appear to be by an unknown artist in Lafreri's workshop, the earlier version with the niche fully convinces as a work by Nicolas Béatrizet.[9] It shows close similarities with Béatrizet's signed prints after ancient sculpture – for example, the equestrian statue of Marcus Aurelius of 1548, a relief of 1553, and the *Oceanus* dated 1560 (FIG. 3).[10] Tightly delineated curly hair and incisively shadowed drapery give these engravings a peculiar energy, enhanced by intense highlights scattered throughout the compositions. Béatrizet gives exaggerated expressions to his faces that sometimes approach caricature. Lafreri's name was added as publisher to the second state of CAT. 23, which hints that the print was not originally made for the *Speculum Romanae Magnificentiae*.

Nicolas Béatrizet was born in Lorraine and sometimes signed his work "Lotharingo." Between 1541 and 1562, he produced nineteen signed prints for Lafreri's *Speculum*.[11] In addition, he made numerous prints after Michelangelo's work, including a reproduction of the *Last Judgment* consisting of ten engravings, which he published himself in 1562.[12] Giorgio Vasari mentions Béatrizet as making "many prints worthy of praise."[13]

Alan Chong

INSCRIPTION

Laochoon. On the plinth: Romae in palatio pont in / loco qui vulgo dicitur / Belvedere. [In the papal palace, Rome, the place popularly known as the Belvedere]

REFERENCES

Illustrated Bartsch, vol. 29, no. 90. Hülsen 1921, p. 168, no. 59d. Brummer 1970, p. 93. Bianchi 2003, p. 4, no. 99. Rebaudo 2007, pp. 85–86, no. DS 44 [2nd state described]. Rubach 2016, no. 325 [attributed to Béatrizet].

1. The best catalogue of the *Speculum* is Rubach 2016. See also: Parshall 2006; Witcombe 2008; Chicago 2008.

2. Rubach 2016, no. 322, repr.

3. Dated 1550. Rubach 2016, no. 323. Rubach states that Antonio Salamanca also issued a print of the *Laocoon* (Biblioteca Apostolica Vaticano, Rome: Cicognara XII.541,75). The print in FIG. 1 has been attributed to Jacob Bos in Hollstein 1949, vol. 3, p. 150, no. 16.

4. *Stanze d'Eurialo d'Ascoli sopra le statue di Lacoonte, di Venere, e d'Apollo* (Rome, 1539), with a woodcut frontispiece of the *Laocoon*. Rome 2006, pp. 158–59, no. 50, repr.; Rebaudo 2007, no. DS 39, fig. 22.

5. Brummer 1970, p. 93, fig. 80; Rebaudo 2007, no. DS 40, fig. 23.

6. Print of the *Laocoon* with no niche: Illustrated Bartsch vol. 29, no. 91; Bianchi 2003, p. 4, no. 98; Rubach 2016, no. 324.

7. Hülsen 1921, p. 168; repeated by Bianchi 2004, vol. 3, p. 4; Rebaudo 2007, pp. 85, 86.

8. It may be derived in part from Cornelis Bos's print (signed and dated 1548, in reverse; Rijksmuseum, Amsterdam, RP-P-BI-2784), which is closer to Dente's print. On Bos's print, see Hülsen 1921, no. 59c; and Bianchi 2003, no. 98.

9. Rubach 2016, nos. 324, 325, identifies both versions of the *Laocoon* as "attributed to Béatrizet." Bianchi 2003, nos. 98, 99, attributes both prints to Béatrizet.

10. Rubach 2016, nos. 310, 273, 328 (signed "Nicolao Beatricio Lotharingo"), repr.

11. Rubach 2016. Also: Bianchi 2003; Bury 1996.

12. Barnes 2010. *Last Judgment*: Barnes 2010, pp. 202–6; Bury and Lockett 2011.

13. Vasari 1966, vol. 5, p. 20: "In Roma, outré ai sopradetti, ha talmente dato opera a questi intagli di bulino Niccolò Beatricio loteringo, che ha fatto molte carte degne di lode."

147

FIG. 2
Laocoon, mid-16th century. Engraving, 49.1 × 32.1 cm. Metropolitan Museum of Art, New York. 41.72(2.77). Made for *Speculum Romanae Magnificentiae*.

FIG. 3
Nicolas Béatrizet, *Oceanus*, 1560. Engraving, 30.7 × 41.8 cm. Rijksmuseum, Amsterdam. RP-P-1926-324. First state. Made for *Speculum Romanae Magnificentiae*.

CAT. 24
Italian
Laocoon
ca. 1600
terracotta, height 68 cm (26 ¾ in.)
Princeton University Art Museum
Museum purchase,
gift of Elias Wolf, Class of 1920, and Mrs. Wolf,
y1968-118

Almost from the moment of its discovery in 1506, the ancient sculpture of Laocoon and his sons being strangled by serpents was copied in various media – proof of its hold on the artistic imagination. In 1510, a competition was held to produce a faithful copy on a small scale of the *Laocoon*. Jacopo Sansovino produced the winning version in wax. The Florentine artist Sandro di Lorenzo made a terracotta reduction of the *Laocoon* that was painted in imitation of bronze, which was recorded in 1523 (see CAT. 16). In 1525, Federico Gonzaga, the marquis of Mantua and builder of the Palazzo Te, commissioned a gesso version of the *Laocoon*, which is said to have been about one *braccia* high (68 centimeters or 27 inches).[1]

Probably made in Rome around 1600, the exhibited terracotta was closely modeled after Giovan Angelo Montorsoli's restoration of the *Laocoon*. Also falling into the category of collectors' items are Stefano Maderno's highly finished terracottas of *Hercules and Telephos* and *Laocoon*, which are signed and dated 1620 and 1630 respectively (State Hermitage Museum, St. Petersburg).[2] Maderno's richly expressive terracotta (FIG. I) demonstrates the uninterrupted fascination with the ancient group in the Baroque era. Ancient sculptures sometimes appear in Netherlandish paintings of the seventeenth century. Abraham Begeyn, for example, depicted the *Laocoon* in reverse in the 1670s in a painting made in England for Ham House, near London, where the work remains.

Alan Chong

FIG. I
Stefano Maderno, *Laocoon*,
1630. Terracotta, height 71 cm.
State Hermitage Museum,
St. Petersburg. 553.

PROVENANCE

This terracotta and another after the *Laocoon* at Princeton (inv. y1968-119) belonged to Ludwig Pollak (1868–1943), the Czech archaeologist who in 1905 discovered the original right arm of Laocoon, four hundred years after the rest of the statue has been found. Pollak, honorary director of the Museo Barracco in Rome, died at Auschwitz in 1943. Adolf Loewy, Los Angeles, sold the work to the museum in 1968.

REFERENCES

Martin 1968. Brummer 1970, pp. 103–7 [perhaps derived from Sansovino]. Winner 1974, p. 112 note 81. Boucher 1991, vol. 2, pp. 314–15 [not connected with Sansovino]. Rossi Pinelli 1993, p. 9. Rebaudo 2007, no. CR 14 [mid-16th century?].

1. Boucher 1991, vol. 1, p. 183.

2. Chicago 1998, nos. 1, 2.

FIG. 2
Back of CAT. 24.

CAT. 25
Nicolò Boldrini (active 1520s to 1566),
after Titian (1485/90–1576)
Caricature of the Laocoon
1540s
woodcut, 27.3 × 40 cm (10 ¾ × 15 ¾ in.)
Illustrated: The Metropolitan Museum of Art,
New York. Rogers Fund, 1922. 22.73.3-125.
Exhibited: Harvard Art Museums / Fogg Museum.
Gift of William Gray from the collection of Francis
Calley Gray, G464. 27 × 35 cm (trimmed).

See page 53 for discussion.

REFERENCES
Ridolfi 1648, vol. 1, p. 183 [after Titian]. Janson
1946. Rosand and Muraro 1976, no. 40 [Boldrini
after Titian; with earlier references]. Barkan 1999,
pp. 11, 13–14, 16. Nadine Orenstein in McPhee
and Orenstein 2011, no. 42.

CAT. 26

Zaccaria Zacchi da Volterra (1473-1544)

Marsyas

ca. 1510

wax, 22 × 10 × 12 cm (8 ⅝ × 4 × 4 ¾ in.)

Carnegie Museum of Art, Pittsburgh

Gift of Herbert DuPuy, 27.10.378

The ancient marble sculpture *Laocoon* influenced innumerable Renaissance works of art within a few years of its discovery in 1506. An early interpretation of the composition is Moderno's bronze plaquette of the Flagellation of Christ (FIG. 1), made around 1510 to 1515, where the pose of Christ is based on Laocoon's expression of extreme physical distress.[1] In turn, the outstretched arm tied to a column bears a close relationship to representations of the Flaying of Marsyas, as seen in this wax sculpture by Zaccaria Zacchi da Volterra, which was very likely made around the same time as Moderno's relief. The wax sculpture gains in significance because the artist is one of the earliest recorded copyists of the *Laocoon*. In 1510, four artists made wax copies of the *Laocoon* in an informal competition (see p. 46).[2] According to Giorgio Vasari, Zaccaria Zacchi was one of the participants.

WAX SCULPTURES IN THE RENAISSANCE

The physical properties of wax made it a favorite medium for sculpture.[3] The pliable material can be easily worked, and it hardens naturally without cracking, as clay sometimes does during firing. Wax also remains stable when applied over wood or metal. However, wax is fragile, making its long-term preservation difficult. Among the most significant surviving Renaissance waxes is Michelangelo's model for the *Young Slave* (Victoria and Albert Museum, London, 4117-1854). Besides preparatory works of this type, wax was also employed for small portraits, ex-voto images, and anatomical studies. And wax was fundamental to the casting of bronzes.

Beeswax is naturally yellow, but loses its color after prolonged exposure to sunlight. Liquefied wax can be colored with powdered additives. Red, orange, and green were preferred by Renaissance artists, since they recalled the metal sculptures cast from wax models. In his autobiography, Benvenuto Cellini described in detail how he made a yellow wax model for his monumental bronze *Perseus* around 1545. Giambologna produced five models in yellow wax for the *Equestrian Monument of Cosimo I de' Medici*, which was cast in 1591.[4] Filippo Baldinucci wrote that modeling wax, usually white or yellow, was often mixed with "tallow, turpentine, fine flour,

and cinnabar, to be used to make models of large and small figures."[5]

The small wax model exhibited here was probably made as a study for a larger version in clay or marble. It was built around a wooden armature, which demonstrates that the wax was not poured into a mold. The wood base is not original.

ATTRIBUTION AND ICONOGRAPHY

The wax *Marsyas* was tentatively connected with Giovan Angelo Montorsoli by Birgit Laschke, who noted similarities with figures on the relief on the tomb of Jacopo Sannazaro (see p. 155).[6] Giorgio Vasari writes that Montorsoli made wax portraits of Leo X and Clement VII, Medici popes whose images were destroyed in 1527 with the expulsion of the Medici from Florence.[7] While the physiognomy of the Marsyas is not dissimilar to Montorsoli's work, the figure is more sparsely handled and the drapery stiffer, factors that suggest that the wax is earlier in date. Indeed it seems closer to the time of the discovery of the *Laocoon* in 1506.

In ancient art, the satyr Marsyas is often represented as an old man without goat's legs, and at the beginning of the sixteenth century such representations became common, especially in Florence and northern Italy.[8] Zaccaria's wax sculpture demonstrates a close familiarity with ancient art, since Marsyas is shown tied to a tree. This detail is absent from Ovid's *Metamorphoses*, and while it is described in the *Fabulae* by Hyginus, the latter was only published in 1535.[9] Therefore, Zaccaria must have

FIG. 1
Moderno, *Flagellation of Christ*, ca. 1510–15. Bronze, 14.2 × 11 cm. Bode-Museum, Staatliche Museen zu Berlin.

FIG. 2
Zaccaria Zacchi, *The Lamentation*,
ca. 1504. Painted terracotta. Santa
Caterina, Colle di Val d'Elsa.

FIG. 3
Zaccaria Zacchi, *Nicodemus*. Detail
of FIG. 2.

taken the motif from ancient works of art such as vases, statues, or carved gems. The ropes that bind Marsyas's hand over his head recall the snakes that encircle Laocoon in the ancient marble.

Born in Volterra, Zaccaria Zacchi worked in Rome, Florence, Bologna, and Trento.[10] The sharp-cornered drapery that falls straight down in tubular forms behind the shoulders of his *Marsyas* is similar to the drapery of the painted terracotta figures of the *Lamentation* in Santa Caterina in Colle di Val d'Elsa (FIG. 2), and in another *Lamentation* group in San Francesco in Volterra, commissioned in 1504.[11] The elongated proportions and exaggerated emotions of Marsyas can be compared with the expressive faces of Joseph of Arimathea and Nicodemus (FIG. 3) in the monumental group in Colle di Val d'Elsa. The figures share characteristic features, including hooked noses with a high hump, deep wrinkles, wide mouths contorted by a grimace, and distinctive curls of the beard and hair. Zaccaria's marble *Nymph and Satyr* (FIG. 4), dated 1506, also has stylistic ties with the *Marsyas*; it

shows similarities in the modeling of the abdomen, with the central muscles in slight relief, and in the rendering of squarish hands with long fingers. Both Zaccaria's Colle di Val d'Elsa *Lamentation* and *Nymph and Satyr* support dating the wax *Marsyas* to around 1506 or slightly later.

The subject of the *Flaying of Marsyas* continued to attract Zaccaria's imagination. An alabaster sculpture of the same subject (FIG. 5) is stylistically related to busts of Christ and the Apostles made by the artist around 1523 to 1525 for San Giovanni in Monte in Bologna (FIG. 6).[12] The alabaster *Marsyas* was probably made around 1530, which explains the differences with the wax in Pittsburgh, evident above all in the greater luxuriance of the beard and hair.

Lorenzo Principi

PROVENANCE

The wax is first recorded in the collection of the art dealer and numismatist Arthur Sambon (1867–1947), Paris, when he placed it at auction at Georges Petit, Paris, May 25–28, 1914 (lot 345, as "Ancien travail italien"); it sold for 75 francs with the buyer recorded as Mellain. Shortly afterward it entered the collection of Herbert DuPuy (1856–1930), Pittsburgh, who gave his extensive collection of small sculptures to the Carnegie Museum of Art in 1927.

REFERENCES

Laschke 1993, p. 55 note 73, fig. 186 [16th-century Italian, Montorsoli?]. Jesse 2017, p. 199, fig. 4 [anonymous, Montorsoli?].

FIG. 4
Zaccaria Zacchi, *Nymph and Satyr*,
1506. Marble, height 54.6 cm.
Metropolitan Museum of Art,
New York. Gift of Irwin Untermeyer,
1964, 64.101.1443.

FIG. 5
Zaccaria Zacchi, *Flaying of Marsyas*,
ca. 1530. Alabaster, height 44.5 cm.
Private collection.

FIG. 6
Detail of CAT. 26.

FIG. 7
Zaccaria Zacchi, *Bust of an Apostle*,
1523–25. Marble. San Giovanni in
Monte, Bologna.

1. Lewis 1989, pp. 129–31; T. Schtrauch in Rome 2006, pp. 155–56. The first version of the composition by Moderno seems to have been a gilded silver plaque (Kunsthistorisches Museum, Vienna), made for Cardinal Domenico Grimani around 1510 to 1515. Grimani also owned the bronze casting of Jacopo Sansovino's wax model of the *Laocoon* of 1510.

2. Vasari 1966, vol. 6, p. 178. On the date of the competition: Mozzati 2007, pp. 569–70.

3. See Penny 1993, pp. 215–18; and Panzanelli 2008.

4. Krahn 2006, p. 45. They are recorded in 1588.

5. Baldinucci 1681, pp. 31–32: modeling wax (*cera da modellare*) is described as "bianca o gialla co[n] sego, trementina, farina sottile, e cinabro; serve per far modelli di figure grandi e piccole."

6. Laschke 1993, p. 55 note 73.

7. Vasari 1966, vol. 5, p. 493. Montorsoli made votive portraits of the king of Bosnia and "Signor Vecchio" of Piombino shortly after this. In the autumn of 1534, he also made a wax portrait of Duke Alessandro de' Medici.

8. Wyss 1996, pp. 93–95; Faticcioni 2007, p. 132, fig. 10.

9. Faticcioni 2007, pp. 139, 141, 143, doc. 16.

10. Lucidi 2012. For Zaccaria's work in Trento, see Bacchi 1995. For his work in Volterra and Tuscany, see La Porta 1998.

11. Gennari 1958, pp. 13–14.

12. Lucidi 2012, pp. 147, 165 note 138. I am grateful to David Lucidi, who wrote an unpublished study of this alabaster, for bringing it to my attention. It was displayed by Mauro Prasedi Antiquario, Legnano; see *Arte Antica '97: Lingotto Fiere, Torino, 15–23 Febbraio 1997* (Turin, 1997), p. 116.

CAT. 27
Silvio Cosini (ca. 1500–1545)
The Flaying of Marsyas
1533
marble, 73 × 60 × 7 cm (28 ¾ × 23 ⅝ × 2 ¾ in.)
Private collection

Jacopo Sansovino may have taken Silvio Cosini on as a pupil in Florence as early as 1515 to 1520. In 1533 Cosini is securely recorded as working at the Santo in Padua, the workshop of which was directed by Sansovino.[1] In the same year, Silvio Cosini and his brother Vincenzo worked at a marble workshop in Venice on Sansovino's tomb, which was being planned for the Frari church in the same city.[2] Cosini arrived in Padua by September 1533 and there is no further description of his work on Sansovino's tomb. The marble components of the monument, including Cosini's sculptures, were still in storage in 1568 and were in fact never assembled in the tomb. The discovery of this relief by Cosini showing the Flaying of Marsyas raises the intriguing possibility that it was intended for Sansovino's tomb.

THE TOMB OF JACOPO SANNAZARO

Cosini's *Flaying of Marsyas* is closely related to *Arcadia*, the central relief of the tomb of the celebrated poet Jacopo Sannazaro (FIG. 1). Close in size and style, the works may also have shared the same decorative role in funerary monuments. The commission for Sannazaro's tomb (FIG. 2) was given to Giovan Angelo Montorsoli at the end of 1536 or beginning of 1537, and completed in 1541.[3] The base of the tomb is signed by Montorsoli, but several other artists were involved in the project. According to Vasari, part of the architectural carving is by Francesco Ferrucci del Tadda,[4] while Borghini reports that Bartolomeo Ammannati made three figures for the project, very likely the two putti holding the epigram and the figure of Saint Nazarius.[5]

Vasari also states that Montorsoli carved a "historical scene with figures in half relief" for the tomb.[6] This may have been selective memory on Vasari's part, since he was keen to emphasize the importance of the art establishment in Florence, which included Montorsoli as the founder of the Accademia, with the result that Cosini's role in the tomb was ignored. Since Montorsoli directed the project and his name appears on the base, there has been an understandable tendency to attribute its major components to him.[7] In fact, Cosini is not documented as working on Sannazaro's tomb, but he did work closely with Montorsoli in Genoa around 1540 to 1544, for example, on the monumental statue of Andrea Doria and the decorations in the church of San Matteo.[8] Since Montorsoli carved the Sannazaro tomb in Carrara and Genoa (when Cosini was also there) and sent the components to Naples in late 1541, Cosini's participation in the project seems very likely.

The *Arcadia* relief is loosely based on the tenth eclogue of *Arcadia*, written by Sannazaro between 1480 and the 1490s, and published in Naples in 1504. The relief is stylistically unlike other works by Montorsoli, being more detailed and varied in texture. Conceived in pictorial terms, the relief subtly blends the figures into the landscape, with the surface worked in a variety of techniques to create a rich sense of light and shadow. The *Arcadia* relates closely to the *Flaying of Marsyas*, which depicts Apollo torturing the satyr Marsyas for daring to challenge him in music, and both can be attributed with confidence to Silvio Cosini.[9] The twisting, flexed figures of Marsyas and Neptune are not only similar in pose, but are carved in an almost identical manner. The rounded forms of the trees are also analogous. It is typical of Cosini to leave drill holes and gradine marks visible to heighten the

FIG. 1
Silvio Cosini, *Arcadia*, 1536/37–41. Marble,
91 × 100.5 cm. Tomb of Jacopo Sannazaro,
Santa Maria del Parto a Margellina, Naples.

FIG. 2
Giovan Angelo Montorsoli and others,
Tomb of Jacopo Sannazaro, 1536–41. Marble,
height 485 cm. Santa Maria del Parto a
Margellina, Naples.

FIG. 3
Silvio Cosini, *Presentation of the Virgin*,
ca. 1540. Marble, 172 × 98 cm.
Cathedral, Savona.

effects of light. The two reliefs can be compared to Cosini's relief of the *Presentation of the Virgin* (FIG. 3) in the cathedral of Savona, which was carved around 1540.[10] The billowing drapery of Apollo in the Marsyas relief is similar to that of Cosini's stucco figures in the Hall of Giants at the Villa del Principe, Genoa (FIG. 4), made from 1531 to 1532.

THE FLAYING OF MARSYAS

If Cosini carved the *Flaying of Marsyas* in 1533 for Sansovino's tomb, then it is possible that a few years later, around 1537, he convinced Montorsoli to adopt the idea of a mythological relief of about the same size, specifically tailored to the poetry of Jacopo Sannazaro. The *Flaying of Marsyas* can therefore be considered the direct precursor of the *Arcadia* relief. Moreover, Cosini's earlier relief influenced artistic developments in Venice. The contortion of Marsyas's body and the features of Apollo's face seem to have inspired Francesco

Salviati's frescos of 1540 in the Camerino of Apollo in the Palazzo Grimani (FIG. 5).[11] The subject is also depicted on the Loggetta of the Campanile in Venice (FIG. 6), a monument planned and directed by Sansovino in the 1540s, although he did not carve the relief, which is poorly preserved.[12] The figure of the satyr is almost precisely quoted from Cosini's version, which demonstrates that his work was well known and commanded respect from Sansovino, who apparently asked his workshop to use his tomb relief as a model.

According to an ancient Greek myth, the satyr Marsyas played a double flute so well that he decided to challenge Apollo, the god of music.[13] The Muses could not decide the winner of the contest until Apollo began to sing and play simultaneously, or, in another version of the story, played his instrument upside down. As punishment for challenging a god, Marsyas was condemned to be skinned alive by Apollo himself.

FIG. 4
Silvio Cosini, *Dance of a Satyr and
Nymphs*, 1531–32. Stucco. Hall of
Giants, Villa del Principe, Genoa.

FIG. 5
Francesco Salviati, *Flaying of Marsyas*,
1540. Fresco. Camerino of Apollo,
Palazzo Grimani, Venice.

FIG. 6
Workshop of Jacopo Sansovino, *Flaying of
Marsyas*, 1540s. Marble. Loggetta, Piazza
San Marco, Venice.

In Cosini's relief, Marsyas is tied to a tree by one hand. Apollo has begun to slice Marsyas's shoulder, drawing blood. In the back at left, two goat-legged satyrs (unlike Marsyas, who is depicted with human legs) lament Marsyas's fate. Ovid, in the *Metamorphoses* (6.392–95), writes: "The country folk, the forest deities, the fauns, and his brother satyrs all wept."[14]

An important source for the tale is the Italian translation of Ovid published in Venice in 1497, which was accompanied by fifty-two woodcuts.[15] In the print showing Apollo flaying Marsyas (FIG. 7), the musical instrument is not the double flute mentioned in most ancient sources, but a bagpipe, exactly as seen in Cosini's relief. Two seated figures play bagpipes in the print, while a third

FIG. 7
Flaying of Marsyas. Woodcut from
Ovidio Methamorphoseos vulgare (Venice,
1497). Signed "ia," perhaps Jacobus
Argentoratensis.

instrument lies on the ground in front of Marsyas. Both the print and the sculpture show Marsyas not as a satyr with goat legs, but as a human, a fairly common form in the sixteenth century.

The story of the Flaying of Marsyas is a reminder that real human dissections often took place in the Renaissance for scientific and artistic purposes. Michelangelo's mastery of art was explained by his "flaying [*scorticando*] dead bodies to study anatomical matters."[16] Giorgio Vasari tells a macabre story that Silvio Cosini went far beyond the mere study of corpses. Cosini took the body of a hanged man and, "after dissecting it in the interests of art, being capricious and perhaps a necromancer and someone who believed in magic and such follies, he flayed it completely, and prepared the skin as he had been taught, and thinking that it had some great power, made a tunic that he wore for a while over his shirt without anyone ever knowing."[17] Unsurprisingly, Vasari considered this "the strangest thing in the world."

LAOCOON

The figures of Neptune and Marsyas in Cosini's two reliefs (CAT. 27 and FIG. 1) are strongly indebted to the ancient sculpture of *Laocoon*, which was restored in 1532 to 1533 by Cosini's close friend and collaborator, Giovan Angelo Montorsoli. In essence, Cosini offers alternative reconstructions of Laocoon's missing arm. In the Sannazaro relief, Neptune's right arm stretches diagonally outward in a manner similar to Montorsoli's reconstruction (p. 49). In contrast, in the Marsyas relief, the right arm is shown sharply bent back. The gesture is close to the original arm (p. 50), although it was only discovered in 1905.[18]

Lorenzo Principi

PROVENANCE

The relief is first recorded in 1966 when the dealer Ettore Viancini, Venice, exhibited it as by Baccio Bandinelli (*3a Mostra nazionale dell'antiquariato: Roma, Palazzo Braschi* [Rome 1966], fig. XVIII). It belonged to Paul and Eula Ganz, and then to Anthony Roth, London. It was sold after his death by Sotheby's, London, December 9, 1993 (lot 71), as attributed to François Marchand.

1. Principi 2014, pp. 112–14.

2. The workshop was near San Silvestro al Canal Grande. Boucher 1991, vol. 1, pp. 233–34, doc. 256 (testament of 1568).

3. Laschke 1993, pp. 16, 53. Principi 2014, pp. 116–17.

4. Vasari 1966, vol. 5, p. 496.

5. Borghini 1584, p. 590. The figures are identified by Davis 1977, pp. 71–73.

6. Vasari 1966, vol. 5, p. 497: "Là dove [to Carrara] andò il frate molto volentieri per tirare innanzi con quell'occasione la detta sepoltura del Sanazaro, e particolarmente una storia di figure di mezzo rilievo."

7. Laschke 1993, pp. 45–57, 160 (with earlier references).

8. Principi 2014, pp. 114–18.

9. The relief is attributed to Cosini by Ciardi Dupré 1961, pp. 11–12; Principi 2014, p. 115–16; Principi 2017, pp. 7–8. It is attributed to Montorsoli by Laschke 1993, pp. 55–56.

10. Principi 2017.

11. Tempestini 2005.

12. Boucher 1991, vol. 2, pp. 334–35, no. 27.

13. On Marsyas in the Renaissance, see Wyss 1996; and Faticcioni 2007.

14. Illum ruricolae, silvarum numina, fauni / et satyri fratres et tunc quoque carus Olympus / et nymphae flerunt, et quisquis montibus illis / lanigerosque greges armentaque bucera pavit.

15. *Ovidio Methamorphoseos vulgare* (Venice, 1497). The Italian translation is by Giovanni Bonsignori (active 14th century). On the woodcuts, see Wyss 1996, pp. 83–85.

16. Vasari 1966, vol. 6, p. 13: "dove molte volte scorticando corpi morti per studiare le cose di notomia, cominciò a dare perfezzione al gran disegno che gl' ebbe poi."

17. Vasari 1966, vol. 4, p. 260: "e dopo averne fatto notomia per conto dell'arte, come capriccioso e forse maliastro, e persona che prestava fede agl'incanti e simili sciocchezze, lo scorticò tutto, et acconciata la pelle secondo che gl'era stato insegnato, se ne fece, pensando che avesse qualche gran virtù, un coietto, e quello portò per alcun tempo sopra la camicia, senza che nessuno lo sapesse già mai." See Campbell 2002, p. 602; Bohde 2003, pp. 28–29.

18. Another coincidence is the similarity of the figure of Marsyas in the 1497 woodcut with the unrestored *Laocoon*, as seen in reverse. The positions of the legs are nearly identical.

CAT. 28
Benedetto da Maiano (1442–1497)
Virgin and Child
ca. 1490
painted terracotta, height 107 cm (42 in.)
Currier Museum of Art, Manchester
Museum Purchase: Currier Funds, 1945.3

Benedetto da Maiano spent much of his career working in Naples and Calabria, as one of the many artists from Florence who travelled to the south. For example, Giovan Angelo Montorsoli also undertook major commissions in Naples and Sicily in the middle of the sixteenth century.

This painted terracotta sculpture of the standing Virgin carrying the infant Christ is closely related to several marble works carved by Benedetto da Maiano for southern Italian patrons.[1] The Currier Museum's *Virgin and Child* is the only known terracotta of this type by the artist, and is especially close to the sculpture in Santa Maria Assunta e San Elia in Terranova Sappo Minulio (40 km northeast of Reggia Calabria), where very similar figures are set against an elaborate rocky landscape (FIG. 1).[2]

The popularity of the standing Virgin holding the Christ Child in small southern Italian towns is striking, especially since no examples of the type by Benedetto exist in his native Tuscany. These commissions are connected with the sculptor's activity in Naples between 1475 and 1497, when

FIG. I
Benedetto da Maiano, *Virgin and Child*
(Madonna della Neve), ca. 1490. Marble. Santa
Maria Assunta e San Elia, Terranova Sappo
Minulio (Calabria).

he worked for the royal court there and for Marino Curiale, a confidant of King Alfonso II of Naples. A large altarpiece in the church of Santa Caterina in Terranova from around 1490 was very likely a commission from Curiale, who was count of Terranova. The central figure of this dispersed altarpiece is a standing Virgin and Child similar to the Currier Museum's work. It has been suggested that this terracotta may be the preparatory model for the marble, as the artist sometimes initiated projects with full-scale terracotta models.[3] On the other hand, the Currier Museum's sculpture does not appear to be a working model since it is highly finished enough for permanent display. Indeed, the artist created other polychromed terracottas of the Virgin and Child in different poses, including a roundel (Isabella Stewart Gardner Museum, Boston) and enthroned figures in the cathedral of Prato and the Bode-Museum, Berlin.[4] Another, less-refined terracotta of the standing Virgin holding the Christ Child has been attributed to Benedetto da Maiano.[5] In sum, the terracotta in the Currier Museum was probably destined for a church in Naples or the surrounding region.
Alan Chong

PROVENANCE

Duveen Brothers, New York, sold the work in 1914 to Elbert H. Gary, New York.[6] Returned to Duveen Brothers, who sold it in March 1928 for $15,000, to Leon Schinasi, New York; to Mrs. Leon Schinasi, New York; auctioned at Parke-Bernet, New York, Nov. 3, 1944 (lot 374), sold for $5,500 to French and Co., New York; sold to the Currier Gallery of Art for a 15% commission in Jan. 1945.

This terracotta was owned by two remarkable American collectors of the early twentieth century. Elbert Gary (1846–1927) was one of the founders of US Steel Corporation and its first president. The planned city of Gary, Indiana, was named after him. Gary apparently did not actually own the sculpture, as it is listed as on approval in Duveen's account books from 1914 to 1928, when it was sold to Leon Schinasi (1890–1930) of New York. Schinasi had

FIG. 2
CAT. 28 in the frame made
for it by the Duveen
Brothers around 1914.

inherited a successful cigarette business from his father, an immigrant from the Ottoman Empire. Leon and his wife, Ruby Smith Salmon Schinasi, were involved in a series of salacious lawsuits with a cousin, Nettie Stoeve, who accused Mrs. Schinasi of doping her husband with morphine to force him to alter his will.[7]

Although this sculpture has always been attributed to Benedetto da Maiano (it was illustrated in Dussler's monograph of 1924 and exhibited in the New York World's Fair in 1939), its value dropped precipitously in the course of the twentieth century. Valued at $48,000 in 1914, it was sold to Schinasi just fourteen years later for a third of that at $15,000, and it made only a third of that in 1944. This is evidence of the decline in appreciation for Quattrocento sculpture, with the exception of the spending sprees that Andrew Mellon and S. H. Kress embarked on in preparation for the opening of the National Gallery of Art in Washington in 1941.

REFERENCES
Dussler 1924, p. 82, no. 37, fig. 29 [Benedetto da Maiano, late 1480s]. New York 1939, no. 414 [lent by Mrs. Schinasi]. Lein 1988, p. 223 [attributed to Benedetto]. Carl 2006, vol. 1, p. 109, pl. 53. Caglioti 2007, pp. 18, 26, 37.

---

1. Carl 2006, pp. 105–11, pls. 32–52. Examples at Nicotera, Morano Calabro, Amantea, Bombile, and Terranova Sappo Minulio, as well as a half-length figure in Pietrapennata.

2. Carl 2006, pp. 108–9.

3. Carl 2006, pls. 157–61. See also Pope-Hennessy 1964, vol. 1, p. 157; Radke 1992.

4. Carl 2006, pls. 23, VI, 26 (a related figure of Charity).

5.   Carlo De Carlo, Florence; see Caglioti 2007, pp. 18, 27.

6.   Duveen Brothers records: client book, G–H, no. 6, for 1914: "1 Terra cotta painted group, The Virgin & Child by Benedetto da Majano. 48,000." However, Duveen carried the object and its costs in its stock books as inventory number 26873 until 1928, with Gary listed as having it only on approval, and with book values declining to $15,000, $12,000, and then $8,000. In the 1927 stock book the sculpture is finally recorded as sold, to Leon Schinasi.

7.   New York Supreme Court AD; *New York Times* (Oct. 23, 1934), p. 8. The suit was settled for a token sum: *New York Times* (Jan. 8, 1936), p. 22.

FIG. 3
Back of CAT. 28.

SIC·ROMAE·EX·MARMORE·SCVLPTO

·LAOCHOON·

·ROMAE·IN·PALATIO·PONT·IN·
·LOCO·QVI·VVLGO·DICITVR·
·BELVEDERE·

168   BIBLIOGRAPHY

Most references from before 1940 are
available through archive.org, europeana.eu,
Gallica, HathiTrust, and other sites.
Journal articles have often been accessed
through JSTOR and DigiZeitschriften, etc.

Achilles-Syndram 1994
Katrin Achilles-Syndram, ed. *Die
Kunstsammlung des Paulus Praun: Die
Inventare von 1616 und 1719*. Nuremberg,
1994.

Ackley 1981
Clifford S. Ackley. *Printmaking in the Age
of Rembrandt*. Exh. Museum of Fine Arts,
Boston; and Saint Louis Art Museum,
1980–81. Boston, 1981.

Albèri 1846
Eugenio Albèri, ed. *Le relazioni degli
ambasciatori veneti al senato*. Series 2, vol. 3.
Florence, 1846.

Alizeri 1870
Federigo Alizeri. *Notizie dei professori del
disegno in Liguria dalle origini al secolo XVI*.
6 vols. Genoa, 1870–80.

Amsterdam et al. 1998
Adriaen de Vries, 1556–1626. Exh.
Rijksmuseum, Amsterdam, et al.
1998–2000. By Frits Scholten et al.

Androsov 2008
Sergei Androsov. *Museo Statale Ermitage:
La scultura italiana dal XIV al XVI secolo*.
Milan, 2008.

Arciniega 2013
Luis Arciniega García. "Las esculturas
encargadas por Carlos V a Leone Leoni en
1549 y su acabado en España por Pompeo
Leoni." *Archivo español de arte* 86 (2013),
pp. 87–106.

Aricò 2013
Nicola Aricò. *Architettura del tardo
Rinascimento in Sicilia: Giovannangelo
Montorsoli a Messina (1547–57)*. Florence,
2013.

Atlanta and Los Angeles 2009
Leonardo da Vinci and the Art of Sculpture.
Exh. High Museum of Art, Atlanta;
and J. Paul Getty Museum, Los Angeles,
2009–10. By Gary M. Radke et al.

Attwood 2003
Philip Attwood. *Italian Medals c.
1530–1600 in British Public Collections*. 2
vols. London, 2003.

Avery 1981
Charles Avery. *Fingerprints of the Artist:
European Terra-Cotta Sculpture from the
Arthur M. Sackler Collections*. Washington,
1981.

Avery 1999
Victoria J. Avery. *Documenti sulla vita e le
opere di Alessandro Vittoria (c. 1525–1608)*.
Trento, 1999.

Avery 2002
Victoria J. Avery. *Renaissance and Baroque
Bronzes from the Fitzwilliam Museum,
Cambridge*. Exh. Daniel Katz Ltd., London,
2002.

Avery 2016
Charles Avery. *Joseph de Levis & Company:
Renaissance Bronze-Founders in Verona*.
London, 2016.

Bacchi 1995
Andrea Bacchi. "Zaccaria Zacchi eccellente
statuario" in *Il Castello del Buonconsiglio*,
vol. 1: *Percorso nel Magno Palazzo* (Trento,
1995), pp. 262–95.

Baccioni 1708
Giuseppi Baccioni. *Ristretto degli obblighi
spirituali che hanno i fratelli d[e]ll'antica,
divota e veneranda compagnia del nome
Santissimo di Giesù, sotto la protezione del
precursore S. Giovanbattista detta lo Scalzo,
della città di Firenze, cavato da' suoi capitoli*.
Florence, 1708.

Baldinucci 1681
Filippo Baldinucci. *Vocabolario toscano
dell'arte del disegno*. Florence, 1681.

Bambach 2017
Carmen C. Bambach. *Michelangelo, Divine
Draftsman and Designer*. Exh. Metropolitan
Museum of Art, New York, 2017–18.

Bardeschi Ciulich and Barocchi 1970
Lucilla Bardeschi Ciulich and Paola
Barocchi, eds. *I ricordi di Michelangelo*.
Florence, 1970.

Barkan 1999
Leonard Barkan. *Unearthing the Past:
Archaeology and Aesthetics in the Making of
Renaissance Culture*. New Haven, 1999.

Barnes 2010
Bernadine Barnes. *Michelangelo in Print:
Reproductions as Response in the Sixteenth
Century*. London, 2010.

Bartalini 2001
Roberto Bartalini. "Sodoma, the Chigi and
the Vatican Stanze." *Burlington Magazine*
143 (2001), pp. 544–53.

Bartoli 1567
Cosimo Bartoli. *Ragionamenti accademici*.
Venice, 1567.

Battisti 1965
Eugenio Battisti. "Disegni inediti del
Montorsoli." *Arte lombarda* 10 (1965),
pp. 143–48.

Bentz 2013
Katherine M. Bentz. "The afterlife of the
Cesi Garden: Family identity, politics, and
memory in early modern Rome." *Journal
of the Society of Architectural Historians* 72
(2013), pp. 134–65.

Berger 1994
Ursel Berger. "Eine Plastiksammlung mit
dem Bildhauernachlass von Johann Gregor
van der Schardt" in Achilles-Syndram
1994, pp. 43–60.

Bertini 2005
Cristina Bertini. "Giovanni degli Alessandri
e la conservazione delle opere d'arte."
Arte musica spettacolo 6/7 (2005–6),
pp. 135–59.

Bianchi 2003
Silvia Bianchi. "Catalogo dell'opera incisa di
Nicola Beatrizet (III parte)." *Grafica d'arte*
14, no. 56 (2003), pp. 3–12. [Article in 4
parts: nos. 54–57.]

Blanco and Lorente 1969
Antonio Blanco and Manuel Lorente.
Museo del Prado: Catálogo de la escultura.
Madrid, 1969.

Bloemacher 2016
Anne Bloemacher. *Raffael und Raimondi:
Produktion und Intention der frühen
Druckgraphik nach Raphael.* Berlin, 2016.

Bober and Rubinstein 2010
Phyllis Pray Bober and Ruth Rubinstein.
*Renaissance Artists and Antique Sculpture: A
Handbook of Sources.* 2nd edition. London,
2010. 1st edition: London, 1986.

Boccardo et al. 2004
Piero Boccardo et al., eds. *España y Génova:
Obras, artistas y coleccionistas.* Madrid,
2004. Italian edition: *Genova e la Spagna:
Opere, artisti, committenti, collezionisti*
(Milan, 2002).

Bodart 2011
Diane Bodart. *Pouvoirs du portrait sous les
Habsbourg d'Espagne.* Paris, 2011.

Bode 1883
Wilhelm Bode. "Die Ausstellung von
Gemälden älterer Meister im berliner
Privatbesitz." *Jahrbuch der Königlich
Preussischen Kunstsammlungen* 4 (1883),
pp. 130–38.

Bode 1890
Wilhelm Bode. "Versuche der Ausbildung
des Genre in der Florentiner Plastik des
Quattrocento." *Jahrbuch der Preussischen
Kunstsammlungen* 11 (1890), pp. 95–107.

Bode 1891
Wilhelm Bode. *Handbücher der Königlichen
Museen zu Berlin: Die Italienische Plastik.*
Berlin, 1891.

Bode 1892
Willhem Bode. *Denkmäler der Renaissance-
Sculptur Toscanas.* Munich, 1892–1905.

Bode 1901
Wilhelm Bode. "Ein florentiner
Thonbildner vom Anfang der
Hochrenaissance." *Zeitschrift für bildende
Kunst* 37 (1901–2), pp. 1–4.

Bode 1902
Wilhelm Bode, ed. *Florentiner Bildhauer der
Renaissance in historischer Anordnung.* 12
vols. Berlin, 1902.

Bode 1904
Wilhelm Bode. *The Art Collection of Mr.
Alfred Beit at His Residence 26 Park Lane,
London.* Berlin, 1904.

Bode 1907
Wilhelm Bode. Assisted by Murray
Marks. *The Italian Bronze Statuettes of the
Renaissance.* 3 vols. London, 1907.

Bode 1913
Wilhelm Bode. *Catalogue of the Collection of
Pictures and Bronzes in the Possession of Mr.
Otto Beit.* London, 1913.

Bode 1980
Wilhelm Bode. Edited by James David
Draper. *The Italian Bronze Statuettes of the
Renaissance.* New York, 1980.

Bohde 2003
Daniela Bohde. "Skin and the search for
the interior: The representation of flaying
in the art and anatomy of the Cinquecento"
in *Bodily Extremities: Preoccupations with
the Human Body in Early Modern European
Culture,* edited by Florike Egmond and
Robert Zwijnenberg (Aldershot, 2003),
pp. 10–47.

Bonn 2015
Der Göttliche: Hommage an Michelangelo.
Exh. Kunst- und Ausstellungshalle der
Bundesrepublik Deutschland, Bonn, 2015.

Boon 1978
K. G. Boon. *Netherlandish Drawings of the
Fifteenth and Sixteenth Centuries.* Catalogus
van de Nederlandse tekeningen in het
Rijksmuseum te Amsterdam, part 2. 2 vols.
The Hague, 1978.

Borghini 1584
Raffaello Borghini. *Il riposo.* Florence, 1584.

Borroni Salvadori 1974
Fabia Borroni Salvadori. "Le esposizioni
d'arte a Firenze dal 1674 al 1767."
*Mitteilungen des Kunsthistorischen Institutes
in Florenz* 18 (1974), pp. 1–166.

Boston and Florence 2003
Raphael, Cellini, and a Renaissance Banker.
Exh. Isabella Stewart Gardner Museum,
Boston; and Museo Nazionale del Bargello,
Florence, 2003–4. Edited by Alan Chong,
Donatella Pegazzano, and Dimitrios Zikos.

Boucher 1991
Bruce Boucher. *The Sculpture of Jacopo
Sansovino.* 2 vols. New Haven, 1991.

Brandt 2001
Aurelia Brandt. "Goltzius and the antique."
Print Quarterly 18 (2001), pp. 135–49.

Brilliant 2000
Richard Brilliant. *My Laocoön: Alternative
Claims in the Interpretation of Artworks.*
Berkeley, 2000.

Brook 2003
Anthea Brook. "Au Département des
sculptures du Louvre, 'Bacchus et un satyre'
de Francesco Susini (1585–v. 1653)." *Revue
du Louvre* 53, no. 1 (2003), pp. 48–58.

Brummer 1970
Hans Henrik Brummer. *The Statue Court
in the Vatican Belvedere.* Stockholm, 1970.

Brun 2014
Brun Fine Art. *A Taste for Sculpture:
Marble, Terracotta and Ivory (16th to
20th Centuries).* Edited by Andrea Bacchi.
London, 2014.

Buranelli 2006
Francesco Buranelli. "La scoperta del
Laocoonte e il Cortile delle Statue in
Vaticano" in Rome 2006, pp. 49–60.

Bury 1996
Michael Bury. "Beatrizet and the 'repro-
duction' of antique relief sculpture." *Print
Quarterly* 13 (1996), pp. 111–26.

Bury and Lockett 2011
Michael Bury and Katharine Lockett.
"Béatrizet's 'Last Judgement', after
Michelangelo, in the Courtauld Gallery."
Print Quarterly 28 (2011), pp. 266–71.

Bustamante and Marías 1991
Agustín Bustamante and Fernando Marías.
"Álbum de Fra Giovanni Vincenzo Casale"
in *Dibujos de arquitectura y ornamentación
de la Biblioteca Nacional, siglos XVI y XVII*
(Madrid, 1991), pp. 213–312.

Butterfield and Franklin 1998
Andrew Butterfield and David
Franklin. "A documented episode in
the history of renaissance 'terracruda'
sculpture." *Burlington Magazine* 140
(1998), pp. 819–24.

Cadenas y Vicent 1977
Vicente de Cadenas y Vicent. *El protecto-
rado de Carlos V en Génova: La "condotta"
de Andrea Doria.* Madrid, 1977.

Caglioti 1996
Francesco Caglioti. "Il perduto 'David
mediceo' di Giovanfrancesco Rustici e il
'David' Pulszky del Louvre." *Prospettiva*, nos.
83/84 (1996), pp. 80–101.

Caglioti 2007
Francesco Caglioti. "Nuove terracotte di
Benedetto da Maiano." *Prospettiva* 126–27
(2007), pp. 15–45.

Caglioti 2012
Francesco Caglioti. "Il 'San Giovannino'
mediceo di Michelangelo, da Firenze
a Úbeda." *Prospettiva*, no. 145 (2012),
pp. 2–81.

Caglioti 2012a
Francesco Caglioti. "Benedetto da
Rovezzano in England: New light on the
Cardinal Wolsey-Henry VIII tomb" in
*The Anglo-Florentine Renaissance: Arts
for the Early Tudors* (New Haven, 2012),
pp. 177–202.

Cambareri 2016
Marietta Cambareri. *Della Robbia:
Sculpting with Color in Renaissance Florence.*
Exh. Museum of Fine Arts, Boston; and
National Gallery of Art, Washington,
2016–17.

Campbell 2002
Stephen J. Campbell. "'Fare una cosa morta
parer viva': Michelangelo, Rosso, and the
(un)divinity of art." *Art Bulletin* 84 (2002),
pp. 596–620.

Campigli 2005
Marco Campigli. "Silvio Cosini: Scultore
di marmo e di stucco tra la Toscana e il
Veneto." PhD thesis: Università degli Studi
di Udine, 2005.

Campigli 2006
Marco Campigli. "Silvio Cosini e
Michelangelo." *Nuovi studi*, no. 12 (2006),
pp. 85–116.

Campigli 2014
Marco Campigli. "Silvio Cosini, Niccolò da
Corte e la scultura a Palazzo Doria." *Nuovi
studi*, no. 20 (2014), pp. 83–104.

Campori 1873
Giuseppi Campori. *Memorie biografiche
degli scultori, architetti, pittori ec. nativi di
Carrara e di altri luoghi della provincia di
Massa.* Modena, 1873.

Capecchi 2017
Gabriele Capecchi. *Ipotesi su Castello:
L'iconografia di Niccolò Tribolo e il giardino
delle origini (1538–1550).* Florence, 2017.

Carl 2006
Doris Carl. *Benedetto da Maiano, A
Florentine Sculptor at the Threshold of the
High Renaissance.* 2 vols. Turnhout, 2006.

Carpi 2009
*Ugo da Carpi: L'opera incisa: Xilografie
e chiaroscuri da Tiziano, Raffaello e
Parmigianino.* Exh. Palazzo dei Pio, Carpi,
2009. Edited by Manuela Rossi.

Carroll 1987
Eugene A. Carroll. *Rosso Fiorentino:
Drawings, Prints, and Decorative Arts.* Exh.
National Gallery of Art, Washington,
1987–88.

Casalini 1974
Eugenio M. Casalini. "Il Montorsoli e le
statue del coro dell'Annunziata di Firenze."
Studi storici dell'ordine dei Servi di Maria 24
(1974), pp. 288–304. Reprinted in Ircani
Menichini 2013.

Catterson 2005
Lynn Catterson. "Michelangelo's 'Laocoön?'"
Artibus et Historiae 26 (2005), pp. 29–56.

Cazzato et al. 2002
Vincenzo Cazzato et al., eds. *Atlante delle
grotte e dei ninfei in Italia: Italia settentrio-
nale, Umbria e Marche.* Milan, 2002.

Cecchi 1986
Alessandro Cecchi. "Profili di amici
e committenti" in *Andrea del Sarto,
1486–1530: Dipinti e disegni a Firenze* (exh.
Palazzo Pitti, Florence, 1986), pp. 42–58.

Cellini 1901
*Vita di Benvenuto Cellini: Testo critico con
introduzione e note storiche.* Florence, 1901.
Edited by Orazio Bacci.

Checa 1987
Fernando Checa Cremades. *Carlos V y la
imagen del héroe en el Renacimiento.* Madrid,
1987.

Chellini 2009
Riccardo Chellini, ed. *Chronica de origine
civitatis Florentiae.* Rome, 2009.

Cherubini 2005
Alessandro Cherubini. "Bartolomeo
Ammannati 'ad hominum utilitatem.'"
Artista (2005), pp. 100–185.

Chicago 1998
*From the Sculptor's Hand: Italian Baroque
Terracottas from the State Hermitage
Museum.* Exh. Art Institute of Chicago
and Philadelphia Museum of Art, 1998.
Organized by Ian Wardropper.

Chicago 2008
The Virtual Tourist in Renaissance Rome: Printing and Collecting in the Speculum Romanae Magnificentiae. Exh. University of Chicago Library, 2008. By Rebecca Zorach et al.

Chicago et al. 2005
Paper Museums: The Reproductive Print in Europe, 1500–1800. Exh. Smart Museum of Art, Chicago, et al. 2005. By Rebecca Zorach, Elizabeth Rodini, et al.

Chong 2009
Alan Chong. "Émile Gavet, patron, collector, dealer" in *Gothic Art in the Gilded Age: Medieval Treasures in the Gavet-Vanderbilt-Ringling Collection* (exh. John and Mable Ringling Museum of Art, Sarasota, 2009), pp. 1–21.

Chretien 1994
Heidi L. Chretien. *The Festival of San Giovanni: Imagery and Political Power in Renaissance Florence.* New York, 1994.

Cianchi 1995
Mario Cianchi, ed. *Pierino da Vinci: Atti della giornata di studio.* Florence, 1995.

Ciardi 2003
John Ciardi, trans. Dante Alighieri. *The Divine Comedy: The Inferno, the Purgatorio, and the Paradiso.* New York, 2003.

Ciardi et al. 1988
Roberto Paolo Ciardi et al., eds. *Scultura del '500 a Volterra.* Volterra, 1988.

Ciardi Dupré 1961
Maria Grazia Ciardi Dupré. "La prima attività dell'Ammannati scultore." *Paragone* 12 (1961), pp. 3–28.

Ciardi Dupré 1963
Maria Grazia Ciardi Duprè. "Giovan Francesco Rustici." *Paragone* 14 (1963), pp. 29–50.

Cinelli et al. 2002
Carlo Cinelli et al. *Il ciclo degli Apostoli nel Duomo di Firenze.* Florence, 2002.

Clark 1956
Kenneth Clark. *The Nude: A Study of Ideal Art.* London, 1956.

Cleveland 1942
Cleveland Museum of Art. *Catalogue of the John L. Severance Collection: Bequest of John L. Severance, 1936.* Cleveland, 1942.

Collareta 1985
Marco Collareta. "Michelangelo e le statue antiche: Un probabile intervento di restauro." *Prospettiva*, no. 43 (1985), pp. 51–55.

Collareta 1992
Marco Collareta. "Intorno ai disegni murali della Sagrestia Nuova." *Studies in the History of Art* 33 (1992), pp. 162–77.

Colnaghi 1965
P. and D. Colnaghi and Co. *Exhibition of Seventeenth and Eighteenth Century Italian Sculpture.* London, 1965.

Coonin 1995
Arnold Victor Coonin. "Portrait busts of children in Quattrocento Florence." *Metropolitan Museum Journal* 30 (1995), pp. 61–71.

Coppel 1998
Rosario Coppel Aréizaga. *Museo del Prado: Catálogo de la escultura de época moderna, siglos XVI–XVIII.* Madrid, 1998.

Cropper 1997
Elizabeth Cropper. *Pontormo: Portrait of a Halberdier.* Los Angeles, 1997.

Dalli Regoli and Turchi 1991
Gigetta Dalli Regoli and S. Taccini Turchi. *Silvius magister: Silvio Cosini e il suo ruolo nella scultura toscana del primo Cinquecento.* Galatina, 1991.

Dal Poggetto 1979
Paolo Dal Poggetto. *I disegni murali di Michelangiolo e della sua scuola nella Sagrestia Nuova di San Lorenzo.* Florence, 1979.

Dal Poggetto 2012
Paolo Dal Poggetto. *Michelangelo: La "stanza segreta": I disegni murali nella Sagrestia Nuova di San Lorenzo.* 2nd edition. Florence, 2012.

Daltrop 1982
Georg Daltrop. *Die Laokoongruppe im Vatikan: Ein Kapitel aus der römischen Museumsgeschichte und der Antiken-Erkundung.* Konstanz, 1982.

D'Amico 1987
John F. D'Amico. "The Raffaele Maffei monument in Volterra: Small town patronage in the Renaissance" in *Supplementum Festivum: Studies in Honor of Paul Oskar Kristeller*, edited by James Hankins et al. (Binghamton, N.Y., 1987), pp. 469–88.

Darr and Roisman 1987
Alan Phipps Darr and Rona Roisman. "Francesco da Sangallo: A rediscovered early Donatellesque 'Magdalen' and two wills from 1574 and 1576." *Burlington Magazine* 129 (1987), pp. 784–93.

Darr et al. 2002
Alan P. Darr, Peter Barnet, and Antonia Boström. *Catalogue of Italian Sculpture in the Detroit Institute of Arts.* 2 vols. London, 2002.

Davis 1976
Charles Davis. "Benvenuto Cellini and the Scuola fiorentina." *North Carolina Museum of Art Bulletin* 13 (1976), pp. 1–70.

Davis 1977
Charles Davis. "The tomb of Mario Nari for the SS. Annunziata in Florence: The sculptor Bartolomeo Ammannati until 1544." *Mitteilungen des Kunsthistorischen Institutes in Florenz* 21 (1977), pp. 69–94.

Davis 1989
John H. Davis. *The Guggenheims (1848–1988): An American Epic.* New York, 1989.

172

Davis 2014
Charles Davis. "Three Roman cardinals: Portrait busts by Leonardo Sormano" in *La festa delle arti: Scritti in onore di Marcello Fagiolo per cinquant'anni di studi*, edited by Vincenzo Cazzato et al. (Rome, 2014), pp. 278–81.

De' Maffei 1964
Fernanda De' Maffei. *Michelangelo's Lost St. John*. New York, 1964.

Delaborde 1888
Henri Delaborde. *Marc-Antoine Raimondi: Étude historique et critique suivie d'un catalogue raisonné des oeuvres du maître*. Paris [1888].

Del Bravo 1992
Carlo Del Bravo. "Silvio e la magia." *Artista* (1992), pp. 8–19.

Detroit and Florence 1974
The Twilight of the Medici: Late Baroque Art in Florence, 1670–1743. Exh. Detroit Institute of Arts and Palazzo Davanzati, Florence, 1974.

Detroit and Fort Worth 1985
Italian Renaissance Sculpture in the Time of Donatello. Exh. Detroit Institute of Arts and Kimbell Art Museum, Fort Worth, 1985–86.

Diemer 2004
Dorothea Diemer. *Hubert Gerhard und Carlo di Cesare del Palagio: Bronzeplastiker der Spätrenaissance*. 2 vols. Berlin, 2004.

Dillon 2018
Sarah M. Dillon. "The problematic 'Baptist': Benedetto da Maiano's Sala dei Gigli doorway." *Burlington Magazine* 160 (2018), pp, 624–29.

Dominici 1860
Giovanni Dominici. *Regola del governo di cura familiare*. Florence, 1860.

Doni 1543
Anton Francesco Doni. *Lettera di m. Antonfrancesco Doni fiorentino, con sonetti d'alcuni gentili huomini piacentini in sua lode*. Piacenza, 1543.

Doni 1970
Anton Francesco Doni. Edited by Mario Pepe. *Disegno: fac simile della edizione del 1549 di Venezia, con una appendice di altri scritti del Doni riguardanti le arti figurative*. Milan, 1970.

Dow 2006
Douglas N. Dow. "Confraternal piety and corporate patronage: A reconstruction of the art and oratory of the Company of San Giovanni Battista dello Scalzo, Florence." Dissertation: Pennsylvania State University, 2006.

Dow 2014
Douglas N. Dow. *Apostolic Iconography and Florentine Confraternities in the Age of Reform*. Burlington, Vt., 2014.

Dunkleman 2005
Martha Levine Dunkleman. "Donatello's Mary Magdalen: A model of courage and survival." *Woman's Art Journal* 26, no. 2 (2005), pp. 10–13.

Dussler 1924
L. Dussler. *Benedetto da Majano, ein florentiner Bildhauer des späten Quattrocentro*. Munich, 1924.

Duveen 1944
Duveen Sculpture in Public Collections of America: A Catalogue Raisonné with Illustrations of Italian Renaissance Sculptures by Great Masters Which Have Passed through the House of Duveen. New York, 1944.

Duveen Records
Duveen Brothers Records, 1876–1981. Getty Research Institute. Online: www.getty.edu/research/tools.

Edinburgh et al. 1978
Giambologna, 1529–1609, Sculptor to the Medici. Exh. Royal Scottish Museum, Edinburgh et al., 1978–79. Edited by Charles Avery and Anthony Radcliffe.

Eiche 1995
Sabine Eiche. "On the layout of the Cesi Palace and gardens in the Vatican Borgo." *Mitteilungen des Kunsthistorischen Institutes in Florenz* 39 (1995), pp. 258–81.

Eisler 1983
William Eisler. "The impact of the Emperor Charles V upon the Italian visual culture, 1529–1533." *Arte lombarda* 65 (1983), pp. 93–110.

Elam 1981
Caroline Elam. "The mural drawings in Michelangelo's New Sacristy." *Burlington Magazine* 123 (1981), pp. 593–602.

Estella 2008
Margarita Estella Marcos. "Adiciones y rectificaciones a noticias sobre esculturas italianas en España." *Archivo español de arte* 81 (2008), pp. 17–30.

Fabriczy 1909
Cornelius von Fabriczy. "Kritisches Verzeichnis toskanischer Holz- und Tonstatuen bis zum Beginn des Cinquecento." *Jahrbuch der Königlich Preussischen Kunstsammlungen* 30: Beiheft (1909), pp. 1–88.

Fadda 2013
Elisabetta Fadda. "Ancora su Bartolomeo Cancellieri, pittore itinerante e sul ritratto di Carlo V attribuito a Parmigianino." *Ricerche d S/confine* 4 (2013), pp. 133–46.

Falomir 2010
Miguel Falomir. "Carlos V, Tiziano y el retrato en armadura" in Madrid 2010, pp. 41–53.

Faticcioni 2007
Lorenzo Faticcioni. "Un volto per Marsia: Modalità di rappresentazione e testi letterari nella fruizione cinquecentesca di un mito antico." *Prospettiva*, nos. 126/127 (2007), pp. 128–48.

Favaretto 1972
Irene Favaretto. "Andrea Mantova
Benavides: Inventario delle antichità di
casa Mantova Benavides, 1695." *Bollettino
del Museo Civico di Padova* 61 (1972),
pp. 35–164.

Favaretto and Menegazzi 2013
Irene Favaretto and Alessandra Menegazzi,
eds. *Un museo di antichità nella Padova del
Cinquecento: La raccolta di Marco Mantova
Benavides all'Università di Padova, Museo di
Scienze Archeologiche e d'Arte*. Rome, 2013.

Ferrara 1974
Placchette e bronzi nelle Civiche Collezioni.
Exh. Palazzina di Marfisa d'Este, Ferrara et
al., 1974–75.

Ferretti 2000
Emanuela Ferretti. "Compagnie e oratori
nella storia e nei documenti" in *I segni del
sacro: Immagini della religiosità popolare nel
Comune di Vinci*, edited by Silvia Ciappi et
al. (Campi Bisenzio, 2000), pp. 13–19.

Ferretti 2016
Emanuela Ferretti. *Acquedotti e fontane del
Rinascimento in Toscana*. Florence, 2016.

ffolliott 1984
Sheila ffolliott. *Civic Sculpture in the
Renaissance: Montorsoli's Fountains at
Messina*. Ann Arbor, 1984.

Fiesole 1998
*I Della Robbia e l'arte nuova' della scultura
invetriata*. Exh. Basilica di Sant'Alessandro,
Fiesole, 1998. Edited by Giancarlo
Gentilini.

Filedt Kok 1993
Jan Piet Filedt Kok. "Hendrick Goltzius:
Engraver, designer and publisher,
1582–1600." *Nederlands Kunsthistorisch
Jaarboek* 42–43 (1991–92) [1993], pp.
157–218.

Fleming 1955
John Fleming. "The Hugfords of Florence
(part I)." *Connoisseur* 136 (1955),
pp. 106–10.

Fleming 1955a
John Fleming. "The Hugfords of Florence
(part II), with a provisional catalogue of
the collection of Ignazio Enrico Hugford."
Connoisseur 136 (1955), pp. 197–206.

Florence 1984
*Raffaello a Firenze: Dipinti e disegni delle
collezioni fiorentine*. Exh. Palazzo Pitti,
Florence, 1984.

Florence 1992
*Il Giardino di San Marco: Maestri e
compagni del giovane Michelangelo*. Exh.
Casa Buonarroti, Florence, 1992. Edited by
Paola Barocchi.

Florence 1996
*L'officina della maniera: Varietà e fierezza
nell'arte fiorentina del Cinquecento fra le due
Repubbliche, 1494–1530*. Exh. Galleria
degli Uffizi, Florence, 1996–97. Edited by
A. Cecchi and A. Natali.

Florence 2006
Giambologna: Gli dei, gli eroi. Exh. Museo
Nazionale del Bargello, Florence, 2006.
Edited by Beatrice Paolozzi Strozzi and
Dimitrios Zikos.

Florence 2008
*I grandi bronzi del Battistero: L'arte di
Vincenzo Danti, discepolo di Michelangelo*.
Exh. Museo Nazionale del Bargello,
Florence, 2008. Edited by Charles Davis
and Beatrice Paolozzi Strozzi.

Florence 2010
*I grandi bronzi del Battistero:
Giovanfrancesco Rustici e Leonardo*.
Exh. Museo Nazionale del Bargello,
Florence, 2010–11. Edited by Tommaso
Mozzati, Beatrice Paolozzi Strozzi, and
Philippe Sénéchal.

Florence 2011
*L'acqua, la pietra, il fuoco: Bartolomeo
Ammannati scultore*. Exh. Museo
Nazionale del Bargello, Florence, 2011.
Edited by Beatrice Paolozzi Strozzi and
Dimitrios Zikos.

Florence 2013
*Diafane passioni: Avori barocchi dalle corti
europee*. Exh. Palazzo Pitti, Florence,
2013. Edited by Eike Schmidt and
Maria Sframeli.

Florence 2014
*Baccio Bandinelli, scultore e maestro
(1493–1560)*. Exh. Museo Nazionale del
Bargello, Florence, 2014. Edited by Detlef
Heikamp and Beatrice Paolozzi Strozzi.

Florence 2016
*"Fece di scoltura di legname e colori": Scultura
del Quattrocento in legno dipinto a Firenze*.
Exh. Galleria degli Uffizi, Florence, 2016.

Florence 2017
*La fabbrica della bellezza: La manifattura
Ginori e il suo popolo di statue*. Exh.
Museo Nazionale del Bargello, Florence,
2017. Edited by Tomaso Montanari and
Dimitrios Zikos.

Florence and Paris 2013
*Springtime of the Renaissance: Sculpture
and the Arts in Florence, 1400–60*. Exh.
Palazzo Strozzi, Florence; and Musée
du Louvre, Paris, 2013–14. Edited
by Beatrice Paolozzi Strozzi and
Marc Bormand.

Francini 2000
Carlo Francini. "L'inventario della collezione Loeser alla Villa Gattaia." *Bollettino
della Società di Studi Fiorentini*, no. 6 (2000),
pp. 95–127.

Freddolini 2016
Francesco Freddolini. "A rediscovered
work by Domenico Pieratti: The bust
of Louis Hesselin." *Mitteilungen des
Kunsthistorischen Institutes in Florenz* 58
(2016), pp. 411–20.

Freedberg 1982
S. J. Freedberg. "A recovered work of
Andrea del Sarto with some notes on a
Leonardesque connection." *Burlington
Magazine* 124 (1982), pp. 281–88.

174

Frey 1923
Karl Frey, ed. *Der literarische Nachlass Giorgio Vasaris*. 3 vols. Munich, 1923–40. Reprint: 1982.

Fulton 1997
Christopher Fulton. "The boy stripped bare by his elders: Art and adolescence in Renaissance Florence." *Art Journal* 56, no. 2 (1997), pp. 31–40.

Fusco and Corti 2006
Laurie Fusco and Gino Corti. *Lorenzo de' Medici, Collector and Antiquarian*. Cambridge, 2006.

Gamba 1920
Carlo Gamba. "Il palazzo e la raccolta Horne a Firenze." *Dedalo* 1 (1920), pp. 162–85.

Gamberini 2015
Diletta Gamberini. "Benedetto Varchi, Giovann'Angelo Montorsoli e il Tempio dei 'Pippi': Un inedito dialogo in versi agli albori dell'Accademia Fiorentina del Disegno." *Mitteilungen des Kunsthistorischen Institutes in Florenz* 57 (2015), pp. 139–44.

Gavet 1889
Collection Émile Gavet: Catalogue raisonné, précédé d'une étude historique et archéologique sur les oeuvres d'art qui composent cette collection. Introduction by Émile Molinier. Paris, 1889.

Gavet 1894
Collection Émile Gavet: Catalogue raisonné, précédé d'une étude historique et archéologique sur les oeuvres d'art qui composent cette collection. Introduction by Émile Molinier. 2 vols. Paris, 1894.

Gaye 1839
Giovanni Gaye. *Carteggio inedito d'artisti dei secoli XIV, XV, XVI, pubblicato ed illustrato con documenti pure inediti*. 3 vols. Florence, 1839–40.

Gennari 1958
Gualberto Gennari. *Zaccaria Zacchi, scultore volterrano, 1473–1544*. Bologna, 1958.

Gentilini 1992
Giancarlo Gentilini. *I della Robbia: La scultura invetriata nel Rinascimento*. 2 vols. Florence, 1992.

Gentilini 2013
Giancarlo Gentilini. "Attualità di Donatello: Alonso Berruguete e l'eredità del Quattrocento fiorentino" in *Norma e capriccio: Spagnoli in Italia agli esordi della "maniera moderna"* (exh. Galleria degli Uffizi, Florence, 2013), pp. 73–85.

Giannattasio and Quartino 1982
Bianca Maria Giannattasio and Luigina Quartino. "Statue antiche e all'antica nei giardini di Villa Scassi a Genova-Sampierdarena." *Xenia* 4 (1982), pp. 37–48.

Giannotti 1974
Donato Giannotti. Edited by Furo Diaz. *Opere politiche*. Opere, vol. 1. Milan, 1974.

Gilbert 1961
Creighton Gilbert. "Tintoretto and Michelangelo's 'St Damian.'" *Burlington Magazine* 103 (1961), pp. 16–20.

Gilbert 1977
Felix Gilbert. "Andrea del Sartos 'Heilige Familie Borgherini' und florentinische Politik" in *Festschrift für Otto von Simson zum 65. Geburtstag*, edited by Lucius Grisebach and Konrad Renger (Frankfurt, 1977), pp. 284–88.

Gioli 2012
Antonella Gioli. "Giovanni degli Alessandri, il Deposito di San Marco e gli inizi della Galleria dell'Accademia di Firenze (1810–1816)" in *Scritti di museologia e di storia del collezionismo in onore di Cristina De Benedictis*, edited by Donatella Pegazzano (Florence, 2012), pp. 183–96.

Giometti 2011
Cristiano Giometti. *Sculture in terracotta: Museo Nazionale del Palazzo di Venezia*. Rome, 2011.

Gnann 2013
Achim Gnann. *In Farbe! Clair-obscur-Holzschnitte der Renaissance aus der Sammlung Baselitz und der Albertina*. Exh. Albertina, Vienna, 2013.

Gnann 2014
Achim Gnann. *Chiaroscuro: Renaissance Woodcuts from the Collections of Georg Baselitz and the Albertina, Vienna*. Exh. Royal Academy of Arts, London, 2014.

Goddard and Ganz 2001
Stephen H. Goddard and James A. Ganz. *Goltzius and the Third Dimension*. Exh. Sterling and Francine Clark Art Institute, Williamstown, et al., 2001–2.

Goldscheider 1962
Ludwig Goldscheider. *A Survey of Michelangelo's Models in Wax and Clay*. London, 1962.

Gómez 2014
Marta Gómez Ubierna. "Entre Italia y España: Las esculturas para Francisco de los Cobos" in *Il San Giovannino di Úbeda restituito*, edited by Maria Cristina Improta (Florence, 2014), pp. 169–82.

Gómez-Moreno 1930
Manuel Gómez-Moreno. "Obras de Miguel Ángel en España." *Archivo español de arte y arqueología* 6 (1930), pp. 189–97.

Gottschewski 1909
Adolf Gottschewski. "Der Modellkopf von der Hand Michelangelos im Besitze des Pietro Aretino." *Monatshefte für Kunstwissenschaft* 2 (1909), p. 399.

Gramaccini and Meier 2009
Norberto Gramaccini and Hans Jakob Meier. *Die Kunst der Interpretation: Italienische Reproduktionsgrafik, 1485–1600*. Berlin, 2009.

Granada 2000
Carlos V: Las armas y las letras. Exh. Palacio Real de la Alhambra, Granada, 2000. Edited by Fernando Marías and Felipe Pereda.

Grapheus 1550
Cornelius Scribonius Grapheus. *Spectaculorum in susceptione Philippi Hispan. princ. divi Caroli V.* Antwerp, 1550.

Guldan 1988
Margarete Merkel Guldan. *Die Tagebücher von Ludwig Pollak: Kennerschaft und Kunsthandel in Rom, 1893–1934.* Vienna, 1988.

Hartt 1992
Frederick Hartt. "Michelangelo, the mural drawings, and the Medici Chapel." *Studies in the History of Art* 33 (1992), pp. 178–211.

Haskell and Penny 1981
Francis Haskell and Nicholas Penny. *Taste and the Antique: The Lure of Classical Sculpture, 1500–1900.* New Haven, 1981.

Heikamp 1990
Detlef Heikamp. "Die Laokoongruppe des Vincenzo de' Rossi." *Mitteilungen des Kunsthistorischen Institutes in Florenz* 34 (1990), pp. 342–78.

Heikamp 2017
Detlef Heikamp. *Il Laocoonte di Vincenzo de' Rossi.* Rome, 2017. Edited by Caterina Napoleone.

Hittorff 1835
J. I. Hittorff. *Architecture moderne de la Sicile, ou, Recueil des plus beaux monuments religieux, et des édifices publics et particuliers les plus remarquables de la Sicile.* Paris, 1835.

Hofacker 2004
Emanuel C. Hofacker. *Rückführung italienischer Kulturgüter nach dem Ende des 2. Weltkriegs.* Berlin, 2004.

Hollstein 1949
F. W. H. Hollstein. *Dutch and Flemish Engravings, Etchings and Woodcuts, ca. 1450–1700.* 58 vols. Amsterdam et al., 1949–2001.

Honnens de Lichtenberg 1991
Hanne Honnens de Lichtenberg. *Johan Gregor van der Schardt, Bildhauer bei Kaiser Maximilian II., am dänischen Hof, und bei Tycho Brahe.* Copenhagen, 1991.

Houston 1945
Catalogue of the Edith A. and Percy S. Straus Collection. Exh. Museum of Fine Arts of Houston, 1945.

Houston and London 2001
Earth and Fire: Italian Terracotta Sculpture from Donatello to Canova. Exh. Museum of Fine Arts, Houston; and Victoria and Albert Museum, London, 2001–2. Edited by Bruce Boucher.

Howard 1959
Seymour Howard. "On the reconstruction of the Vatican Laocoon group." *American Journal of Archaeology* 63 (1959), pp. 365–69.

Howard 1989
Seymour Howard. "Laocoon rerestored." *American Journal of Archaeology* 93 (1989), pp. 417–22.

Hülsen 1921
Christian Hülsen. *Das Speculum Romanae Magnificentiae des Antonio Lafreri.* Munich, 1921.

Hykin 2007
Abigail Hykin. "The conservation and technical analysis of a glazed terracotta figure of St. John the Baptist attributed to Giovanni Francesco Rustici" in *La statua e la sua pelle: Artifici tecnici nella scultura dipinta tra Rinascimento e Barocco,* edited by Raffaele Casciaro (Lecce, 2007), pp. 81–99.

Illustrated Bartsch
The Illustrated Bartsch. New York, 1978– . Based on Adam von Bartsch, *Le peintre graveur,* 21 vols. (Vienna, 1803–21).

Impruneta 1980
La civiltà del cotto: Arte della terracotta nell'area fiorentina dal XV al XX secolo. Exh. Impruneta, 1980.

Ircani Menichini 2013
Paola Ircani Menichini, ed. *L'"infinito amore" alle arti e agli artisti: La Cappella dei Pittori e il p. Montorsoli nel 450° anniversario della morte (1563–2013).* Florence, 2013.

Jacquot 1960
Jean Jacquot, ed. *Fêtes et cérémonies au temps de Charles Quint. Les fêtes de la Renaissance,* vol. 2. Paris, 1960. Reprint: 1975.

Jansen 2000
Katherine Ludwig Jansen. *The Making of the Magdalen: Preaching and Popular Devotion in the Later Middle Ages.* Princeton, 2000.

Janson 1946
H. W. Janson. "Titian's *Laocoon Caricature* and the Vesalian-Galenist controversy." *Art Bulletin* 28 (1946), pp. 49–53.

Jesse 2017
Darja Jesse. "'und wegen der Wunde versagt dem Marmor der Atem': Die Reflexionen des Laokoon in der Skulptur und Plastik der Renaissance" in *Laokoon: Auf der Suche nach einem Meisterwerk,* edited by Susanne Muth (Rahden, 2017), pp. 195–200.

Joannides 1997
Paul Joannides. "Michelangelo *bronzista:* Reflections on his mettle." *Apollo* 145 (June 1997), pp. 11–20.

Katz 1996
European Sculpture: Daniel Katz. Exh. New York and London, 1996. By Johannes Auersperg.

Katz 2001
Daniel Katz: European Sculpture. Exh. New York and London, 2001. By Katherine Zock.

Katz 2013
Daniel Katz: 45 Years of European Sculpture. London, 2013.

176

Kauffmann 1931
Hans Kauffmann. "Donatellos Jünglingsstatuen, David und Johannes." *Sitzungsberichte: Kunstgeschichtliche Gesellschaft zu Berlin* (1931–32), pp. 1–4.

Kim 2014
David Young Kim. *The Traveling Artist in the Italian Renaissance: Geography, Mobility, and Style.* New Haven, 2014.

Klapisch-Zuber 1985
Christiane Klapisch-Zuber. *Women, Family, and Ritual in Renaissance Italy.* Chicago, 1985.

Kleiner 1981
Diana E. E. Kleiner. "Second-century mythological portraiture: Mars and Venus." *Latomus* 40 (1981), pp. 512–44.

Kornell 1989
Monique Kornell. "Rosso Fiorentino and the anatomical text." *Burlington Magazine* 131 (1989), pp. 842–47.

Krahn 2006
Volker Krahn. "I bozzetti del Giambologna" in Florence 2006, pp. 45–61.

Krahn 2018
Volker Krahn. "A bronze after Michelangelo's model for 'Earth.'" *Burlington Magazine* 150 (2018), pp. 462–69.

Kubler 1978
George Kubler. "Drawings by G. A. Montorsoli in Madrid" in *Collaboration in Italian Renaissance Art*, edited by Wendy Stedman Sheard and John T. Paoletti (New Haven, 1978), pp. 143–64.

Landau and Parshall 1994
David Landau and Peter W. Parshall. *The Renaissance Print, 1470–1550.* New Haven, 1994.

Lanzarini 1998
Orietta Lanzarini. "Il codici cinquecentesco di Giovanni Vincenzo Casale e i suoi autori." *Annali di architettura* 10–11 (1998–99), pp. 183–202.

La Porta 1998
Patrizia La Porta. "Zaccaria Zacchi: Proposte per gli esordi." *Prospettiva*, nos. 91–92 (1998), pp. 115–26.

Larsson 1984
Lars-Olof Larsson. "Från Florens till Prag" in *Bruegels tid: Nederländsk konst, 1540–1620* (exh. Nationalmuseum, Stockholm, 1984–85), pp. 16–40.

Laschke 1987
Birgit Laschke. "Montorsolis Entwürfe für das Siegel der 'Accademia del Disegno' in Florenz." *Mitteilungen des Kunsthistorischen Institutes in Florenz* 31 (1987), pp. 392–402.

Laschke 1993
Birgit Laschke. *Fra Giovan Angelo da Montorsoli, ein Florentiner Bildhauer des 16. Jahrhunderts.* Berlin, 1993.

Laschke 1998
Birgit Laschke. "Die Arme des Laokoon" in Winner et al. 1998, pp. 175–86.

Lavin 1955
Marilyn Aronberg Lavin. "Giovannino Battista: A study in Renaissance religious symbolism." *Art Bulletin* 37 (1955), pp. 85–101.

Lavin 1961
Marilyn Aronberg Lavin. "Giovannino Battista: A supplement." *Art Bulletin* 43 (1961), pp. 319–26.

Lavin 1998
Irving Lavin. "*Ex uno lapide*: The Renaissance sculptor's *tour de force*" in Winner et al. 1998, pp. 191–210.

LeBrooy 1972
Paul James LeBrooy. *Michelangelo Models Formerly in the Paul von Praun Collection.* Vancouver, 1972.

Leesberg 2012
Marjolein Leesberg. *The New Hollstein: Dutch and Flemish Etchings, Engravings and Woodcuts, 1450–1700: Hendrik Goltzius, Part II.* Ouderkerk aan den IJssel, 2012. Edited by Huigen Leeflang.

Lein 1988
Edgar Lein. *Benedetto da Maiano.* Frankfurt, 1988. Dissertation: Bochum, 1987.

Levin 2005
William R. Levin. "'Tanto goffe e mal fatte ... dette figure si facessino ... belle': The Trecento overdoor sculptures for the Baptistry in Florence and their Cinquecento replacements," *Studies in Iconography* 26 (2005), pp. 205–42.

Lewis 1989
Douglas Lewis. "The plaquettes of 'Moderno' and his followers." *Studies in the History of Art* 22 (1989), pp. 105–41.

Lillie 2003
Sophie Lillie. *Was einmal war: Handbuch der enteigneten Kunstsammlungen Wiens.* Vienna, 2003.

Liverani 2006
Paolo Liverani. "Il Laocoonte in età antica" in Rome 2006, pp. 23–40.

Liverpool 1983
Lady Lever Art Gallery, Port Sunlight. *Catalogue of Foreign Paintings, Drawings, Miniatures, Tapestries, Post-Classical Sculpture and Prints.* Liverpool, 1983.

Loeser 1928
Charles Loeser. "Gianfrancesco Rustici." *Burlington Magazine* 52 (1928), pp. 260–72.

Loffredo 2012
Fernando Loffredo. "La vasca del *Sansone* del Giambologna e il *Tritone* di Battista Lorenzi in un'inedita storia di duplicati (con una nota sul *Miseno* di Stoldo per la villa dei Corsi)." *Saggi e memorie di storia dell'arte* 36 (2012), pp. 57–114.

Loh 2011
Maria H. Loh. "Outscreaming the Laocoön: Sensation, special affects, and the moving image." *Oxford Art Journal* 34, pp. 393–414.

Lomazzo 1584
Giovanni Paolo Lomazzo. *Trattato dell'arte de la pittura*. Milan, 1584.

López 1997
Rosa López Torrijos. "Obras, autores y familias genovesas en España." *Archivo español de arte* 70 (1997), pp. 247–56.

Los Angeles 1949
Leonardo Da Vinci Loan Exhibition. Exh. Los Angeles County Museum, 1949.

Los Angeles 2018
The Chiaroscuro Woodcut in Italy. Exh. Los Angeles County Museum of Art and National Gallery of Art, Washington, 2018–19. By Naoko Takahatake et al.

Lucidi 2012
David Lucidi. "Zaccaria Zacchi volterrano: Una nota sulla formazione e qualche aggiunta al catalogo dello scultore." *Nuovi studi*, no. 18 (2012), pp. 133–66.

Luijten 2003
Ger Luijten. "The art of Italy: The fruits of the journey to Italy, 1590–1591" in *Hendrick Goltzius (1558–1617): Drawings, Prints and Paintings* (exh. Rijksmuseum, Amsterdam; Metropolitan Museum of Art, New York; Toledo Museum of Art, 2003–4), pp. 117–44.

Madrid 2007
Tintoretto. Exh. Museo Nacional del Prado, Madrid, 2007. Edited by Miguel Falomir Faus.

Madrid 2010
El arte del poder: La Real Armería y el retrato de corte. Exh. Museo Nacional del Prado, Madrid, 2010. Edited by Álvaro Soler del Campo.

Madrid 2015
Teresa de Jesús: La prueba de mi verdad. Exh. Biblioteca Nacional de España, Madrid, 2015. Edited by Rosa Navarro Durán and Juan Dobado Fernández.

Magi 1961
Filippo Magi. *Il ripristino del Laocoonte*. Rome, 1961.

Magnani 2005
Lauro Magnani. *Il tempio di Venere: Giardino e villa nella Cultura genovese*. 2nd edition. Genoa, 2005. 1st edition: 1987.

Malgouyres 2007
Philippe Malgouyres. "Charles d'Urfé, Montorsoli, Giulio Camillo, Charles Quint et quelques autres." *Bulletin de la Société de l'Historie de l'Art français* (2007), pp. 9–25.

Manara 1959
Carla Manara. *Montorsoli e la sua opera genovese*. Genoa, 1959.

Manchester 2016
Marcantonio Raimondi, Raphael and the Image Multiplied. Exh. The Whitworth, Manchester, U.K., 2016–17. Edited by Edward H. Wouk with David Morris.

Mantua and Vienna 1999
Rapahel und der klassischen Stil in Rom, 1515–1527. Exh. Palazzo Te, Mantua; and Graphische Sammlung Albertina, Vienna, 1999. Edited by Konrad Oberhuber; catalogue by Achim Gnann.

Marabottini 1988
Alessandro Marabottini. *Jacopo di Chimenti da Empoli*. Rome, 1988.

Marciari 2002
John Marciari. "Girolamo Muziano and the dialogue of drawings in Cinquecento Rome." *Master Drawings* 40 (2002), pp. 113–34.

Marías 2004
Fernando Marías. "La magnificencia del mármol: La escultura genovesa y la arquitectura española (siglos XV–XVI)" in Boccardo et al. 2004, pp. 55–68.

Martin 1968
John Rupert Martin. "Two terra-cotta replicas of the Laocoon Group." *Record of the Art Museum, Princeton University* 27, no. 2 (1968), pp. 68–71.

McPhee and Orenstein 2011
Constance C. McPhee and Nadine M. Orenstein. *Infinite Jest: Caricature and Satire from Leonardo to Levine*. Exh. Metropolitan Museum of Art, New York, 2011–12.

Meijer 1987
Bert W. Meijer. "Una commissione medicea per Cornelis Cort." *Mitteilungen des Kunsthistorischen Institutes in Florenz* 31 (1987), pp. 168–76.

Merli and Belgrano 1874
Antonio Merli and L. T. Belgrano. "Il Palazzo del Principe d'Oria a Fassolo in Genova." *Atti della Società Ligure di Storia Patria* 10 (1874), pp. v–xv, 1–118.

Middeldorf 1932
Ulrich Middeldorf. "Unknown drawings of the two Sansovinos." *Burlington Magazine* 60 (1932), pp. 236–45.

Middeldorf 1935
Ulrich Middeldorf. "New attributions to G. F. Rustici." *Burlington Magazine* 66 (1935), pp. 71–81.

Middeldorf 1976
Ulrich Middeldorf. *Sculptures from the Samuel H. Kress Collection: European Schools, XIV–XIX Century*. London, 1976.

Middione 2001
Roberto Middione. *Museo Nazionale di San Martino: Le raccolte di sculptura*. Naples, 2001.

Miedema 1969
H. Miedema. "Het voorbeeldt niet te by te hebben: Over Hendrick Goltzius' tekeningen naar de antieken" in *Miscellanea I. Q. van Regteren Altena* (Amsterdam, 1969), pp. 74–78.

Miedema 1994
Hessel Miedema, ed. *Karel van Mander, The Lives of the Illustrious Netherlandish and German Painters, from the First Edition of the Schilder-boeck (1603–1604)*. Doornspijk, 1994.

178

Migliorato 2014
Alessandra Migliorato. *Nel segno di Michelangelo: La scultura di Giovan Angelo Montorsoli a Messina*. Palermo, 2014.

Mitchell 1986
Bonner Mitchell. *The Majesty of State: Triumphal Progresses of Foreign Sovereigns in Renaissance Italy (1494-1600)*. Florence, 1986.

Molonia 1995
Giovanni Molonia. "Una medaglia di Montorsoli." *Quaderni dell'attività didattica del Museo Regionale di Messina*, no. 5 (1995), pp. 45–52. [Miscellanea di studi e ricerche sulle collezioni del Museo.]

Mongan and Sachs 1940
Agnes Mongan and Paul J. Sachs. *Drawings in the Fogg Museum of Art*. Cambridge, Mass., 1940.

Monte San Savino 2016
Andrea Sansovino, profeta in patria. Exh. Monte San Savino, 2016. Edited by Paola Refice et al.

Morani 1539
Eurialo Morani d'Ascoli. *Stanze Deurialo d' Ascoli sopra le statue di Laocoonte, di Venere et d' Apollo, al gran Marchese Del Vasto*. Rome, 1539.

Morselli 1982
Piero Morselli. "Florentine sixteenth-century artists in Prato: New documents for Baccio da Montelupo and Francesco da Sangallo." *Art Bulletin* 64 (1982), pp. 52–59.

Möseneder 1979
Karl Möseneder. *Montorsoli: Die Brunnen*. Mittenwald, 1979.

Moskowitz 1986
Anita Fiderer Moskowitz. *The Sculpture of Andrea and Nino Pisano*. Cambridge, 1986.

Mozzati 2007
Tommaso Mozzati. "Alonso Berruguete a Roma: Un conto corrente e gli itinerari del soggiorno italiano." *Mitteilungen des Kunsthistorischen Institutes in Florenz* 51 (2007), pp. 568–75.

Mozzati 2008
Tommaso Mozzati. *Giovanfrancesco Rustici: Le Compagne del paiuolo e della cazzuola: Arte, letteratura, festa nell'età Maniera*. Florence, 2008.

Mozzati and Sénéchal 2010
Tommaso Mozzati and Philippe Sénéchal. "Giovanfrancesco Rustici, un percorso" in Florence 2010, pp. 35–63.

Murr 1797
Christophe Théophile de Murr. *Description du Cabinet de Monsieur Paul de Praun à Nuremberg*. Nuremberg, 1797.

Naples 1964
Museo di San Martino: Mostra di oggetti d'arte e di documenti storici scelti dalle raccolte dei depositi. Naples, 1964. Edited by Marina Causa Picone and Anna Maria Bonucci.

Naples 2006
Tiziano e il ritratto di corte da Raffaello ai Carracci. Exh. Museo di Capodimonte, Naples, 2006.

Nesselrath 1998
Arnold Nesselrath. "Il cortile delle statue: Luogo e storia" in Winner et al. 1998, pp. 1–16.

Nesselrath 1998a
Arnold Nesselrath. "Montorsolis Vorzeichnung für seine Ergänzung des Laokoon" in Winner et al. 1998, pp. 165–74.

New York 1939
Catalogue of European Paintings and Sculpture from 1300–1800: Masterpieces of Art, New York World's Fair. Exh. New York, 1939. By George Henry McCall.

Nichols 2015
Tom Nichols. *Tintoretto: Tradition and Identity*. London, 2015.

Nickel et al. 1982
Helmut Nickel, Stuart W. Pyhrr, and Leonid Tarassuk. *The Art of Chivalry: European Arts and Armor from The Metropolitan Museum of Art*. New York, 1982.

Nocchi 2015
Livia Nocchi. "Gli scultori del Cardinale Pier Donato Cesi a Roma (1570–1586): Documenti e ipotesi." *Bollettino d'arte*, no. 25 (2015), pp. 77–96.

Oberhuber 1999
Konrad Oberhuber. *Raphael: The Paintings*. Munich, 1999. First edition in Italian: Milan, 1982.

O'Brien 2004
Alana O'Brien. "Andrea del Sarto and the Compagnia dello Scalzo." *Mitteilungen des Kunsthistorischen Institutes in Florenz* 48 (2004), pp. 258–67.

O'Brien 2011
Alana O'Brien. "Apostles in the Oratory of the Compagnia dello Scalzo: 'Adornata da e mia frateli academizi.'" *I Tatti Studies in the Italian Renaissance* 14/15 (2011), pp. 209–62.

O'Brien 2013
Alana O'Brien. "'Maestri d'alcune arti miste e d'ingegno': Artists and artisans in the Compagnia dello Scalzo." *Mitteilungen des Kunsthistorischen Institutes in Florenz* 55 (2014), pp. 359–433.

O'Grody 1999
Jeannine O'Grody. "*Un semplice modello*: Michelangelo and his three-dimensional preparatory works." Dissertation: Case Western Reserve University, 1999.

O'Grody 2001
Jeannine O'Grody. "Michelangelo, the master modeler" in Houston and London 2001, pp. 33–42.

Ortenzi 2006
Francesco Ortenzi. "Per il giovane
Francesco da Sangallo." *Nuovi studi*,
no. 12 (2006), pp. 71–84.

Ortenzi 2009
Francesco Ortenzi. "Formazione e ascesa
di Francesco da Sangallo." *Proporzioni* 7/8
(2006–7) [2009], pp. 49–66.

Ottawa 2005
*Leonardo da Vinci, Michelangelo, and the
Renaissance in Florence.* Exh. National
Gallery of Canada, Ottawa, 2005. Edited
by David Franklin.

Paci 1877
G. Paci. *Notizie istoriche e religiose di Santa
Maria a Petrojo.* Empoli, 1877.

Pacini 1999
Arturo Pacini. *La Genova di Andrea Doria
nell'impero di Carlo V.* Florence, 1999.

Panzanelli 2008
Roberta Panzanelli, ed. *Ephemeral Bodies:
Wax Sculpture and the Human Figure.* Los
Angeles, 2008.

Paolozzi Strozzi 2006
Beatrice Paolozzi Strozzi. "Donatello
and Desiderio: A suggestion and some
reflections on the Martelli Saint John" in
Paris et al. 2006, pp. 60–73.

Paolozzi Strozzi 2013
Beatrice Paolozzi Strozzi. "Saints and
infants" in Florence and Paris 2013,
pp. 119–29.

Paris et al. 2006
*Desiderio da Settignano, Sculptor of
Renaissance Florence.* Exh. Musée du
Louvre, Paris; Museo Nazionale del
Bargello, Florence; and National Gallery of
Art, Washington, 2006–7. Edited by Marc
Bormand et al.

Paris 2012
D'Agostino di Duccio à Caffieri. Exh. Galerie
Charles Ratton et Guy Ladrière, Paris,
2012.

Parker 2014
Deborah Parker. *Michelangelo and the Art
of Letter Writing.* Cambridge, 2014.

Parronchi 2003
Alessandro Parronchi. *Opere giovanili
di Michelangelo.* Vol. 6: *Con o senza
Michelangelo.* Florence, 2003.

Parshall 2006
Peter Parshall. "Antonio Lafreri's 'Speculum
Romanae Magnificentiae.'" *Print Quarterly*
23 (2006), pp. 3–28.

Pellegrini 2014
E. Pellegrini. "Gli scambi di opere d'arte
nella politica del Ventennio: I busti
Vanchetoni per la Pietà di Palestrina e il
caso Ventura-Goering" in *Storia dell'arte
come impegno civile: Scritti in onore di
Maria Dalai Emiliani*, edited by A. Cipriani
et al. (Rome, 2014), pp. 245–51.

Penny 1992
Nicholas Penny. *Catalogue of European
Sculpture in the Ashmolean Museum, 1540
to the Present Day.* 3 vols. Oxford, 1992.

Penny 1993
Nicholas Penny. *The Materials of Sculpture.*
New Haven, 1993.

Petrioli Tofani 2003
Annamaria Petrioli Tofani. "Appunti per
un corpus grafico di Giovanni Angelo
Montorsoli." *Artista* (2003), pp. 150–63.

Petrioli Tofani 2014
Annamaria Petrioli Tofani. *L'inventario
settecentesco dei disegni degli Uffizi di
Giuseppe Pelli Bencivenni: Trascrizione e
commento, III, Parte II, cc. 1–233.* Florence,
2014.

Pillsbury 1971
Edmund Pillsbury. *Florence and the Arts:
Five Centuries of Patronage.* Exh. Cleveland
Museum of Art, 1971.

Pina 2014
Marco Pina. "Dante and the *Florentine
Chronicles*." Dissertation: University of
California, Berkeley, 2014.

Pisani 2007
Linda Pisani. "San Giovannino Battista
nei busti del Rinascimento Fiorentino" in
*Kopf/Bild: Die Büste in Mittelalter und
Früher Neuzeit*, edited by Jeanette Kohl
and Rebecca Müller (Munich, 2007),
pp. 211–33.

Pizzorusso 2013
Claudio Pizzorusso. "Aspetti della
scultura del Cinquecento alla Santissima
Annunziata: Una visita di Giambologna."
in *La Basilica della Santissima Annunziata:
Dal Duecento al Cinquecento*, vol. 1
(Florence, 2013), pp. 219–36.

Poggi 1965
Giovanni Poggi with Paola Barocchi
and Renzo Ristori, eds. *Il carteggio di
Michelangelo.* 5 vols. Florence, 1965–83.

Poleggi 1972
Ennio Poleggi. *Strada Nuova: Una lottizza-
zione del Cinquecento a Genova.* 2nd edition.
Genoa, 1972. 1st edition: Genoa, 1968.

Pollak 1994
Ludwig Pollak. Edited by Margarete
Merkel Guldan. *Römische Memoiren:
Künstler, Kunstliebhaber und Gelehrte,
1893–1943.* Rome, 1994.

Pon 2004
Lisa Pon. *Raphael, Dürer, and Marcantonio
Raimondi: Copying and the Italian
Renaissance Print.* New Haven, 2004.

Ponz 1776
Antonio Ponz. *Viage de España, en que
se da noticia de las cosas mas apreciables, y
dignas de saberse, que hay en ella.* 13 vols.
Madrid, 1776–88.

Pope-Hennessy 1964
John Pope-Hennessy. Assisted by Ronald
Lightbown. *Catalogue of Italian Sculpture
in the Victoria and Albert Museum.* 3 vols.
London, 1964.

Pope-Hennessy 1985
John Pope-Hennessy. *Italian High Renaissance and Baroque Sculpture*. An Introduction to Italian Sculpture, part 3. New York, 1985. First published: London, 1970.

Pope-Hennessy 1993
John Pope-Hennessy. *Donatello*. New York, 1993.

Pressouyre 1969
Sylvia Pressouyre. "Les fontes de Primatice à Fontainebleau." *Bulletin Monumental* 127 (1969), pp. 223–39.

Principi 2014
Lorenzo Principi. "Un altare a Portovenere e altre novità per il secondo soggiorno genovese di Silvio Cosini, tra Padova e Milano." *Nuovi studi*, no. 20 (2014), pp. 105–44.

Principi 2016
Lorenzo Principi. *The Master of the Unruly Children: River God and Bacchus*. London, 2016.

Principi 2017
Lorenzo Principi. "Silvio Cosini a Savona." *Paragone* 68 (2017), pp. 3–26.

Principi 2018
Lorenzo Principi. *Il Maestro dei bambini turbolenti: Sandro di Lorenzo scultore in terracotta agli albori della Maniera*. Perugia, 2018.

Radke 1992
Gary M. Radke. "Benedetto da Maiano and the use of full scale preparatory models in the Quattrocento" in *Verrocchio and Late Quattrocento Italian Sculpture*, edited by Steven Bule and Alan Phipps Darr (Florence, 1992), pp. 217–24.

Ramiro 2016
Sergio Ramiro Ramírez. "La fuente regalada por Antonio Doria a Francisco de los Cobos en 1541: Una posible obra de Giovanni Angelo Montorsoli y un error de Vasari" in *El legado hispánico: Manifestaciones culturales y sus protagonistas*, edited by Abel Lobato Fernández et al. (Léon, 2016), pp. 275–93.

Rebaudo 2007
Ludovico Rebaudo. *Il braccio mancante: I restauri del Laooconte (1506–1957)*. Trieste, 2007. [An earlier version appeared in Settis 1999.]

Reznicek 1961
E. K. J. Reznicek. *Die Zeichnungen von Hendrick Goltzius mit einem beschreibenden Katalog*. Utrecht, 1961.

Riccetti 2014
Lucio Riccetti. "Le terrecotte invetriate nella collezione di Alexandre Imbert." *Faenza* 100 (2014), pp. 49–61.

Richa 1754
Giuseppe Richa. *Notizie istoriche delle chiese fiorentine*. 10 vols. Florence, 1754–62.

Richardson 1722
Jonathan Richardson the Elder and Jonathan Richardson the Younger. *An Account of Some of the Statues, Bas-reliefs, Drawings and Pictures in Italy, &c, with Remarks*. London, 1722.

Richter 1992
Simon Richter. *Laocoon's Body and the Aesthetics of Pain: Winckelmann, Lessing, Herder, Moritz, Goethe*. Detroit, 1992.

Ridolfi 1648
Carlo Ridolfi. *Le maraviglie dell'arte, overo Le vite de gl'illustri pittori veneti, e dello stato*. 2 vols. Venice, 1648.

Robey 2013
Tracey E. Robey. "Damnatio memoriae: The rebirth of condemnation of memory in Renaissance Florence." *Renaissance and Reformation* 36, no. 3 (2013), pp. 5–32.

Rome 1999
Villa Medici: Il sogno di un cardinale: Collezioni e artisti di Ferdinando de' Medici. Exh. Académie de France, Rome, 1999–2000. Edited by M. Hochmann.

Rome 2006
Laocoonte alle origini de Musei Vaticani. Exh. Musei Vaticani, Rome, 2006–7

Rosand and Muraro 1976
David Rosand and Michelangelo Muraro. *Titian and the Venetian Woodcut*. Exh. National Gallery of Art, Washington, et al., 1976–77.

Rosenberg 2003
Raphael Rosenberg. "The reproduction and publication of Michelangelo's Sacristy: Drawings and prints by Franco, Salviati, Naldini and Cort" in *Reactions to the Master: Michelangelo's Effect on Art and Artists in the Sixteenth Century*, edited by Francis Ames-Lewis and Paul Joannides (Aldershot, 2003), pp. 114–36.

Roskill 2000
Mark W. Roskill. *Dolce's Aretino and Venetian Art Theory of the Cinquecento*. 2nd edition. Toronto, 2000. 1st edition: New York, 1968.

Rossi 1711
Domenico de Rossi. *Studio d'architettura civile sopra vari ornamenti di cappelle, e diversi sepolcri tratti da più chiese di Roma*. Rome, 1711. Part 2 of *Studio d'architettura civile*; reprint: Brookfield, Vt., 1972.

Rossi 1975
Paola Rossi. *I disegni di Jacopo Tintoretto*. Florence, 1975.

Rossi Pinelli 1986
Orietta Rossi Pinelli. "Chirurgia della memoria: Scultura antica e restauri storici" in *Memoria dell'antico nell'arte italiana*, edited by Salvatore Settis (Turin, 1986), vol. 3, pp. 183–250.

Rossi Pinelli 1993
Orietta Rossi Pinelli. *Imitazione e modelli dall'antico nella scultura del Quattrocento: Artisti, opere, trattati, problemi*. Rome, 1993.

Rubach 2016
Birte Rubach. *Ant. Lafreri formis Romae: Der Verleger Antonio Lafreri und seine Druckgraphikproduktion.* Berlin, 2016.

Rubinstein 1987
Nicolai Rubinstein. "Classical themes in the decoration of the Palazzo Vecchio in Florence." *Journal of the Warburg and Courtauld Institutes* 50 (1987), pp. 29–43.

Rubinstein 1995
Nicolai Rubinstein. *The Palazzo Vecchio, 1298–1532: Government, Architecture, and Imagery in the Civic Palace of the Florentine Republic.* Oxford, 1995.

Rubinstein 1998
Ruth Rubinstein. "The statue of the river god Tigris or Arno" in Winner et al. 1998, pp. 275–85.

Saint Louis 2017
Learning to See: Renaissance and Baroque Masterworks from the Phoebe Dent Weil and Mark S. Weil Collection. Exh. Saint Louis Art Museum, 2017. By Judith W. Mann and Elizabeth Wyckoff.

Sancho 2000
José Luis Sancho. *Las fuentes de los tritones y las conchas en el Palacio Real de Madrid.* Madrid, 2000.

Sarica 1997
Antonino Sarica. "Una medaglia con l'effigie di Montorsoli in una collezione privata messinese." *Archivio storico messinese* 72 (1997), pp. 31–39.

Sassu 2007
Giovanni Sassu. *Il ferro e l'oro: Carlo V a Bologna (1529–1530).* Bologna, 2007.

Schmidt 2003
Eike D. Schmidt. "'Furor' und 'Imitatio': Visuelle Topoi in den Laokoon-Parodien Rosso Fiorentinos und Tizians" in *Visuelle Topoi: Erfindung und tradiertes Wissen in den Künsten der italienischen Renaissance,* edited by Ulrich Pfisterer and Max Seidel (Munich, 2003), pp. 351–83.

Scholten 2008
Frits Scholten. "Johan Gregor van der Schardt and the moment of self-portraiture in sculpture." *Simiolus* 33 (2007/2008), pp. 195–220.

Schottmüller 1933
Frida Schottmüller. *Staatliche Museen zu Berlin: Die italienischen und spanischen Bildwerke der Renaissance und des Barock.* Vol. 1: *Die Bildwerke in Stein, Holz, Ton und Wachs.* 2nd edition. Berlin, 1933.

Scolaro 1994
Michela Scolaro. "Verso la maniera moderna: L'incoronazione di Carlo V a Bologna e la genesi del ritratto di corte" in *La pittura in Emilia e in Romagna: Il Cinquecento,* edited by Vera Fortunati (Bologna, 1994), vol. 1, pp. 73–101.

Seelig-Teuwen 2003
Regina Seelig-Teuwen. "Large bronzes in France during the sixteenth century." *Studies in the History of Art* 64 (2003), pp. 114–27.

Sellink 2000
Manfred Sellink. Edited by Huigen Leeflang. *The New Hollstein: Dutch and Flemish Etchings, Engravings and Woodcuts, 1450–1700: Cornelis Cort, Part III.* Rotterdam, 2000.

Sénéchal 2007
Philippe Sénéchal. *Giovan Francesco Rustici, 1475–1554, un sculpteur de la Renaissance entre Florence et Paris.* Paris, 2007.

Sénéchal 2009
Philippe Sénéchal. "Giovan Francesco Rustici, with and without Leonardo" in Atlanta and Los Angeles 2009, pp. 161–93.

Serie 1773
Serie degli uomini i più illustri nella pittura, scultura, e architettura. Vol. 6. Florence, 1773.

Settis 1999
Salvatore Settis. *Laocoonte: Fama e stile.* Rome, 1999.

Setton 1976
Kenneth M. Setton. *The Papacy and the Levant, 1204–1571.* 4 vols. Philadelphia, 1976–84.

Seymour 1961
Charles Seymour Jr. *Art Treasures for America: An Anthology of Paintings and Sculpture in the Samuel H. Kress Collection.* London, 1961.

Seymour 1966
Charles Seymour Jr. *Sculpture in Italy, 1400–1500.* The Pelican History of Art. Harmondsworth, 1966.

Shearman 1967
John Shearman. *Mannerism.* Harmondsworth, 1967.

Shearman 1975
John Shearman. "The Florentine *Entrata* of Leo X, 1515." *Journal of the Warburg and Courtauld Institutes* 38 (1975), pp. 136–54.

Shearman 1977
John Shearman. "Raphael, Rome, and the Codex Escurialensis." *Master Drawings* 15 (1977), pp. 107–46.

Shoemaker 1981
Innis H. Shoemaker. "Marcantonio and his sources: A survey of his style and engraving techniques" in Shoemaker and Broun 1981, pp. 3–18.

Shoemaker and Broun 1981
Innis H. Shoemaker and Elizabeth Broun. *The Engravings of Marcantonio Raimondi.* Exh. Spencer Museum of Art, Lawrence, Kans., et al., 1981–82.

Siena 1989
La scultura: Bozzetti in terracotta, piccoli marmi e altre sculture dal XIV al XX secolo. Exh. Palazzo Chigi-Saraceni, Siena, 1989. Edited by Giancarlo Gentilini and Carlo Sisi.

Siracusano 2011
Luca Siracusano. "'Cose tutte piene d'invenzioni, capricci e varietà': Proposte per Tiziano Minio a Padova e altrove." *Nuovi studi,* no. 17 (2011), pp. 79–97.

182

Smith 1981
Graham Smith. "Tintoretto and Michelangelo's 'St Damian.'" *Burlington Magazine* 123 (1981), p. 614.

Solum 2015
Stefanie Solum. *Women, Patronage, and Salvation in Renaissance Florence: Lucrezia Tornabuoni and the Chapel of the Medici Palace*. Farnham, 2015.

Stagno 2017
Laura Stagno. "Triumphing over the enemy: References of the Turks as a part of Andrea, Giannettino and Giovanni Andrea Doria's artistic patronage and public image" in *Changing the Enemy, Visualizing the Other: Contacts between Muslims and Christians in the Early Modern Mediterranean Art* (Il capitale culturale, vol. 6, 2017), pp. 145–88. Online: http://riviste.unimc.it.

Stedman Sheard 1979
Wendy Stedman Sheard. *Antiquity in the Renaissance*. Exh. Smith College Museum of Art, Northampton, Mass., 1978. Northampton, 1979.

Steinmann 1907
Ernst Steinmann. *Das Geheimnis der Medicigraeber Michel Angelos*. Leipzig, 1907.

Stevenson 1997
Michael Stevenson. "Old masters and aspirations: The Randlords, art and South Africa." PhD thesis: University of Cape Town, 1997.

Summers 1969
David Summers. "The sculptural program of the Cappella di San Luca in the Santissima Annunziata." *Mitteilungen des Kunsthistorischen Institutes in Florenz* 14 (1969), pp. 67–90.

Tejero 1998
Beatriz Tejero Villarreal. "Las fuentes genovesas en los jardines de Felipe II" in *Jardín y naturaleza en el siglo XVI: Felipe II, el rey íntimo* (Aranjuez, 1998), pp. 399–420.

Tempestini 2005
Anchise Tempestini. "Apollo e Marsia nel Camerino di Apollo del Palazzo Grimani a Santa Maria Formosa" in *Der unbestechliche Blick: Festschrift zu Ehren von Wolfgang Wolters zu seinem siebzigsten Geburtstag*, edited by M. Gaier et al. (Trier, 2005), pp. 383–86.

Testaverde Matteini 1991
Annamaria Testaverde Matteini. *L'officina delle nuvole: Il Teatro Mediceo nel 1589 e gli Intermedi del Buontalenti nel Memoriale di Girolamo Seriacopi*. Milan, 1991.

Thode 1908
Henry Thode. *Michelangelo: Kristische Untersuchungen über seine Werke*. 3 vols. Berlin, 1908–13.

Toker 1976
Franklin Toker. "A baptistery below the Baptistery of Florence." *Art Bulletin* 58 (1976), pp. 157–67.

Tolnay 1943
Charles de Tolnay. *The Youth of Michelangelo*. Princeton, 1943.

Tolnay 1948
Charles de Tolnay. *The Medici Chapel*. Princeton, 1948.

Tomasso 2018
Important European Terracottas: Tomasso Brothers Fine Art. Exh. New York, 2018.

Tormen 2015
Gianluca Tormen. "Appunti sulle terrecotte invetriate nella collezione (e nelle memorie di viaggio) di Tommaso degli Obizzi." *Jahrbuch des Kunsthistorischen Museums Wien* 17/18 (2015–16), pp. 104–17.

Torraca 1986
Giorgio Torraca. "Momenti nella storia della conservazione del marmo: Metodi e attitudini in varie epoche." *OPD restauro* 1 (1986), numero speciale, pp. 32–45.

Trento 2009
L'uomo del concilio: Il cardinale Giovanni Morone tra Roma e Trento nell'età di Michelangelo. Exh. Museo Diocesano Tridentino, Trento, 2009.

Trexler 1991
Richard C. Trexler. *Public Life in Renaissance Florence*. Ithaca, 1991.

Trunk 2002
Markus Trunk. *Die Casa de Pilatos in Sevilla: Studien zu Sammlung, Aufstellung und Rezeption antiker Skulpturen im Spanien des 16. Jhs.* Mainz, 2002.

Urrea 1981
Jesús Urrea Fernández. *Antiguo Partido Judicial de Villalón de Campos*. Valladolid, 1981.

Valentiner 1938
William R. Valentiner. "Michelangelo's lost Giovannino." *Art Quarterly* 1 (1938), pp. 25–39.

Varchi 1564
Benedetto Varchi. *Oratione funerale di M. Benedetto Varchi fatta, e recitata da lui pubblicamente nell'essequie di Michelagnolo Buonarroti*. Florence, 1564.

Vasari 1550
Giorgio Vasari. *Le vite de piu eccelenti architetti, pittori, et scultori italiani, da Cimabue insino a' tempi nostri*. Florence, 1550.

Vasari 1568
Giorgio Vasari. *Le vite de' piu eccelenti pittori, scultori, e architettori*. 3 vols. Florence, 1568.

Vasari 1966
Giorgio Vasari. Edited by Rosanna Bettarini and Paola Barocchi. *Le vite de' più eccellenti pittori scultori e architettori nelle redazioni del 1550 e 1568*. 11 vols. Florence, 1966–94. Online text: http://vasari.sns.it.

Venturi 1935
Adolfo Venturi. *Storia dell'arte italiana*. Vol. 10: *La scultura del Cinquecento*. 3 vols. Milan, 1935–37.

Verdon et al. 2000
Timothy Verdon, Alessandro Coppellotti, and Patrizia Fabbri. *Churches of Florence.* Venice, 2000.

Verellen 1979
Till Verellen. "Cosmas and Damian in the New Sacristy." *Journal of the Warburg and Courtauld Institutes* 42 (1979), pp. 274–77.

Vienna 2010
Der Fürst als Sammler: Neuerwerbungen unter Hans-Adam II. von und zu Liechtenstein. Exh. Liechtenstein Museum, Vienna, 2010. Edited by Johann Kräftner.

Viljoen 2001
Madeleine Viljoen. "Raphael and the restorative power of prints." *Print Quarterly* 18 (2001), pp. 379–95.

Viljoen 2007
Madeleine Viljoen. "Laocoon's snakes: The reception of the group in Renaissance Italy" in *Towards a New Laocoon* (exh. Henry Moore Institute, Leeds, 2007), pp. 21–25.

Villani 1991
Giovanni Villani. Edited by Giovanni Porta. *Nuova cronica.* 3 vols. Parma, 1991.

Visconti 1818
Ennio Quirino Visconti. *Il Museo Pio Clementino illustrato e descritto.* 7 vols. Milan, 1818.

Vitzthum 1963
Walter Vitzthum. "The Accademia del Disegno at the Uffizi." *Master Drawings* 1 (1963), pp. 57–58.

Voraigne 1993
Jacobus de Voragine. *The Golden Legend.* Translated by William Granger Ryan. New York, 1993.

Vossilla 1997
Francesco Vossilla. "Baccio Bandinelli e Benvenuto Cellini tra il 1540 ed il 1560: Disputa su Firenze e su Roma." *Mitteilungen des Kunsthistorischen Institutes in Florenz* 41 (1997), pp. 254–313.

Waldman 2004
Louis A. Waldman. *Baccio Bandinelli and Art at the Medici Court: A Corpus of Early Modern Sources.* Philadelphia, 2004.

Waldman 2005
Louis A. Waldman. "Sculptor and perfumer in early Cinquecento Florence: The career of Sandro di Lorenzo." *Mitteilungen des Kunsthistorischen Institutes in Florenz* 49 (2005), pp. 119–32.

Waldman 2006
Louis A. Waldman. "A drawing by Tribolo for Montorsoli's lost Hercules and Antaeus at Castello." *Bulletin du Musée Hongrois des Beaux-Arts* 105 (2006), pp. 93–100.

Wallace 1987
William E. Wallace. "Two presentation drawings for Michelangelo's Medici Chapel." *Master Drawings* 25 (1987), pp. 242–60.

Wallace 1994
William E. Wallace. *Michelangelo at San Lorenzo: The Genius as Entrepreneur.* Cambridge, 1994.

Wallace 2005
William E. Wallace. "Clement VII and Michelangelo: An anatomy of patronage" in *The Pontificate of Clement VII: History, Politics, Culture,* edited by Kenneth Gouwens and Sheryl E. Reiss (Aldershot, 2005), pp. 189–98.

Wardropper 1991
Ian Wardropper. "A new attribution to Francesco Mochi." *Art Institute of Chicago Museum Studies* 17 (1991), pp. 102–19.

Wardropper 2011
Ian Wardropper. *European Sculpture, 1400–1900 in the Metropolitan Museum of Art.* New York, 2011.

Warren 1996
Jeremy Warren. "Bode and the British." *Jahrbuch der Berliner Museen* 38: Beiheft (1996), pp. 121–42.

Warren 2016
Jeremy Warren. *The Wallace Collection: Catalogue of Italian Sculpture.* 2 vols. London, 2016.

Washington 1941
National Gallery of Art. *General Information and List of Paintings and Sculpture.* Washington, 1941.

Washington 2009
The Art of Power: Royal Armor and Portraits from Imperial Spain. Exh. National Gallery of Art, Washington, 2009. By Álvaro Soler del Campo.

Washington and New York 2011
Antico: The Golden Age of Renaissance Bronzes. Exh. National Gallery of Art, Washington; and Frick Collection, New York, 2011–12. By Eleonora Luciano et al.

Waźbiński 1987
Zygmunt Waźbiński. *L'Accademia Medicea del Disegno a Firenze nel Cinquecento: Idea e istituzione.* 2 vols. Florence, 1987.

Weinberger 1963
Martin Weinberger. "Portrait busts by Montorsoli" in *Scritti di storia dell'arte in onore di Mario Salmi* (Rome, 1961–63), vol. 3, pp. 39–48.

Wethey 1971
Harold E. Wethey. *The Paintings of Titian: Complete Edition.* Vol. 2: *The Portraits.* London, 1971.

Whitaker 1997
Lucy Whitaker. "Tintoretto's drawings after sculpture and his workshop practice" in *The Sculpted Objects, 1400–1700,* edited by Stuart Currier and Petra Motture (Aldershot, 1997), pp. 177–91.

Wiles 1933
Bertha Harris Wiles. *The Fountains of Florentine Sculptors and Their Followers, from Donatello to Bernini.* Cambridge, 1933.

Winner 1974
Matthias Winner. "Zum Nachleben des Laokoon in der Renaissance." *Jahrbuch der Berliner Museen* 16 (1974), pp. 83–121.

184

Winner 1998
Matthias Winner. "La collocazione degli dei fluviali nel Cortile delle Statue e il restauro del Laocoonte del Montorsoli" in Winner et al. 1998, pp. 117–28.

Winner 1998a
Matthias Winner. "Paragone mit dem Belvederischen Apoll: Kleine Wirkungsgeschichte der Statue von Antico bis Canova" in Winner et al. 1998, pp. 227–52.

Winner et al. 1998
Matthias Winner et al., eds. *Il cortile delle statue: Der Statuenhof des Belvedere im Vatikan.* Mainz, 1998.

Wischermann 1979
Heinfried Wischermann. "Ein pommer-sches 'Schandgemälde' auf Papst Paul III. von 1546: Ein Beitrag zur Bildpolemik der Reformationszeit." *Jahrbuch der Berliner Museen* 21 (1979), pp. 119–35.

Witcombe 2008
Christopher L. C. E. Witcombe. *Print Publishing in Sixteenth-Century Rome: Growth and Expansion, Rivalry and Murder.* London, 2008.

Wixom 1975
William D. Wixom. *Renaissance Bronzes from Ohio Collections.* Exh. Cleveland Museum of Art, 1975.

Wright 1976
David Roy Wright. "The Medici villa at Olmo a Castello: Its history and iconography." Dissertation: Princeton University, 1976.

Wright 1993
David H. Wright. *The Vatican Vergil: A Masterpiece of Late Antique Art.* Berkeley, 1993.

Wyss 1996
Edith Wyss. *The Myth of Apollo and Marsyas in the Art of the Italian Renaissance: An Inquiry into the Meaning of Images,* Newark, Del., 1996.

Yates 1975
Frances A. Yates. *Astraea: The Imperial Theme in the Sixteenth Century.* London, 1975.

Zeri 1978
Federico Zeri. "Un pittore del Cinquecento ferrarese: Bartolomeo Cancellieri." *Antologia di belle arti* 2 (1978), pp. 112–13.

Zikos 2003
Dimitrios Zikos. "Benvenuto Cellini's Bindo Altoviti and its predecessors" in Boston and Florence 2003, pp. 133–72.

Zikos 2012
Dimitrios Zikos, ed. *Marks of Identity: New Perspectives on Sixteenth-Century Italian Sculpture.* Boston, 2012.

Zucker 1984
Mark J. Zucker. *Early Italian Masters.* The Illustrated Bartsch, vol. 25: *Commentary.* New York, 1984.

189

PHOTOGRAPHY CREDITS

The Currier Museum of Art respects fair use and copyright in a manner consistent with its nonprofit, educational mission. All of the works of art illustrated in this book are in the public domain.

Mauro Magliani: frontispiece: left and lower right; pp. 6–9: FIGS. 1, 4, 5; pp. 13–21: FIGS. 2, 3, 5, 7, 9, 10, 12, 14–16, 19, 23, 28; pp. 62–72: FIGS. 1, 2, 5, 7, 8, 10, 25, 30; p. 93: FIG. 1; pp. 124, 157, 158.

Jeffrey Nintzel: p. 7: FIG. 2; pp. 15–16: FIGS. 11, 13, 17; p. 34: fig. 16; pp. 117, 162, 165.

Rijksmuseum, Amsterdam: p. 21: FIG. 28; p. 78: FIGS. 1, 2; p. 81: FIG. 11.
Carnegie Museum of Art, Pittsburgh, photo: Bryan Conley: p. 84: FIG. 18; pp. 136, 156; p. 155: FIG. 3.
J. Paul Getty Museum, Los Angeles: pp. 42, 44: FIGS. 1, 5; p. 49: FIG. 17.
Genevra Kornbluth: p. 30: FIG. 8; p. 105: FIG. 1.
Magi 1961: p. 50: FIG. 20.

CAPTIONS
Cover: CAT. 8.
Frontispiece: details of p. 14: fig. 7; cat. 8; CAT. 11.
Page 90, clockwise from top: CATS. 2, 4, 24, 16.
Page 167: cat. 19.
Page 168: p. 145.

This exhibition and book would not have been possible without the critical advice of Dimitrios Zikos and Sergio Ramiro Ramírez. Marietta Cambareri and Valentine Talland kindly contributed entries for the catalogue. Technical analysis of Montorsoli's *John the Baptist* was conducted by Richard Newman, Mary Kate Donais, and Valentine Talland.

Warm thanks are due Giancarlo Gentilini and Irving Lavin, as well as Katherine Bentz, Fausto Calderai, Maichol Clemente, Victor Coelho, Douglas N. Dow, Clario Di Fabio, Maria Grazia Di Natale, James Fenton, Davide Gambino, Francesca Girelli, Alex Kader, Geoff Kaplan, Laura Kraus, Stuart Lochhead, David Lucidi, Mauro Magliani, Giacomo Montanari, Tommaso Mozzati, Giambattista Oneto, Clement Onn, Annamaria Petrioli Tofani, Darryl Pinckney, Assunta Procopio, Frits Scholten, Philippe Sénéchal, Carlo Sobrero, Tong Wee Sian, Louis Waldman, and Alison Whiting.

We owe a debt of gratitude to our museum colleagues: Erik M. Lee, Nadine Orenstein, C. D. Dickerson, Betsy Wieseman, Betsy Rosasco, Sarah Cartwright, Fabio Speranza, Anna Imponente, Rita Pastorelli, Giandomenico Spinola, Helga Aurisch, Marietta Cambareri, Michael Belman, Xavier Salomon, Lloyd DeWitt, Denise Allen, Judy Mann, Timothy Verdon, Susanne Blöcker, and Guido Cornini.

At the Currier Museum, we thank Rachel Kase, the exhibition's research assistant, and Andrew Spahr, Karen Papineau, Karen Graham, Jeff Allen, Meghan Petersen, Karl Hutchins, Carol Fabricant, and Barbara Jaus. Production of this book was in the hands of Geoff Kaplan, Kristin Swan, and Linus Lee. Christie's and Stuart Lochhead have kindly supported the scholarly conference accompanying the exhibition.

The editors are especially grateful to the museums and collectors that furnished high-resolution photographs for this book free of charge. The book has not used images from commercial rights agencies, as we regard them as restrictions on scholarship. Open access to images is now as important as any public museum program, and images should not be treated as income generators. Scholars, students, and other nonprofit institutions are heavily penalized, often with the result that charitable contributions are transferred from one organization to another. Leading the way in open access are the British Museum, the Metropolitan Museum of Art, the Getty Museum, and especially the Rijksmuseum, which has encouraged the public to use images of the highest possible resolution as a contribution to the free exchange of ideas. We strongly encourage other museums to follow these examples.

The research and publication of this book have been generously supported by Rose-Marie and Eijk van Otterloo. We warmly thank our exhibition sponsors: M. Christine Dwyer and Michael Huxtable, and Thomas Silvia and Shannon Chandley.

AC, LP, KS

Carnegie Museum of Art, Pittsburgh
Cleveland Museum of Art
Currier Museum of Art, Manchester
Harvard Art Museums, Cambridge
John and Mable Ringling Museum of Art, Sarasota
The Metropolitan Museum of Art, New York
Morgan Library and Museum, New York
Museo Nazionale della Certosa di San Martino, Naples
Museum of Fine Arts, Boston
Museum of Fine Arts, Houston
National Gallery of Art, Washington
Princeton University Art Museum
Worcester Art Museum
Private collectors

LORENZO PRINCIPI received his PhD from the University of Genoa for his study of Silvio Cosini, a pupil of Michelangelo and collaborator of Montorsoli and Jacopo Sansovino. He recently completed a study of Sandro di Lorenzo, the Master of the Unruly Children.

KURT SUNDSTROM, curator at the Currier Museum of Art, wrote his dissertation on the Chiostro Grande of Monte Oliveto Maggiore. He has curated an exhibition on Jan de Bray and written on Frank Lloyd Wright's Zimmerman House.

ALAN CHONG, director of the Currier Museum of Art, has curated exhibitions on Christianity in Asia and the patronage of Bindo Altoviti.

SERGIO RAMIRO RAMÍREZ will receive his PhD from the Complutense University of Madrid. His dissertation focuses on the artistic patronage of Francisco de los Cobos at the court of Charles V.

MARIETTA CAMBARERI, curator of decorative arts and sculpture at the Museum of Fine Arts, Boston, organized the exhibition *Della Robbia: Sculpting with Color in Renaissance Florence*.

VALENTINE TALLAND is an independent objects conservator and a regular collaborator with the Currier Museum of Art.